Monetary Policy
and Modern
Money Markets

Monetary Policy and Modern Money Markets

Fixed versus Market-Determined Deposit Rates

Michael G. Hadjimichalakis
University of Washington and
Board of Governors of the
Federal Reserve System

LexingtonBooks
D.C. Heath and Company
Lexington, Massachusetts
Toronto

332.4
H129m

Library of Congress Cataloging in Publication Data

Hadjimichalakis, Michael G.
   Monetary policy and modern money markets.

   Includes index.
   1. Monetary policy—United States. 2. Money—United States. I. Title.
HG540.H32 1982   332.4′973   82-47638
ISBN 0-669-05550-6   AACR2

Copyright © 1982 by D.C. Heath and Company

Published simultaneously in Canada.

Printed in the United States of America.

International Standard Book Number: 0-669-05550-6

83-6612

Library of Congress Catalog Card Number: 82-47638

In memory of my parents,
Maria Palos Hadjimichalakis
and
Gregory Hadjimichalakis

Contents

Figures

Tables

Preface

While I pondered the issues examined herein and formulated a plan for this book, my intention was always to present monetary policy in a framework that is recognizable to participants in money markets, to the practitioners of monetary policy, and to observers—whether academics or Fed watchers. This effort accelerated during my two-year tenure as a visiting scholar at the Federal Reserve Board. Furthermore, my plan had to be modified because any attempt to provide a framework that is consistent with the real world must now incorporate the new financial environment effected by three recent and drastic institutional changes: financial innovations, regulatory changes, and changes in Federal Reserve operating procedures.

Two key characteristics of this emerging financial environment are (1) the increasing reliance on market-determined interest rates for the assets held and especially for the liabilities issued by financial institutions, and (2) the emergence of managed liabilities as the primary instrument for attracting funds by financial intermediaries. Incorporating these two characteristics into a stylized financial system requires a new monetary framework—one in which the supply of demand deposits (and, hence, of money) is on an equal footing with the demand. This framework, in turn', must be contrasted with the current framework—one in which the quantity of money (that is, demand deposits) is demand determined.

The great difference in this framework can be seen in its implication that a cost-reducing, supply-augmenting financial innovation that increases the quantity of money is contractionary rather than expansionary and, hence, in the attendant implication that financial innovations may be either inflationary or deflationary, depending on whether demand-side or supply-side effects predominate. This difference can also be seen in the implication that a demand-side shock either reduces volatility in monetary aggregates and in interest rates or increases volatility in both but will never effect a trade-off in those volatilities.

In this book, the models representing the current, fast-disappearing regime and the emerging new regime are deliberately simple. That is, they envision an environment with only three financial assets: one kind of deposits (collectively called demand deposits), one kind of earning assets (often collectively called Treasury bills), and base money, or reserves. These models are designed to be compatible with the Federal Reserve's own monthly model and with the models used by academic economists. In particular, these models are also designed to be special cases of those explored by J. Tobin and W.C. Brainard and associates and to be consistent with the models used by K. Brunner and A.H. Meltzer, who have consistently been among the Fed's severest critics.

I hope that this book will contribute toward a dialogue between these practitioners of monetary policy and their critics. I also hope that the book will help to answer an often-voiced complaint—sometimes justified—by the practitioners of monetary policy that academics fail to design models applicable to the real world. I have had the good fortune to be at the Federal Reserve Board for two years—a period sufficient for learning the institutional aspects of money markets and of monetary policy that are necessary to do justice to the real world.

In conveying the analytical results discussed in this book, I have made a conscious effort to avoid drawing too many policy implications. Also, I have abstained from using these results to explain current issues, such as recent misses in monetary aggregate targets, current high and rising interest rates, and a recession that is deeper than anticipated—although all of these subjects can be explained by the analytical results of our framework. Instead, I shall leave these applications to research papers designed specifically to examine these issues and merely present in this book a theory on which future empirical research can be based. In chapter 7, I shall present a simple linear version of this work, a model that can be estimated as new and more reliable data become available. In the meantime, this linear version can be used for simulations under a variety of assumptions.

The book is organized into three sections. Part I, consisting of chapters 1 and 2, sets the stage by examining the institutional changes that have formed the new financial environment. Part II, consisting of chapters 3–7, forms the core of the book. This section examines the financial markets in isolation from the real sector and compares the old and disappearing regime with the emerging monetary regime. Part III, consisting of chapters 8–10, integrates the financial system of Part II with a particular version of the real sector and of inflationary expectations. As an illustration of such an integration, I have examined a fully employed real sector, which permits us to concentrate exclusively on inflation. As an expectations-formation mechanism, I have chosen an adaptive scheme. I must emphasize, however, that we can attach to this system a different expectations scheme, a real sector that permits unemployment, or we can permit both.

Acknowledgments

This book is the most visible product of my two-year stay as a visiting scholar at the Federal Reserve Board. It is therefore natural that my list of acknowledgments consists almost exclusively of economists associated with the Federal Reserve System. My plan to write this book was brought to fruition and my efforts accelerated when Jerry Enzler asked me to examine monetary issues associated with a market-determined deposit rate. I am most grateful to Jerry—both for his penetrating comments and for his support throughout this project. Without his monitoring of my progress, this project would still be unfinished.

In the early stages of my work I also profited from important comments made by Lewis O. Johnson, Dale Henderson, and Karma G. Hadjimichalakis. Their comments and interest continued until this work was completed.

Equally important, although perhaps less visible, is my indebtedness to the many specialists at the Federal Reserve who cheerfully gave so much of their time to explain the facts and the institutional aspects of money markets, bank credit, bank profitability, discount-window borrowings, and data gathering; that is, the essentials of monetary policy in a real-world financial environment. I am especially grateful to Marcelle Arak of the Federal Reserve Bank of New York and to Ed Fry, Barbara Opper, John Spitzer, and Neva Van Peski of the Federal Reserve Board. Further gratitude is due to Neva Van Peski who meticulously went over chapter 2. Finally, colleagues in Special Studies at the Federal Reserve Board who made helpful comments include, Bill Cleveland, Dave Pierce, and Clif Wilson.

The contents of this book have been presented in seminars at the University of Pennsylvania, the Federal Reserve Board, the Federal Reserve Bank of New York, and the Philadelphia meeting of the Committee on Financial Analysis of the Federal Reserve System. I have benefited from the comments of the participants—especially Anthony Santomero and Jeremy Siegel of the University of Pennsylvania—at those seminars.

In this book—even more than in my previous writings—I am most grateful to my wife and colleague, Karma G. Hadjimichalakis, who is also a visiting professor at the Federal Reserve Board; she has read and commented on all versions of this manuscript.

I am indebted, once again, to Dollmarvelene Flood Pardi for editing the manuscript. I also owe thanks to Marian G. Bolan for her typing.

Finally, the views in this book are entirely my own and do not necessarily reflect those of the Board of Governors or the staff of the Federal Reserve System.

Part I
The New Financial
Environment

1 Overview

There is an acute and growing need for a book on monetary policy that can be of interest to its practitioners—that is, to policymakers, Wall Street analysts, and Fed watchers, as well as academicians. Such a book should construct a framework capable of deriving the effects of monetary policy on interest rates and on monetary aggregates from the interaction of decisions by financial intermediaries, the nonfinancial business and household sector, and the Federal Reserve.

The role of financial intermediaries in monetary control was examined in the classic work of Gurley and Shaw (1960). During the two decades since this work was written, important changes have occurred that must be incorporated into a new monetary framework. These changes first concern advances in monetary theory—mostly in work by Tobin and Brainard, and by associates of the Yale school and by Brunner and Meltzer of the Rochester-Carnegie-Mellon school. But perhaps more important in establishing the need for a new monetary framework is the drastic change in the financial environment in which financial institutions operate. Financial innovations, regulatory changes, and new Federal Reserve operating procedures all contributed to this fundamental change in the financial environment. This new environment has witnessed the increasing—or even the exclusive—reliance on market-determined interest rates. Another key characteristic of the new financial environment is the advent of "managed liabilities" as the primary instruments for attracting funds by financial intermediaries.

These two characteristics suggest that we are moving toward a monetary regime of market-determined interest rates on demand deposits and on other deposits. In modeling such a regime, the role of the supply of deposits must be brought to the forefront. Until recently the amount of demand deposits was considered to be—and was in fact—demand determined. Supply did not matter. But now we see that a new norm has emerged, namely, that the suppliers, the financial institutions themselves, offer managed liabilities; that is, these institutions design and actively market liabilities (say, deposits) as opposed to letting them be demand determined. Hence in the emerging regime the supply of deposits, based on the profit-maximizing decisions of financial institutions, must be on equal footing with the demand for such deposits. In other words, supply matters and this should be reflected in or captured by the monetary framework. This is the main innovation in this book—and it is a fundamental one.

3

When the supply of demand deposits and other deposits is on equal footing with the demand, the model becomes richer in that it permits the posing and answering of questions that have far-reaching implications. For example, the effects of financial innovations on monetary control have been examined exclusively from the demand side. In particular, it has been argued that financial innovations reduce the need to hold demand deposits and therefore their demand falls. The consequence, then, is that the quantity of demand deposits and therefore the quantity of money falls. But this fall is expansionary because the interest rate also falls. Even when it is recognized that there are cost-reducing innovations that increase the supply of demand deposits, the existing framework implies that they do not matter. In such a framework it can be argued that because supply does not matter, an increase in the supply will leave both the interest rate and the quantity of demand deposits unchanged. However, when supply matters, the increase in supply will increase the deposit rate, causing the other interest rates to rise. The rise in interest rates is contractionary even though there will be an increase—not a decrease—in the quantity of demand deposits.

In this book, we shall compare the implications of letting the interest rate on demand deposits be market determined as opposed to being determined by Central Bank decree. This comparison will be undertaken in two settings: first, when the financial markets are examined in isolation from the real sector; and second, when the financial sector is integrated with the real sector. Chapters 3 through 7 examine the effects of deliberate and inadvertent monetary shocks on interest rates and on reserves and monetary aggregates when only the financial markets are in equilibrium. A real sector consisting of a goods-and-services market and an expectations-formation mechanism is added to the models, and the implications are examined and compared in chapters 8 through 10. The real-sector equations were designed to reflect neoclassical results—that is, they assume full employment and use an adaptive-expectations mechanism. In such a setting we determine and examine movements in the price level, interst rates, and in actual and expected inflation. We must emphasize, however, that the financial framework of chapters 3 through 7 can be attached to any other modeling of the real sector. For example, the model can be extended to permit unemployment. Alternatively, one could use any other expectations-formation mechanism. But the full-equilibrium results of this study would remain unaffected.

Chapter 2 sets the stage for the analysis to follow by examining institutional changes brought about by either private or governmental initiative. This examination is not intended to be exhaustive; rather, it is meant to identify and concentrate on only those institutional changes that have altered the financial system fundamentally—especially as it concerns the conduct of monetary policy.

Three broad categories of institutional changes are responsible for the fundamental transformation of the financial environment: (1) financial innovations; (2) regulatory changes; and (3) changes in the Federal Reserve's operating procedures.

1. Financial Innovations

In the discussion on financial innovations in chapter 2 we distinguish three categories as follows: (1) innovations in liabilities offered; (2) innovations in assets held; and (3) innovations in the array and the cost of services offered. Innovations in the liabilities offered developed mostly from the initiative of the financial intermediaries in their efforts to (1) circumvent the prohibition of paying explicit interest on demand deposits; (2) circumvent Regulation Q ceilings on interest rates on other deposits; and (3) circumvent (high) reserve requirement ratios; or (4) combinations of 1 through 3. Of course, high and rising interest rates were a contributing factor. Whatever the reason, an increasing portion of the deposits of financial intermediaries is of the "managed liability" variety, which brings the role of the supply of deposits to the forefront.

Financial innovations in the array of assets held took the form of diversification aimed mostly at shortening the average maturity of assets. Shortening of the maturity was mostly achieved by an increased percentage of long-term bank loans with a floating rate (which is tied to either the prime rate or to the London Interbank Offer Rate [LIBOR]). Adjustable-rate mortgages offered by the thrifts also contributed to the shortening of the maturity of assets. In short, financial innovations have created a greater uniformity in the asset sides of financial intermediaries, a uniformity that reflects market-determined interest rates.

Financial innovations in the services offered have affected both the array of the services and the cost of producing these services. Technological progress in data processing was a major factor in both aspects of these innovations. The increased array of services has helped to decrease the need for cash and, hence, to decrease the demand for money. On the other hand, cost-reducing innovations have increased the supply of deposits by financial institutions by decreasing the cost of servicing these deposits. In other words, technological progress caused shocks on the supply side as well as on the demand side of the market for deposits.

In summary, financial innovations have created a trend toward market-determined interest rates—for the assets that financial intermediaries hold and for the deposit liabilities they supply. As a corollary, financial innovations have brought into focus the role of the supply of as well as of the demand for deposits. Further, financial innovations in services have created shocks, or shifts, originating in the supply of as well as in the demand for deposits.

2. **Regulatory Changes**

The trend toward market-determined interest rates, initiated by the financial institutions themselves, has been largely ratified by the second category of changes, namely, regulatory changes examined in the section of the same name in chapter 2. However, regulatory changes have also been initiated by regulatory agencies and by legislatures. These changes, of which the Depository Institutions Deregulation and Monetary Control Act of 1980 is the most important, have permitted diversification in the structure of both the asset and the liability side of the balance sheets of financial institutions. But the unifying theme of this second category of institutional changes is, again, the movement toward market-determined interest rates—both for the assets in the portfolios of financial institutions and for their deposits.

3. **The New Federal Reserve Operating Procedures**

The third important institutional change, discussed in the section titled Change in the Federal Reserve's Operating Procedures, arose in October 1979 when the Central Bank (that is, the Federal Reserve) changed its operating procedures in an effort to better control the quantity of money. It now targets base money (that is, nonborrowed reserves) rather than interest rates. The essence of this institutional change is that interest rates have resumed their asset-market-clearing role. Of course, this is consistent with the theme of the two preceding institutional changes— namely, that the trend is toward market-determined interest rates. Moreover, because the new operating procedures rely on increased volatility in interest rates, financial innovations have increased.

The section called A Stylized Financial System in chapter 2 distills the key characteristics of the new financial environment and presents a stylized model of the fast-disappearing current regime and a stylized model of the emerging monetary system. The current monetary regime is analyzed in chapter 3, and the emerging regime is discussed in chapters 4 and 5.

For the remainder of this book, we assume that the Federal Reserve pursues a reserves operating target, that is, that the Federal Reserve controls nonborrowed reserves, referred to here as the nonborrowed reserve base. Also, beginning with chapter 3, and in line with the stylized facts of chapter 2, we examine a financial-sector model that consists of only three assets: (1) base money (that is, currency plus reserves), (2) demand deposits, and (3) earning assets, collectively called "T-Bills." Our choice of such a model is based on two considerations: the first is simplicity, and the second is the desire to use a model that is similar to the ones used by both the Federal Reserve and by some of its critics. In particular, this three-asset model is a special case of the Tobin-Brainard framework; it is consistent with the Federal Reserve's monthly model and with the basic model that Brunner and Meltzer, who are among the Federal Reserve's severest critics, have established and have been using for a long time.

In the second section of chapter 3 we develop the financial model in abstraction from the real sector. The key assumption is that the nominal interest rate on demand deposits is fixed and is binding. This assumption, in turn, implies that the quantity of demand deposits is demand determined. This is true whether we rely on equilibrium of the deposit market by means of a perfectly elastic supply schedule or whether we rely on disequilibrium of this market.

In the discussion titled Monetary Policy and Stochastic Shocks, we determine the market-clearing interest rate (for earning assets, or T-bills). We then proceed to examine the effect on this interest rate of changes in various instruments of monetary control—the reserve base, the discount rate, the reserve-requirement ratio—and of various other deliberate or inadvertent shocks. The effects of the same changes on monetary aggregates, the quantity of demand deposits, borrowed reserves, and on total reserves are derived, respectively, in the sections called Effects on the Quantity of Demand Deposits and Effects on Borrowed and Total Reserves. In the final section we examine the scope of shocks and, in particular, where they originate and where they have their initial impact.

In chapter 4 we modify the model of chapter 3 to permit market determination of an additional interest rate—namely, the deposit rate, ζ. As shown in chapter 2, this is the direction toward which the money markets are inexorably driven. Both the financial innovations and the governmental deregulation of the last few years point toward a financial environment in which all deposit rates will be market determined and, therefore, in which active liability management will become the norm.

In order to focus on the issue of monetary control in such an environment, we shall examine a situation in which financial institutions supply only one liability, which is managed actively. In other words, the supply of this liability is based on profit-maximizing decisions by the financial firm. We call this single financial liability demand deposits. However, the framework can be extended to incorporate additional managed liabilities, such as negotiable certificates of deposit, which can be analyzed using the techniques introduced here for market-determined demand deposits.

Chapter 4 concentrates on development of the new financial model and on detailed examination of the market for demand deposits. This model is derived from microeconomic principles—that is, its behavioral (or structural) relations reflect profit-maximizing behavior of some firm. In the second section we introduce a very simple profit-maximizing theory of the financial, or banking, firm to derive the behavioral relations we use in the model—that is, the supply of demand deposits, the demand for borrowed reserves, and the demand for earning assets. Of course, the supply of demand deposits is the new ingredient of the model that is developed in the section titled The Model. In developing the model we focus on the key feature, that the deposit rate is determined in the market for demand deposits, by supply as well as by demand.

In this new financial regime, not only the deposit rate but also the quantity of demand deposits is market determined. This attribute confronts the researcher with a mathematical difficulty: Should the demand for or the supply of demand deposits be used to calculate required reserves? The answer is, of course, both. To resolve this difficulty, we appeal to clearance of the deposit market to make the quantity demanded equal to the quantity supplied. For this reason, in Determination of the Market-Clearing Deposit Rate, we examine in detail deposit market clearance, determination of the deposit rate, determination of the quantity of demand deposits, and the effect on these variables of changes in policy and other shocks.

Chapter 5 continues the analysis of the new regime. In this chapter we examine the determination of interest rates and aggregates when all financial markets are cleared—that is, the markets for reserves, for "T-bills," and for demand deposits. Also, we proceed to find the effects of changes in instruments of monetary control and the effects of shocks on the (two) interest rates and on monetary and reserves aggregates.

In the section Full Financial Equilibrium we show that by exploiting the technique introduced in Chapter 4 we can reduce the full equilibrium of the entire financial system to one qualitatively indistinguishable from the equilibrium of the fixed-deposit-rate regime. Then we proceed to determine the effects of monetary policy and shocks on the bills interest rate when all financial markets are cleared. It is interesting to note here that the interest rate rises whether there is an increase in the demand function for or in the supply function of demand deposits.

Our result—that the bill rate rises when there is a positive shift in the demand for demand deposits—is expected; in fact, it is standard in the literature. What is unexpected and, in fact, what exemplifies the fundamental difference between the two regimes is the following: An increase in the supply of demand deposits—that is, an increase in the supply of money—will *increase* the bill rate. In other words, an increase in the supply of money is, in this case, contractionary. The reason for this drastic departure in results is simple: A positive shift—that is, an increase—in the supply function of demand deposits causes excess supply of demand deposits, which is eliminated only when the (variable) deposit rate rises. This rise shifts wealth away from other earning assets—that is, away from bills—causing excess supply of bills, which, in turn, is eliminated only if the bills rate rises.

In the third section, Effects on the Deposit Rate, we explore whether the effects of policy and of other monetary shocks on the deposit rate will change when all asset markets—not merely the deposit market as in chapter 4—are required to equilibrate. We see that the key difference occurs when we consider the effect of an increase in the demand function for demand deposits. When the demand deposit market alone is required to clear, the positive shift in the demand function lowers the deposit rate; but when all financial markets are required to clear, this negative effect may or may not prevail. However, we specify the conditions for either case. (In chapter 6 we shall see that variability of interest rates and in aggregates depends on these same conditions.)

In the remainder of chapter 5 we examine the effects of the same deliberate and inadvertent shocks on monetary and on reserves aggregates, namely, on the quantity of market-determined demand deposits and on the quantities of borrowed and total reserves. The effects on demand deposits (money) are important, especially if the Central Bank follows the procedure of intermediate targeting as is currently the case in the United States. Knowledge of the effects of changes in monetary instruments and of shocks on the quantity of demand deposits is obviously necessary for monetary control. This knowledge is also important to those who try to interpret the actions of the Central Bank—the so-called Fed watchers—by deciphering the releases of monetary data. Furthermore, knowledge of the effects on the reserves aggregates are useful for similar purposes.

The fourth section of chapter 5, Effects on Demand Deposits, examines the effects on the quantity of demand deposits. Particularly interesting is the result that positive shifts in either the demand function or the supply function of demand deposits will lead to an increase in the quantity of demand deposits. Since, as noted, these same shocks also increase the interest rate, there is a conflict between the signals provided by interest rates and by monetary aggregates as indicators of economic activity. Although the quantity of money increases in these two cases, it is contractionary.

The section Effects on Borrowed and on Total Reserves examines the effects of the same shocks on these entities. Finally, in Concluding Comments we apply our analysis of demand and supply shocks to the issue of financial innovations.

Furthermore, we consider some questions that are crucial to the conduct of monetary policy: Are there any qualitative differences in the effects of shocks on the interest rate when the deposit rate is market determined as opposed to when the deposit rate is fixed by the Central Bank? In the absence of qualitative differences, are there any quantitative differences? Similar questions can be posed for the monetary aggregates: Are there any qualitative or quantitative differences in the effects of shocks on monetary aggregates—that is, on demand deposits and on borrowed reserves? These are the questions we consider in chapter 6.

The sensitivity of monetary aggregates to monetary shocks is crucial to a Central Bank committed to achieving targets expressed in monetary aggregates. The sensitivity of interest rates is crucial to those who consider changes in interest rates as the key indicator of the state of the entire economy. Similarly, the effects of shocks on interest rates are crucial to portfolio holders or to consultants to portfolio holders.

Under the heading, Comparison of Interest-Rate Responses, we compare interest-rate responses to deliberate and inadvertent shocks when the deposit rate is fixed and when it is market determined. The comparison is qualitative and, more important, quantitative. We find that when a comparison is legitimate, the two regimes give the same qualitative results; that is, the direction of change in the interest rate because of shocks is the same with fixed and with flexible deposit rates. The responses differ quantitatively, however. In particular—with one important possible exception—interest rates are more responsive to shocks when the deposit rate is flexible than when it is fixed. The possible exception refers to responsiveness of the interest rate to demand-side (for demand deposits) shocks. The relative responsiveness of the interest rate to demand-side shocks depends on the sign of the overall effect of demand-side shocks on the deposit rate when the latter is flexible. If a positive shift in money demand lowers (raises) the deposit rate, the interest-rate responsiveness to this shock is lower (greater) under a flexible deposit rate than it is under a fixed deposit rate. We specify the conditions that permit each of these results.

Another difference occurs in the effects of a positive shift in the supply of demand deposits; this occurs by default. Under a fixed deposit rate the supply side does not matter. Hence an increase in supply will leave the interest rate unchanged when the deposit rate is fixed. But under a flexible deposit rate, the increase in supply will raise both rates and, in particular, it will raise the bills interest rate.

In the section Comparison of Demand-Deposit Variability, we compare the responses of the quantity of demand deposits to the same shocks. As expected, there is a smaller response (variability) in this quantity when the deposit rate is market determined than when it is fixed—with one definite and one possible exception. Exceptions aside, this result establishes a trade-off between variability (volatility) in interest rates and variability in the quantity of money (demand deposits). In this sense, the move toward a market-determined deposit rate strengthens the precision of control of monetary aggregates, at the price of greater volatility in interest rates.

The exceptions concern genuine shocks in demand and in supply. A positive shock in the supply of demand deposits increases the quantity of demand deposits under a flexible deposit rate but leaves demand deposits unchanged under a fixed deposit rate. Hence under a flexible deposit rate there will be greater response of monetary aggregates to shifts in the supply of demand deposits. Combining this result with the corresponding greater interest rate response to the same shock, we can say that if the economy is prone to financial supply-side shocks, the move to a market-determined deposit rate will increase the variability of both aggregates and interest rates.

As in the preceding section, the consequences of a (positive) shift in the demand for demand deposits are not as clear-cut. The response of the quantity of demand deposits to demand-side shocks may increase or decrease when we move to the market-determined deposit-rate regime. However, the response of this aggregate will increase when the response of the interest rate increases; and the response of this aggregate will be reduced when the response of the interest rate is reduced. And we know from the preceding section that the relative response of the interest rate hinges on whether the deposit rate falls or rises when the demand for demand deposits rises. That is, the conditions that guarantee a reduction (increase) in the deposit rate when there is a positive shift in the demand function also guarantee a smaller, (larger) increase in both the interest rate and in the quantity of demand deposits with such a shift.

Next we compare variability in the reserves aggregates under the two regimes. Because the quantity of borrowed reserves depends on the interest rate, the greater variability in the interest rate under a flexible deposit rate also manifests itself as a greater variability in borrowed reserves—again, with some exceptions. Of course, the case of demand shocks is obvious: The variability of borrowed reserves will imitate the variability of the interest rate—greater or smaller. The true exceptions occur in shocks that originate in the borrowings function itself. In particular, borrowings variability caused by a change in the discount rate is smaller under a flexible deposit rate than under a fixed deposit rate. So is the variability caused by a change in the administration of the discount window. Finally, we compare the variability in total reserves, and we find that its pattern coincides with that of demand deposits.

In chapter 7, we examine an example based on the analysis of the preceding four chapters. We use a linear model that purports to reenact and illustrate both the techniques and the results in these chapters. In fact, this simple model in chapter 7 can also be helpful in checking the accuracy of the preceding analysis. Moreover, the linear model is conducive to applications, that is, it can be estimated as more and more data are coming in and in the meantime it can be used for simulations, stochastic or otherwise.

Up to this point we examined the financial sector in isolation. Beginning with chapter 8 we extend the model to include the real sector as well. In this chapter we add the real sector to the financial system characterized by a fixed deposit rate; in other words, we extend the analysis of chapter 3 to include the real sector. In chapter 9, we shall attach the same real sector to the financial sector that permits a market-determined deposit rate; and in chapter 10, we compare the implications of the two regimes.

We undertake completion of the model in the second section of chapter 8. The real sector consists of a price-adjustment mechanism based on the goods-and-services market and a simple expectations-adjustment mechanism, that is, an adaptive expectations mechanism. In this book we are interested in designing a full-employment, neoclassical model that emphasizes inflation and the neutrality of inflation with respect to the real rate of interest (that is, the Fisher hypothesis). For this reason—that is, in order to guarantee such properties—we assume that investment and savings depend only on the real interest rate on bills, which is defined as the nominal interest rate on bills minus the expected rate of inflation. In particular, we deliberately avoid assuming that investment and saving—and, hence, consumption—depend on the real reserve base or, more generally, on the real reserve base plus the real quantity of earning assets, or bills. Shocks originating in the real sector can be considered by strategically incorporating a shift parameter in the investment function—to represent, say, "animal spirits."

In chapter 8, as well as in the rest of this book, we shall examine two variants of the model. The first concentrates on the *level* of the nominal reserve base, that is, on the case where its rate of growth is zero which permits determination of the price level and the expected rate of inflation. Such a model is useful in examining once-and-for-all shocks in the nominal reserve base or in any other parameter. In the second variant of the model, we assume a nonzero rate of growth in the nominal reserve base, which permits a nonzero expected and actual rate of inflation. This model is also useful for examining comparative dynamics—that is, the effects of continuous changes in the nominal reserve base and, in particulr, effects of a change in the rate of growth—not simply a change in the level of the nominal reserve base.

In the third section, we explain the method of solution for the entire model—a method that permits us to use the results derived when we examined the corresponding financial sector in isolation—(that is, the results of chapter 3). The method permits equilibrium and disequilibrium analysis, but it assumes that the financial markets clear considerably faster than the goods market. Of course, for equilibrium analysis and for the comparative statics of the remaining chapters, the assumption of different speeds of response is immaterial.

In Stability, we derive the stability properties of both variants of the model and show that they are identical. Moreover, we prove that the entire model can be stable if a Cagan-type stability condition is satisfied. This Cagan stability condition imposes, as usual, an upper limit on the speed of revision of expectations of inflation.

In the next section of chapter 8, Comparative Statics, we derive the full-equilibrium, comparative-statics effects of one-shot shocks on the price level, on expected inflation, and on the interest rate. These shocks can be one-shot changes in a monetary instrument or one-shot stochastic shocks originating in the financial or in the real sector. The derived results are standard. We show, for example, that a one-shot increase in the nominal reserve base causes an equiproportionate increase in the price level but no change in expectations. The ultimate effect on the interest rate is zero. This means that the initial decrease in the interest rate is eventually matched by the increase in the interest rate caused by the consequent increase in the price level.

Finally, in Comparative Dynamics we examine the effects of a change in the *rate of growth* of the nominal reserve base on expected and actual inflation, on the real reserve base, and on the nominal and real interest rate. An important result is derived here, namely, that an increase in the rate of growth of the nominal reserve base will affect a real variable; in particular, it will diminish the real reserve base. In other words, money cannot be superneutral.

In chapter 9 we add the same real sector as in chapter 8 to the financial sector that relies on a market-determined deposit rate in addition to a market-determined bills interest rate. In other words, we extend the model and the analysis of chapters 4 and 5 to incorporate feedbacks from and to the real sector.

In the second section of chapter 9, Development of the Models, we undertake a detailed derivation of the two basic models: One concentrates on levels of monetary instruments and, hence, on the price level and zero equilibrium inflation (actual and expected): the other concentrates on a continuous change in the nominal reserve base that permits examination of nonzero, equilibrium, and expected and actual inflation.

In the next section, we examine the consistency of the two models by establishing their stability properties. As in the previous chapter, we establish that the models are stable provided some Cagan-type restriction is imposed on the speed of revision of expectations. Then we further examine the consistency of the models by deriving the comparative statics effects on the price level of one-shot shocks. We again show the expected result that an increase in the level of the nominal reserve base causes an equiproportionate increase in the price level and has no lasting effect on expected inflation. Similarly, any one-shot monetary shock—such as a change in the discount rate, a change in the administration of the dicount window, or a change in the demand for excess reserves—changes the price level by a percentage equal to the consequent percentage change in nominal reserves. Finally, we show that a positive shift in the *supply* of demand deposits—say, because of cost-reducing financial innovations—is contractionary because it reduces the equilibrium price level. This confirms a partial result noted earlier in chapter

5. Of course, a positive shift in the *demand* for demand deposits is also contractionary, as expected.

In the section titled The Price Level and Interest Rates—still using the model that assumes zero growth in the nominal reserve base and, hence, zero equilibrium inflation—we examine the effects of one-shot shocks on the interest rate. As expected, we find that no one-shot monetary shock has any lasting effect on the bills rate. Only a shock emanating from the real sector can affect this rate. This is not true for the second interest rate that we must also examine in this chapter, namely, the deposit rate. In particular, we find that one-shot shocks in the demand for or in the supply of demand deposits will have a lasting effect on the deposit rate; changes in the reserve-requirement ratio may have a lasting effect on the deposit rate; and one-shot changes in the remaining parameters will have no ultimate effect on the deposit rate.

In Inflation and Interest Rates, we examine the consequences of a change in the rate of growth of the nominal reserve base. Of course, we use the second variant of our model. We find that an increase in the rate of growth of the nominal reserve base by a given percentage will increase the expected and actual rate of inflation by the same percentage. Because of the way we constructed the real sector, however, the change in the rate of growth of the nominal reserve base will have no effect on the real bills rate; that is, it will increase the nominal bills rate by the same percentage.

However, we show that there are two nonneutralities. First, we find that an increase in the rate of growth of the nominal reserve base will erode the real reserve base. Second, we find that the same increase in the rate of growth of the nominal reserve base increases the nominal deposit rate by a greater percentage, thereby increasing the real deposit rate. In this sense, money—or more precisely, reserves—cannot be superneutral, as we also saw in chapter 8.

Chapter 10 compares the consequences of shocks under the two monetary regimes. Recall that in chapters 8 and 9 we showed that the effects of one-shot financial shocks on the price level, on expected inflation, and on the bills interest rate are identical whether the deposit rate is fixed or market determined. Therefore, in chapter 10 we shall compare the consequences of only one of the two kinds of one-shot shocks, namely, the ones originating in the real sector.

In One-Shot Shocks in the Real Sector, we show that the price level is less sensitive to and, therefore, more immune from shocks originating in the real sector when the deposit rate is market determined than when it is fixed. Next, we compare the consequences of the aforementioned continuous monetary shock. We show that an increase in the rate of growth of the nominal reserve base—and, hence, an increase in the equilibrium rate of inflation—reduces the real reserve base by less under a flexible deposit rate than under a fixed deposit rate. In other words, inflation erodes the real reserve base by less when the deposit rate is market determined than when it is fixed by the Central Bank.

However, the most important difference lies in the dynamic structure of the models. In chapters 8 and 9 we have seen that the two models are stable under some reasonable Cagan-type stability conditions. In the last section of chapter 10 we prove that the entire model is more stable under a market-determined than under a fixed-deposit rate. In particular, we prove that the economy moves faster from one equilibrium to another when the deposit rate is flexible than when it is fixed. This stability property has profound policy implications. With a flexible deposit rate, monetary policy is more effective in the sense that it achieves results faster. Of course, the effects of inadvertent shocks also disappear faster.

2 The New Financial Environment

The financial environment in which banks and other financial institutions operate has changed drastically during the last twenty years—and it continues to change. In this chapter, we set the stage for our analysis by examining institutional changes brought about by either private or governmental initiative. This examination is not meant to be exhaustive. Rather, we shall identify and concentrate on only those institutional changes that have altered fundamentally the financial system, especially as it concerns the conduct of monetary policy.

Three broad categories of institutional changes are responsible for the fundamental transformation in the financial environment. The first is financial innovations in the liabilities offered, in the array of assets held, and in the array and cost of services offered by the financial institutions. These financial innovations suggest that we are moving toward a regime of market-determined interest rates, especially of market-determined interest on demand and other deposits. In such a regime the supply of deposits, based on profit-maximizing decisions by financial institutions, is on equal footing with the demand for such deposits. This, as we shall see, has profound effects on the conduct of monetary policy. Until recently, the amount of demand deposits was considered—and in fact was—demand determined; supply did not matter. Hence innovations were thought of as shifting the demand curve for demand deposits alone: because the supply side did not matter, a cost-reducing innovation that shifts (increases) the supply curve for demand deposits does not matter either. However, when the supply of demand deposits is on equal footing with the demand, any shift on the supply side, caused by innovations, will have important consequences.

The trend toward market-determined interest rates initiated by the financial institutions themselves, has largely been ratified by the second category of changes, namely, regulatory changes. However, regulatory changes have also been undertaken at the initiative of regulatory agencies and legislatures. These regulatory changes—of which the Depository Institutions Deregulation and Monetary Control Act of 1980 is the most important—have permitted diversification in the structure of both the asset and the liability side of the balance sheets of financial institutions. But the unifying theme of this second category of institutional change is, again, the movement toward market-determined interest rates—both for the assets in the portfolios of financial institutions and for their deposits.

Finally, the third important institutional change arose when the Central Bank (that is, the Federal Reserve) changed its operating procedures in an effort to better control the quantity of money; it now targets base money (that is, nonborrowed reserves) rather than interest rates. The essence of this institutional change is that interest rates have resumed their asset-market-clearing role. Of course, this is consistent with the theme of the two preceding institutional changes—that the trend is toward market-determined interest rates. Moreover, because the new operating procedures rely on increased volatility in interest rates, financial innovations have intensified.

The next section examines financial innovations; then we examine regulatory changes; the fourth section examines the changes in the Federal Reserve's operating procedures. And the final section distills the key characteristics of the new financial environment and, based on these characteristics, presents both a stylized model of the disappearing current regime and a stylized model of the emerging monetary system.

Financial Innovations

Financial innovations accelerated in the 1970s and early 1980s. These innovations encompassed the array of liabilities offered by financial institutions, the array of assets that these same institutions hold, and the array of services offered by them.[1]

Liabilities of Financial Institutions

The decade of the 1970s and the early 1980s have witnessed an explosion in the array of liabilities offered to investors by financial institutions—both depository institutions and other financial intermediaries. We shall abstract a key common property of the seemingly bewildering array of liabilities offered by financial institutions. In general, these liabilities are more and more becoming "managed liabilities"; that is, they are designed and actively marketed by the suppliers—the financial institutions themselves—as opposed to being demand determined.

The trend toward managed liabilities, which has intensified recently, is attributable to three factors. First, new liabilities that circumvent the prohibition of interest on demand deposits have been invented and designed to compete with demand deposits. In this category we include overnight repurchase agreements (overnight RPs), negotiated orders of withdrawal (NOW accounts), automatic transfer services (ATS), credit-union share drafts and most important, recently, money market mutual funds (MMFs).

The second reason for the dramatic increase in the array of managed liabilities is attributable to efforts by financial institutions to compete with liabilities whose interest rates fall under Regulation Q ceilings. Examples of these managed liabilities are term repurchase agreements (term RPs), negotiable certificates of deposits (negotiable CDs), and money market certificates (MMCs).

Circumventing reserve requirements was the third reason for creating new managed liabilities. This involved switching from liabilities subject to high required reserve ratios to liabilities subject to low or even to zero reserve requirements. Of course, these efforts combined the two previous reasons. For example, trying to move out of demand deposits, which are subject to a zero deposit rate, also involves trying to move from high to low reserve-requirement ratios; after all, demand deposits are subject to the highest reserve-requirement ratio.

Circumventing the Prohibition of Interest on Demand Deposits. For member banks, prohibition of interest on demand deposits was mandated, by the Banking Act of 1933, and for nonmember banks by the Banking Act of 1935. This prohibition was only a part of legislation that imposed strict regulation on the financial industry in the aftermath of the Great Depression and the bankruptcy of thousands of financial institutions. This regulation in general and the prohibition of interest on demand deposits, in particular, aimed at protecting the safety and stability of financial institutions, especially by reducing their costs.

Of course, the zero ceiling on explicit pecuniary interest payments on demand deposits has caused excess supply of demand deposits. That is, at this binding ceiling the suppliers of demand deposits—the banks—were willing to offer more demand deposits than were demanded. According to the law of supply and demand, competition among banks normally eliminates this excess supply. But because banks were prohibited from competing by offering higher explicit, pecuniary interest payments, they were induced to offer higher implicit, usually nonpecuniary (in kind) payments. These implicit payments usually took the form of financial services offered.

Recent research has shown that for many years banks have paid substantial implicit interest on demand deposits. Although this implicit deposit rate was still binding—that is, below its estimated market clearing level—it has also been consistently rising during the last twenty years.[2]

But financial institutions have become increasing more innovative in circumventing the prohibition of interest on demand deposits. They have introduced other liabilities that for all practical purposes are demand deposits, but they nevertheless pay interest on them. We shall examine briefly the most important among these demand deposit substitutes.

NOW Accounts and Credit-Union Share Drafts—Other Checkables. NOW NOW accounts and credit-union share drafts are the instruments closest to traditional demand deposits. These are accounts on which interest is paid and accounts that can be withdrawn by negotiable drafts rather than, say, in person. The concept of a NOW account was born in Massachusetts in 1970 when a mutual savings bank petitioned that state's commissioner of banking for authority to offer NOW accounts. Although the petition was denied, in May 1972 the state supreme court overturned the denial, thereby establishing the authority of financial institutions to issue these accounts. In September of the same year state-chartered mutual savings banks in New Hampshire were authorized to offer NOW accounts. By 1976, depository institutions in all New England states were authorized by Congress to offer these accounts, and by 1979 New York and New Jersey were added to that list. Finally, nationwide introduction of NOW accounts was authorized as of December 31, 1980, by a provision of the Depository Institutions Deregulation and Monetary Control Act of 1980.

It must be noted that although interest is paid on NOW accounts and share drafts, the rate of interest is regulated by the authorities; it is not market determined. However, according to the provisions of the Depository Institutions Deregulation and Monetary Control Act of 1980, this interest rate will be totally deregulated by 1986. It is also interesting that this same act will nevertheless continue to prohibit the payment of interest on demand deposits. One must expect that these demand deposits will disappear or be reduced substantially, at least in their present form.

NOW accounts are the backbone of a new monetary category called "other checkable deposits," to distinguish them from the regular "demand deposits." Other checkables include, in addition to NOW accounts, credit-union share drafts, which first came into existence in 1974 and for which legislative authorization was granted by the MCA of 1980. This act also provided permanent authorization for the other important component of "other checkable deposits," namely, Automatic Transfer Service (ATS) accounts.[3]

ATSs came into existence in November 1978, when commercial banks were authorized to offer their customers automatic transfers from savings accounts that earn interest to checking accounts that, presumably, do not, thereby permitting in effect interest on demand deposits. This occurs because there is always a zero balance in the customer's checking account until the moment that funds must be transferred to cover a check, and then money is transferred from the savings account. Until recently the category "other checkable deposits" was reported separately and was part of M1-B but not of M1-A. But as of January 1982 this distinction between M1-A and M1-B has been dropped; M1-B is now considered as M1.

As expected, the introduction of these other checkables has cut deeply into the amount of demand deposits. In January 1982, for every dollar in demand deposits, thirty-five cents were in other checkables. By comparison, in June 1980 only eight cents were in other checkables for every dollar in demand deposits.

Of course, not all this shift came at the expense of demand deposits. Other instruments also have suffered. Savings and other time deposits, still under the same Regulation Q ceilings, became less desirable than before. Even such instruments as Treasury bills and credit (loans) have been influenced. In general, the introduction of other checkables has, in effect, increased the explicit deposit rate from zero, which has attracted wealth away from all other assets. This shift in wealth causes excess supply of all other assets, thereby raising their rate of return.[4]

Money Market Mutual Funds. Money market funds (MMFs) are mutual funds that invest in short-term money market instruments thereby earning market-determined rates and that allow redemption of shares by check. In effect, they are a combination of an investment asset and a checking account that earns interest—and market-determined interest at that. These funds were available as early as 1970, but they did not catch on until the mid-1970s; they have skyrocketed since 1979. By January 1982, $187 billion were invested in MMFs as compared with $12 billion in January 1979. Figure 2-1 traces the history of MMFs since 1960. The great appeal of these MMFs lies in both their "checkability" and their high interest rates, which are market rates minus a small management fee. Individuals or institutions can open an account for a sum as small as one-thousand dollars, but there is a lower limit to the size of checks (usually five-hundred dollars). The mutual funds pool these sums and invest in large-demonination instruments, such as Treasury bills, negotiable certificates of deposit, and commercial paper. Because certificates of deposit are issued by financial institutions and because commercial paper is usually underwritten by banks, the risk of these instruments is relatively small and so is the risk to the depositors.

The Federal Reserve subdivides MMFs into two categories: institutional and noninstitutional funds. Institutional funds are those that are available to institutional investors only; they are part of M3. The reasoning behind the exclusion of institutional MMFs from M2 seems to be the assumption that most competing assets to these institutional MMFs are in M3 and not in M2. On the other hand, noninstitutional funds are available to all investors and are recorded in two subcategories: the general purpose funds and the broker/dealer funds. Both subcategories are part of M2, again on the assumption that they are closer substitutes to components of this aggregate—namely, savings and small-time deposits—than to demand deposits and other checkables.[5]

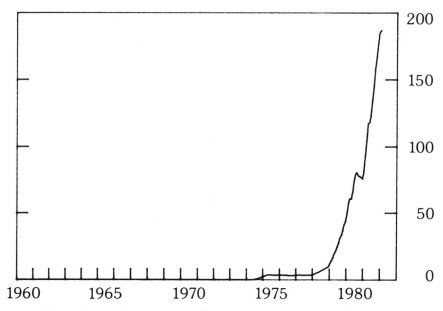

Source: *Federal Reserve Bulletin.*

Figure 2–1. History of Money Market Mutual Funds (MMFs), 1960–1982

Repurchase Agreements, RPs, and Federal Funds. Originally RPs or REPOs were exactly what their name suggests: They were sales of securities, in order to acquire funds, with the understanding that the securities would be repurchased for a specified price and at a specified time. They originated with brokers/dealers purchasing securities from the government and vice versa. Eventually, they came to be used as a source of funds by all financial institutions and in fact as a collaterized loan to financial institutions. In 1969, by an amendment of Regulation D, reserve requirements were imposed on RPs except when the collateral is Treasury securities.

RPs are a particularly useful instrument for nonfinancial firms and individuals to earn market interest rates for available funds and, of course, for financial institutions to acquire such funds. There are two basic kinds of RPs: short-term (usually overnight) RPs and long-term or simply term RPs. The difference is akin to the difference between demand deposits and time deposits. Overnight RPs are, in effect, demand deposit accounts drawn down to zero balance at the end of the day and invested in RPs so that these funds earn interest at the collaterized securities rate until the next day, when they revert to being deposits. Term RPs, of course, earn interest at the collaterized securities rate for the entire term of the agreement. For automatic transfer of deposits at the end of the day, the technique known as continuing contract is used. Overnight (and continuing contract) RPs are considered a component of M2, whereas term RPs are a component of M3. In the statistical releases, overnight RPs are lumped with overnight Eurodollars, which are those issued by Caribbean branches of member banks to U.S. residents, other than depository institutions and MMFs.

RPs fall in the category of purchased funds. Other purchased funds, similar to RPs, are federal funds, which are loans of immediately available funds, that is, funds that can be transferred or withdrawn during the same business day.[6] Like RPs, federal funds are not subject to Regulation Q ceilings. Unlike RPs, however, most federal funds transactions are not secured. When they are secured by a collateral of securities, the title to these securities is not transferred, thereby retaining the distinction between federal funds and repurchase agreements. Nevertheless, in the statistical releases federal funds are usually lumped with RPs. Since 1976 RPs have grown considerably, although recently (1981–1982) their growth rate has slowed down. Figure 2-2 traces the history of overnight RPs alone since 1960.

Circumventing Regulation Q Ceilings. We have seen that wholesale term RPs are considered a component of M3, which also includes large time deposits. Because these RPs pay market levels of interest rates, they are a

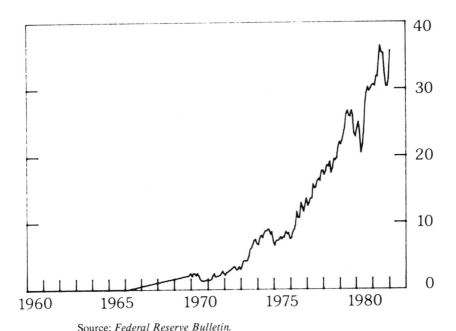

Source: *Federal Reserve Bulletin.*

Figure 2–2. History of Overnight RPs, 1960–1982

means by which financial institutions can circumvent Regulation Q ceilings on savings and on other time deposits. In recent years, we have witnessed the birth of retail RPs, which are small denomination RPs for the benefit of individuals. Because term RPs are similar in structure to overnight RPs, which we have already examined, we shall not examine them further here. Instead we shall concentrate first on the primary tool of circumventing Regulation Q ceilings—namely, the negotiable certificates of deposit (CD)—and second on the money market certificates (MMC).

Negotiable CDs. Negotiable Certificates of Deposit, as the name suggests, are certificates for funds deposited for a specified period of time, of minimum duration of thirty days and for a specified rate of interest. Were it not for the fact that these certificates are *negotiable*—that is, marketable—they would not differ from any other large-denomination time deposits. Negotiable CDs were born in 1961 when the First National City Bank of New York introduced these liabilities and when simultaneously a major securities dealer, the Discount Corporation of New York, announced the establishment of a secondary market for these liabilities. The establishment of the secondary market was, of course, instrumental because it effectively reduces the maturity of a CD, which by law is a minimum of thirty days. Now, if a corporation wants to hold a CD with a maturity of only three days, it simply buys in the secondary market a twenty-seven-day-old CD with a thirty-day original maturity.

When first introduced, negotiable CDs were subject to both Regulation D and Regulation Q; that is, they were subject to a reserve requirement and subject to an interest-rate ceiling. At present, negotiable CDs are subject to reserve requirements but not subject to a Regulation Q ceiling. Because CDs are for deposits of large denominations, it is clear that they are aimed (and were aimed from the very beginning) at attracting funds from corporations. CDs have grown to be a substantial source of funds for financial institutions. It is estimated that, as of December 1980, CDs constitute more than 30 percent of interest-bearing liabilities of large commercial banks and 15 percent of interest-bearing liabilities of small banks. Figure 2–3 traces the history of CDs since 1960.

Money Market Certificates (MMCs) and Small Saver Certificates (SSCs). MMCs are nonnegotiable certificates of deposits with a minimum amount of $10,000 that bear interest almost identical to that of a six-month Treasury bill. Three important properties are the following: their small denomination, which makes them available to the average household; their six-month maturity, which makes them similar to time deposits; and their market-level interest rate, which makes them in effect immune from Regulation Q ceilings.

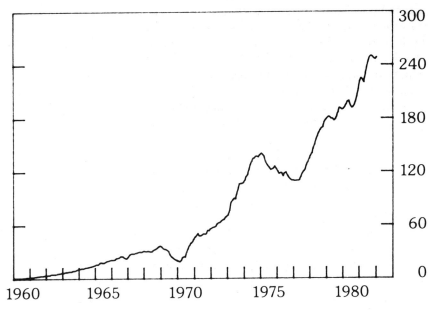

Source: *Federal Reserve Bulletin.*
Figure 2–3. History of Certificates of Deposit (CDs), 1960–1982

The interest rate on these certificates is fixed for the duration of the certificate, but it is variable at the time of the purchase, reflecting that week's Treasury auction of six-month bills. MMCs have become a major source of funds for small banks and for thrift institutions (about 30 percent of their interest-bearing liabilities in 1980). Even for large commercial banks they represent a significant source of funds: in 1980 about 16 percent of their interest-bearing liabilities.[7]

SSCs are similar to MMCs. Like MMCs, they are nonnegotiable certificates with a yield tied to that of Treasury securities; they are currently tied to the (variable) yield of thirty-month Treasury securities. SSCs have become a significant source of funds for small commercial banks and for thrift institutions (8 to 9 percent of their interest-bearing liabilities in 1980) but, as expected, not for large commercial banks.[8]

As a summary, we can abstract from the seemingly bewildering array of new liabilities, caused mostly by innovations, the following key characteristic: An ever-increasing proportion of the liabilities of financial institutions consists of deposits earning close to market-determined rates. In other words, an increasing proportion of the liabilities of the financial sector are "managed liabilities"—that is, liabilities actively sought by their suppliers, the financial

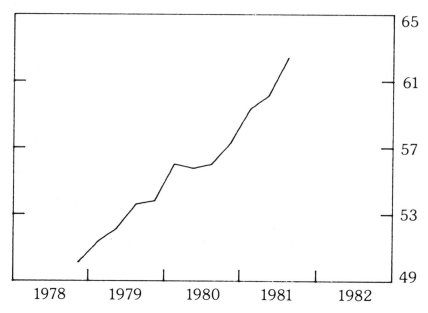

Source: *Federal Reserve Bulletin.*

Figure 2–4. History of Percentage of Net Liabilities Not Subject to Interest
Prohibitions or Interest Ceilings, 1978–1982

institutions themselves. This is shown in figure 2–4 that traces, from the
fourth quarter of 1978 to the third quarter of 1981, the percentage of
commercial bank net liabilities[9] that are *not* subject to prohibitions or ceilings
on the payment of interest. In less than three years this percentage rose from
50 percent to 62.4 percent.[10] This chart also illustrates vividly the
diminishing importance of demand and savings deposits as a source of funds
to the financial sector.[11]

As an abstraction, we can say, then, that changes in the composition of
the liability side of financial institutions suggest that we are moving toward a
monetary regime with market-determined interest on demand and other
deposits. For this reason, we shall assume in this work that there is only one
kind of liability—demand deposits, or simply deposits.[12] This assumption is
not made mainly for simplicity but rather as a way of cutting through the
maze of unnecessary complication implied by the existence of several
measures of monetary aggregates. Such a multiplicity of monetary
aggregates—necessitating continuous monitoring of shifts from one aggregate
to another—eventually and unnecessarily obstructs the vision of the
policymaker.

Assets

The asset side of financial institutions also has undergone a substantial restructuring, though not as far-reaching as the liability side. One character- istic common to this change in the structure of assets held is a shortening of the maturity of these assets to bring them more in line with the maturity of liabilities. We saw that the movement in liabilities is toward more short-term debt with market-determined interest rates. In periods of rising interest rates, financial institutions incur substantial losses unless they change (that is, shorten) the maturity of the assets held.

This match-funding activity led to diversification of the credit supplied by financial intermediaries. For example, for thrifts it led to the birth of adjustable-rate mortgages. Regulatory authorities had to permit this kind of loan to prevent the collapse of thrift institutions. Table 2–1 traces the percentage of home-mortgage loans made by thrift institutions at adjustable rates for the period that the Federal Home Loan Bank Board has kept these data. We see that for the fourth quarter of 1981 this has exceeded 40 percent. On the other hand, for banks, the efforts to reduce the risk of interest-rate variability concentrated on providing long-term loans with variable interest rates to reflect the market-determined rates on their liabilities. This variability in loan rates was achieved by tying the loans rate to either the prime rate or to the London Interbank Offer Rate (LIBOR). Floating-rate long-term loans are now the rule for banks. As is shown in table 2–2, the estimate of the percentage of long-term commercial and industrial loans made at a floating rate at all commercial banks has risen from an average of

Table 2–1
Proportion of Conventional Home-Mortgage Loans Closed with Adjustable-Rate Features
(percent)

	Type of Lender	
Period	*Savings and Loans*	*Mutual Savings Banks*
1981		
September	31.9	53.1
October	35.1	53.8
November	37.7	50.3
December	40.5	61.8
1982		
January	45.3	43.6

Source: Federal Home Loan Bank Board (FHLBB) unpublished data for first mortgages financing home purchases.

Table 2–2
Percentage of Dollar Amount of Long-Term Commercial and Industrial
Loans Made at Floating Rates at All Banks

Year	Percent
1977	48.60
1978	51.90
1979	57.40
1980	69.25
1981	72.00

Source: Federal Reserve Bulletin.

48.6 percent in 1977 to an average of 72 percent in 1981—almost a 50-percent increase.[13]

If anything can be extracted from this evidence, it is that the trend toward more uniformity (homogeneity) on the asset side of the balance sheets of financial institutions reflects the market-determined interest rates on their short-term liabilities. In other words, financial innovations have tended to blur the distinctions between the different assets that financial institutions hold.

It is partly for this reason that our stylized model examines only one kind of asset; we shall refer to this asset collectively as earning assets of financial institutions or simply as T-bills. However, we must emphasize that this is not the primary distinguishing feature of this book. We could have examined—as we do elsewhere—a richer version of assets, as in Tobin-Brainard.[14]

Cost-Reducing Innovations in Services Offered

Innovations in the services offered have been very visible and have received a lot of attention in the literature. Most of these innovations are attributed to technological progress in data processing—that is, in storing and transmitting information. These innovations permitted the provision, by financial institutions, of cash-management services to nonfinancial firms and to the public. Moreover, the electronic funds transfer system (EFTS) is becoming more standard, and point of sale (POS) terminals (or remote-service units [RSUs]) have made their appearance. POSs and RSUs are terminals that are linked to bank computers and are located in retail and in other stores so that automatic payments for purchases can be made.

All of these technological innovations have one common characteristic: They reduce the public's need of or reliance on demand deposits for transactions purposes. In fact, these and other innovations have always been mentioned as the primary reason for the consistent overprediction of the narrow monetary aggregates. The explanation offered is the following: Financial innovation reduces the need for holding transaction balances, thereby shifting inward the demand for demand deposits. With an upward sloping supply of money, because of borrowed reserves, the fall in the demand curve reduces the observed quantity of demand deposits and, therefore, the observed quantity of narrow monetary aggregates. Of course, additional reasons for the inward shift in money demand have been offered. The most prominent among these is the one based on financial innovations in liabilities previously mentioned. The creation of these instruments—that is, those that are part of the higher aggregates—shifts funds away from demand deposits, thereby shifting inward the narrow money-demand curve.[15]

All these explanations rely on the demand side for demand deposits. Supply-side effects of innovations have not been examined previously because the traditional monetary framework assumes that demand deposits are demand determined. This is the consequence of a fixed and binding interest rate on demand deposits. In other words, the deposit rate is fixed at such a low rate—say, at zero—that banks gladly offer whatever amount of demand deposits is demanded by the nonfinancial sector. In this framework, the supply side plays only a passive role. Another implication of technological progress, however, is the cost reduction in the services offered by financial institutions, which will shift the *supply function* for demand deposits. But if supply does not matter, a shift in supply will not have any effect. An important aspect of this work is that it puts the supply side on equal footing with the demand side.[16] In chapter 4 we shall establish that in the emerging regime, in which the deposit rate is market determined, the supply of demand deposits by profit-maximizing financial institutions is an increasing function of net profitability of deposits; this profit rate is equal to the marginal cost of servicing the deposits. Hence cost-reducing financial innovations shift the supply of demand deposits; this shift has profound effects for monetary control.

Regulatory Changes: The Depository Institutions Deregulation and Monetary Control Act of 1980

We have already mentioned several provisions of the Depository Institutions Deregulation and Monetary Control Act of 1980—especially those that ratified innovations initiated by the financial institutions themselves. But this act, signed into law on March 31, 1980, is so far-reaching that it constitutes the charter of the new regulatory environment in which financial institutions operate. It has been hailed as the most significant banking and financial legislation since the 1930s—even since the Federal Reserve Act of 1913 itself.

Of particular importance and interest for our purposes are the first five titles of the act.[17] Title I, or the Monetary Control Act of 1980, has blurred significantly the distinction between member and nonmember banks by phasing in uniform reserve requirements for all depository institutions and by providing and charging fees for services rendered by the Federal Reserve System to all depository institutions. In fact, from the standpoint of reserve requirements, all depository institutions—not only banks—are alike.

Titles II and III of the act deal with the liability side of depository institutions. Title II, or the Depository Institutions Deregulation Act of 1980, phases out Regulation Q ceilings on interest rates that may be paid on savings and time deposits. This provision essentially eliminates the distinction between those deposits and "managed liabilities." Depository institutions may then—by 1986—compete by offering higher interest rates to attract such deposits.

Title III, or the Consumer Checking Account Equity Act of 1980, authorized the nationwide introduction of interest-earning checking accounts as of December 31, 1980. At first this interest is fixed at 5.25 percent, but this ceiling will be lifted by 1986. This provision will transform checking accounts also into managed liabilities.

Titles IV and V deal with the asset side of financial institutions. Title IV permits substantial diversification of assets held by *nonbank* financial institutions. This provision further blurs the distinction among financial institutions by overriding state usury laws that limit interest rates paid on a variety of loans. Taken together, Titles IV and V make the interest rates charged by all financial institutions reflect current market conditions.

Title I: Uniform Reserve Requirements, Provision and Pricing of Services

This title was designed to improve the Federal Reserve's ability to conduct monetary policy—hence its name, the Monetary Control Act. There are three major provisions in Title I: (1) universal reserve requirements, (2) universal provision and pricing of Federal Reserve services, and (3) data-reporting requirements.

Reserve Requirements. Title I extends reserve requirements to all depository institutions, not simply to member banks. These reserve requirements will be phased in by 1988 for nonmember institutions and by 1984 for member banks. When fully implemented, reserve requirements will differ by the category of deposits rather than by membership or nonmembership in the Federal Reserve System.

Universal reserve requirements will blur the distinction between member and nonmember institutions and solve or at least alleviate the membership problem. Until now only member banks were required by the Federal Reserve to hold any reserves; reserves are either deposited with the Federal Reserve System and earn no interest or are held in the bank's own vault and, again, earn no interest. This reserve requirement is akin to taxation. For example, if there is a k-percent reserve requirement for every dollar deposited, only $1-k$ cents can be used as a loan. And if the interest rate on the loan is i percent, then the true after-tax (that is, after-reserve requirement) interest rate accruing to the bank is $(1-k)i$.

Title I makes membership in the Federal Reserve less burdensome by reducing the reserve requirement k. On the other hand, nonmember financial institutions will see their reserve requirements increase. (For very small financial institutions [that is, with deposits of $25 million or less] the reserve requirement is likely to be nonbinding at 3 percent.) Thus there will be less incentive for member banks to defect to nonmembership status.

To further strengthen monetary control, Title I permits the Federal Reserve Board to impose *any* level of reserve requirements on any liability of depository institutions for up to 180 days—if extraordinary circumstances require it. Furthermore, if it is "essential for the conduct of monetary policy," the board is permitted to impose an interest-bearing "supplemental reserve requirement" up to 4 percent on every depository institution.

Provision and Pricing of Federal Reserve Services. Until this act, Federal Reserve services—such as provision of currency and coin, check clearing and collection, wire services, automated clearing-house services, settlement, securities safekeeping, and float—were provided to member banks free of charge. Title I requires the Federal Reserve to charge for these and for any new services offered. It also requires that all services be priced explicitly and, more important, that all such services be available to nonmember depository institutions on the same terms that they are available to member banks. The title further requires the Federal Reserve to publish a fee schedule (which has already been published) and to implement fees by September 1981. It is clear that the provision and pricing of Federal Reserve services further blurred the distinction between financial institutions.

Data Reporting. Finally, Title I requires all depository institutions to report their assets and liabilities at such intervals as the Board of Governors of the Federal Reserve System may prescribe. Of course, this reporting requirement is a consequence of extending the reserve requirement to cover all depository institutions.

Titles II and III: Liabilities of Depository Institutions:
Phasing out of Regulation Q Ceilings on Interest Rates
and Interest on Checking Accounts

Title II: Abolition of Regulation Q Ceilings. Title II, or the Depository Institutions Deregulation Act of 1980, reverses the fifty-year history of interest-rate regulation. It states:

> It is the purpose of this title to provide for the orderly phase-out and the ultimate elimination of the limitations on the maximum rates of interest and dividends which may be paid on deposits and accounts by depository institutions by extending the authority to impose such limitations for 6 years, subject to specific standards designed to ensure a phase-out of such limitations to market rates of interest.

In other words, the Regulation Q ceilings on interest rates will be eliminated within six years. The actual timetable of the phaseout is left mostly to the discretion of the Depository Institutions Deregulation Committee (DIDC), consisting of the Secretary of the Treasury, the chairman of the Board of Governors of the Federal Reserve System, the chairman of the Board of Directors of FDIC, the chairman of the Federal Home Loan Bank Board, and the chairman of the National Credit Union Administration Board as voting members, and the Comptroller of the Currency as a nonvoting member.

It is the stated purpose of Title II that depository institutions may compete for funds by raising the interest rates they offer and that depositors—particularly those with modest savings—are entitled to receive a market rate of return on their savings. When the phaseout is complete, the active solicitation of funds by depository institutions will have turned all such deposit accounts into managed liabilities.

Title III: Interest on Checking Accounts. Title III, or the Consumer Checking Account Equity Act of 1980, authorizes the nationwide introduction of interest-bearing checking accounts as of December 31, 1980. In particular, most depository institutions are authorized to offer NOW accounts. Banks may continue to offer ATS accounts. Credit unions are authorized to offer share drafts. Deposit insurance at banks, savings and loan associations, and at credit unions is increased from $40,000 to $100,000. In addition, savings and loan associations are authorized to establish RSUs.

It must be noted that the term *demand deposits* will continue to mean checking accounts on which interest is not paid because the 1933 prohibition of payment of interest on demand deposits remains in effect. The quantity of funds in demand deposits is expected to shrink considerably, unless, of course, implicit payments of interest continue.

The goals of Title III are: First, to make market rates of interest available to individuals and to nonprofit organizations so that they may be on equal footing with corporations, which already have achieved this goal. Second, to provide new sources of funds for depository institutions by allowing them to compete in terms of interest rates offered. This competition in terms of interest rates will be fully implemented by 1986 when the currently pegged (at 5.25 percent) rate on checking accounts will be totally variable.

Therefore, we see that Titles II and III together effectively eliminate the distinction between deposits, making them, in effect, all managed liabilities.

Titles IV and V: Asset Diversification and Abolition of Usury Laws

Titles IV and V focus on the asset side of depository institutions. Title IV encourages shortening the maturity of the assets of nonbank financial institutions by permitting diversification of the assets in their portfolios. For savings and loans associations this title permits:

1. Investment in consumer loans, commercial paper, and corporate debt securities (up to 20 percent of their assets).
2. Investment in shares of certificates of investment companies whose portfolios are restricted to the same instruments that savings and loans associations are allowed to hold.
3. Investment in education and community development (up to 5 percent).
4. Issuing of credit cards and credit on credit cards.

For mutual savings banks Title IV permits:

1. Investment in commercial, corporate, and business loans (up to 5 percent).
2. Acceptance of demand deposits related to their commercial, corporate, and business-loan activities.

These measures were initiated mainly to prevent further deterioration in the health of the thrift institutions. Earlier regulation that segmented the financial industry, combined with rising interest rates, created a problem for the thrift institutions, which experienced an imbalance between the maturities of the asset and the liability side of their balance sheets. The thrifts by law specialized in mortgages, an asset with a long initial maturity. But their liabilities were deposits with much shorter maturity. The situation has deteriorated as new liability instruments that paid rising market rates were introduced and authorized in a piecemeal fashion. Of these liabilities, the six-month money market certificate (MMC) was instrumental in further reducing the maturity of the liability side and further enhancing the imbalance. The diversification of the asset side, introduced by Title IV, permits *match-funding*—that is, shortening the maturity of one side to match the shorter maturity of the other side of the balance sheets of thrifts.

Title V overrides existing state usury laws that limit the interest rates financial institutions may charge on loans. Title V also overrides state laws that limit interest rates on deposits. This establishes market determination of interest rates that financial institutions charge as well as offer.

Change in the Federal Reserve's Operating Procedures

The third important institutional change that has transformed the financial environment concerns the Federal Reserve's own operating procedures. Since October 6, 1979, the Federal Reserve has switched from targeting interest rates to targeting reserve aggregates (that is, nonborrowed reserves, also called the reserve base) as a means of achieving its targets for the monetary aggregates. The change in operating procedures involves an interchange between instruments and endogenous variables. Under the earlier operating procedures, the federal funds (or bills) interest rate was an instrument, or exogenous variable, whereas the reserve base (that is, nonborrowed reserves) was an endogenous variable. Under that procedure, the Federal Reserve fixed the federal funds interest rate at whatever level was thought necessary and sufficient to achieve its target of a monetary aggregate (say, M1). In turn, the quantity of nonborrowed reserves was allowed to move to whatever level was consistent with asset market clearance at the selected (that is, fixed) federal funds rate of interest. In practice, of course, a small variation around the selected level of interest rate was permitted.

Since October 6, 1979, however, the operating procedure relies on selecting the quantity of nonborrowed reserves that is necessary (and sufficient) to achieve the monetary target. The federal funds interest rate is then allowed to reach whatever level is consistent with the selected reserve aggregate and with market clearance. In other words, under the new operating procedures, the federal funds rate and other interest rates have resumed their role as endogenous, market-clearing, variables.[18] Of course, this switch toward market determination of interest rates is in line with the implications of the other two institutional changes. Furthermore, the pegging of reserves, rather than of interest rates, suggests more interest variability under the new regime than under the old. Financial innovations that allow financial institutions to take advantage of these characteristics or that protect these institutions from them are, of course, expected and are in line with our earlier observations.

Beginning with chapter 3, the analysis in this book will be conducted exclusively in terms of the new, reserves-oriented operating procedure. For this reason we shall examine briefly and compare the implications of the two operating regimes in the remainder of this section. We shall highlight the change in the structure of the financial system that has occurred because of the switch to the new operating procedure, and we shall provide some examples of the implications of this change in the structure. The underlying model for our discussion is a financial system that represents the current, fixed-deposit-rate regime, but it is a system with four asset markets, namely, equity capital, bank loans, interest-bearing government securities (T-bills), and reserves. Financial equilibrium requires that all these asset markets be cleared. But only three of these markets need to be examined explicitly for the immediate determination of three endogenous variables.

Now, which variables are endogenous and which are exogenous, or policy instruments, depends on the operating procedures that are followed. Under the old regime the federal funds rate, which we identify with the T-bill rate, r_B, was not allowed to move according to the law of supply and demand to clear the bills market; the amount of nonborrowed reserves, R, performed this function. Under the new regime the federal funds (or bills) rate moves to clear the bill market whereas R is an exogenous variable, that is, an instrument. Of course, the monetary system possesses other instruments also, such as the discount rate, d, and the reserve requirement, k. In the model under discussion the equity rate, r_K, and the bank loan rate, r_L, are market-clearing endogenous variables under either the federal funds or the reserves operating procedure.

Given these proximate, market-clearing endogenous variables—that is, given the triplet, $(R,\ r_L,\ r_K)$, under the federal funds operating procedure, and given the triplet $(r_B,\ r_L,\ r_K)$ under the new, reserves-operating procedures—we can determine other endogenous variables, such as demand deposits, D; required reserves, $R_R = kD$; borrowed reserves, R_B; and total reserves, $R_T = R + R_B$.

The relation between instruments and endogenous variables for the old regime is captured by the following schema:

$$\textit{Instruments} \quad \textit{Endogenous Variables}$$

$$\left.\begin{array}{c} r_B \\ d \\ k \end{array}\right\} \rightarrow R,\ r_L,\ r_K,\ D,\ R_R,\ R_B,\ R_T$$

We can also depict schematically the new operating procedure:

$$\begin{array}{c} Instruments \quad Endogenous\ Variables \\[6pt] \left.\begin{array}{c} R \\ d \\ k \end{array}\right\} \ \rightarrow\ r_B,\ r_L,\ r_K,\ D,\ R_R,\ R_B,\ R_T \end{array}$$

We should note that r_B and R change positions when the operating procedure changes.

Open-Market Operations

We can compare the money-creation mechanisms of the two regimes by first examining an expansionary open-market operation. Under the new regime this is achieved by an increase in nonborrowed reserves, R, effected by a purchase of bills by the Federal Reserve. The purchase of government securities by the Federal Reserve causes excess demand for those securities which, in turn, forces the bill rate (that is, federal funds rate) down so that the market may be cleared. The fall in the bill rate makes loans and capital more desirable assets, thereby causing excess demands in those markets; these excess demands are eliminated when the loan rate and the equity rate also fall. The fall in these rates and, especially, in the bill (federal funds) rate reduces borrowed reserves because the "spread," $r_B - d$, between the bill rate and the discount rate narrows. This establishes a negative relation between borrowed and nonborrowed reserves, $\Delta R_B/\Delta R < 0$, which has important implications for precision (or its lack) in monetary control The increase in the one component of total reserves, namely in nonborrowed reserves, R, causes a decrease in its other component, R_B. However, total reserves increase and, hence, demand deposits also increase. Therefore, we have established these results,

$$\frac{\Delta r_B}{\Delta R} < 0, \quad \frac{\Delta r_L}{\Delta R} < 0, \quad \frac{\Delta r_K}{\Delta R} < 0,$$

and

$$\frac{\Delta R_B}{\Delta R} < 0, \quad \frac{\Delta R_T}{\Delta R} > 0, \quad \frac{\Delta D}{\Delta R} > 0,$$

as well as the process by which these results were derived.

Let us again examine an expansionary open-market operation, but now under a federal funds, or bill, rate operating procedure.

The Federal Reserve first lowers the target bill rate. To achieve this lower target rate, the Federal Reserve must create excess demand for bills. It does this by buying bills in the open market—that is, by increasing nonborrowed reserves until the target bill rate is achieved. We have therefore established. $\Delta R/\Delta r_B < 0$. On the other hand, we could have developed our explanation by relying on the market for reserves: To achieve the lower target bill rate, the Federal Reserve must create excess supply of reserves; that is, the quantity of nonborrowed reserves must rise. However, regardless of the explanation we give, we have illustrated that the old (federal funds) regime relies on *quantity adjustment* whereas the new regime relies on *interest-rate adjustment*.

Continuing the exercise, we see next that the lower bill rate again causes excess demands in the other two asset markets and, hence, lowers their rates. Furthermore, the spread, $r_B - d$, again narrows, lowering the amount of borrowed reserves. But we can show that total reserves and, hence, deposits, increase. Thus we have established these (algebraic) results:

$$\frac{\Delta R}{\Delta r_B} < 0, \quad \frac{\Delta r_L}{\Delta r_B} > 0, \quad \frac{\Delta r_K}{\Delta r_B} > 0$$

$$\frac{\Delta R_B}{\Delta r_B} > 0, \quad \frac{\Delta R_T}{\Delta r_B} < 0, \quad \frac{\Delta D}{\Delta r_B} < 0.$$

Comparing the results of the two regimes we see that, as far as open-market operations are concerned, the two operating procedures are *analytically* similar but *operationally* different. This difference has much to do with the negative relation between borrowed and nonborrowed reserves, $\Delta R_B/\Delta R$. Precision of monetary control depends significantly on recognizing and employing this relation because a serious underestimation—say—of borrowed reserves causes a serious error in the amount of nonborrowed reserves deemed necessary to achieve a particular target. This problem is very acute under the new regime. Of course, a negative relation between borrowed and nonborrowed reserves was present under the old, federal funds, operating regime, as we can infer from $\Delta R/\Delta r_B < 0$ and $\Delta R_B/\Delta r_B > 0$, but this problem was minor or even nonexistent then. The negative relation between borrowed reserves and nonborrowed reserves is derived from the effect of nonborrowed reserves on the interest rates coupled with the effect of interest rates on borrowed reserves. But under the old regime, the interest rate was pegged as a parameter and hence borrowed reserves were fairly stable, whereas the new regime relies on the variability, and even the volatility, in interest rates that results in greater volatility of borrowed reserves. It is not surprising, then, that precision of monetary control—that is, achieving monetary targets—hinges on successful forecasting of the borrowings relation.[19]

Discount-Rate Policy

The introduction of nonborrowed-reserves targeting that relies on interest-rate adjustments rather than on quantity adjustment to clear markets has had an even greater impact on the structure of the system when we consider supplemental instruments of monetary control such as the discount rate. We can see this change in structure by examining separately the effects of an increase in the discount rate under each regime.

Under the new regime an increase in the discount rate—other things being equal—narrows the spread, $r_B - d$, which reduces borrowed reserves, thereby causing excess demand for reserves. Of course, the bills, or securities, market registers excess supply because the increase in the discount rate lowers the profitability of bills and, hence, decreases their demand. This excess supply of bills (and excess demand for reserves) moves the bill rate, r_B, upward to clear the market and consequently affects the other rates—that is the loan rate, r_L, and the equity rate, r_K—which also rise in sympathy as we saw in the preceding exercise.

But under a federal funds rate regime—that is, under a regime that relies on quantity adjustment—the excess supply of bills must be eliminated by a reduction in the quantity of bills supplied, or available, to the public. This is accomplished by a purchase of bills by the Fed in the open market, that is, by an increase in nonborrowed reserves. The result that under a federal funds rate operating procedure an increase (decrease) in the discount rate must be accompanied by an increase (decrease) in nonborrowed reserves has serious repercussions on precision of monetary control: Because supplemental policies, such as discount-rate policy, have always been used in conjunction with the primary instrument—open-market operations—the accompanying endogenous change in nonborrowed reserves has contaminated the data. In particular, it has distorted the multiplier relation between nonborrowed reserves and money and, hence, it has rendered multipliers estimated from data generated by the old regime less useful or even useless as a guide for current conduct of monetary policy.[20]

NOW Accounts

It is interesting to combine the innovation of nationwide introduction of NOW accounts with the new operating procedures. Until December 31,

1980, NOW accounts were authorized only in the New England states. The nationwide introduction of this account, with a 5.25-percent deposit rate, amounted to an increase from one fixed deposit rate to another.

The increase in the deposit rate makes all other assets less desirable, thereby causing excess supply. Under the new operating procedure, this implies that all three interest rates rise to clear the markets. Of course, the increase in the interest rates raises borrowed reserves and, hence, total reserves and deposits. This is precisely what happened within one month from the nationwide introduction of NOW accounts.[21] On the other hand, under the old regime the excess supply of Treasury securities, or bills, and the consequent excess demand for reserves must be eliminated by a quantity adjustment, a reduction in the supply of bills, and an increase in nonborrowed reserves, that is, by an open-market purchase of bills by the Fed. When NOW accounts were introduced in the New England states the Federal Reserve was still following a federal funds operating procedure. Therefore, if one relied on past experience to predict the consequences of the nationwide introduction of NOW accounts, one would have committed errors, because in January 1981 the Fed was already following reserve targeting.

A Stylized Financial System

In the preceding sections we distilled three important characteristics of the new financial environment. Two of these characteristics concern the trend toward market-determined interest rates. First, on the liability side of the balance sheet of financial institutions, there is an array of deposits that are mostly *managed liabilities* and whose interest rates are largely market determined. Second, on the asset side of the balance sheet there are assets whose rates of return are also market determined. Third, the distinction between financial institutions is blurred. Although there is still considerable market segmentation and specialization of financial institutions in terms of the sources of funds and in types of loans financed with those funds, there is far greater and increasing homogeneity among financial institutions than existed in the decade of the 1970s.

These characteristics will form the backbone in our modeling of a stylized financial system. We shall assume three sectors: the Federal Reserve System, the nonfinancial sector (that is, nonfinancial businesses and individuals), and the financial sector. We shall assume that the financial sector consists of only one kind of financial institutions, collectively called banks, or banking firms. Unless we explicitly state otherwise, the terms *bank, banking firm, financial institution,* and *depository institution* will be used interchangeably in this work.

The balance sheet of this financial sector resembles the following:

Balance Sheet of Financial Sector

Assets	Liabilities
Earning Assets	Deposits
Reserves	Borrowed reserves

In words, we assume that the asset side of financial institutions consists of reserves and of a single kind of earning asset which will, occasionally, also be called T-bills. This assumption of a single kind of earning asset is an abstraction, an idealization, of the characteristic that there is increasingly greater uniformity in the assets of financial institutions. However, this assumption of a single earning asset is made only for convenience, and it is not essential to either the framework of our financial system or the results of this analysis; elsewhere we examine a multiple-asset framework.[22]

On the liability side of their balance sheets, financial institutions have borrowed reserves (that is, reserves from the Central Bank) and a single category of deposits. In the new and emerging financial system, those deposits will be considered as managed liabilities. In the old and fast-disappearing financial system these deposits are treated as demand-determined liabilities. The assumption of a single category of deposit liabilities is made not primarily to simplify but rather to avoid the need to examine issues associated with shifts between or among different kinds of monetary aggregates. Although these issues are sometimes important, they may entangle policymakers in a maze of irrelevant detail that prevents clear vision and identification of the most important issues.

Notes

1. For more detailed and, in several instances, more specialized treatments of recent financial innovations, the reader is referred to W.L. Silber (1975); P. Cagan (1979); R.D. Porter, T.D. Simpson, and E. Mauskopf (1979); M. Goodfriend, J. Parthemos, and B. Summers (1980); T.D. Simpson and R.D. Porter (1980); D. Hester (1981); M. Arak (1982); and A.M. Solomon (1982).

2. See, for example, R.J. Barro and A.M. Santomero (1972); Board of Governors of the Federal Reserve System (1977); and R. Startz (1979).

3. As of 1980, there is one more item in "other checkables"—namely, demand deposits at thrift institutions. Until recently, in general only commercial banks were allowed to offer demand deposits.

4. See M.G. Hadjimichalakis (1980a, 1981a).

5. For an extensive examination of MMFs see M. Dotsey, S. Englander, and J.C. Partlan (1982). New issues related to MMFs are developing so fast that even that paper is becoming dated. For example, the Federal Reserve now recommends the imposition of reserve requirements on MMFs. (See L.E. Gramley [1982]). More important, a new innovation is unfolding—namely "sweep" accounts between MMFs and depository institutions or even between MMFs and retail businesses. Under such agreements, demand balances are "swept" into MMFs at the end of the day, thereby earning MMF interest rates and also circumventing reserve requirements. Such arrangements are not limited to MMFs, however. Sweep accounts for "leftover" demand balances can be arranged and, in fact, are arranged for a variety of interest-yielding instruments.

6. The term *federal* reflects the origin of these funds: They were transactions between banks of balances held at the Federal Reserve. Now the term *federal funds* is broader: It encompasses transfers of immediately available funds, whether or not they are at the Federal Reserve and whether or not they are between banks.

7. See B.N. Opper (1981).

8. See B.N. Opper (1981).

9. Net liabilities are found by netting the liabilities of banks to each other.

10. We have defined "net liabilities *not* subject to prohibitions or interest ceilings" so that they include "small time deposits." A small fraction of these deposits is subject to fixed ceilings and the rest is subject to either no ceiling or subject to market-determined ceilings. The bulk of small time deposits consists of MMCs (and, secondarily, of SSCs) which are subject to market-determined ceilings. It is because they pay (primarily short-term) market interest rates that we chose to consider them as managed liabilities. Besides, there is strong evidence that a significant number of financial institutions offer rates *below* the ceilings. At any rate, had we excluded all small time deposits, the percentage of net liabilities not subject to prohibitions or ceilings would have risen from 28 percent in 1978 to 36 percent in 1981. We have used data from the *Federal Reserve Bulletin*.

11. For the history of the importance of demand and savings deposits from 1960 to 1978 see M. Goodfriend, J. Parthemos, and B. Summers (1980), p. 24.

12. Of course, in the real world—as distinct from the stylized model—it is likely that when all innovative activity comes to an equilibrium (and when all regulatory changes are in place), a wide variety of liabilities tailored to the needs of the public will be offered. But these liabilities will bear market-determined interest rates—their most important characteristic.

13. Since 1977 the Federal Reserve staff has been conducting a

quarterly survey to estimate the percentage of business loans at banks made at floating rates. The numbers in table 2–2 depict the average of each year's published figures.

14. In K.G. Hadjimichalakis and M.G. Hadjimichalakis (1982) several assets and several managed liabilities are examined.

15. Both of these reasons have been emphasized in the recent literature on "financial innovations and monetary control," especially in the work of P. Cagan (1979); T.D. Simpson and R.D. Porter (1980); and D.D. Hester (1981). The earlier work of J. Enzler, L. Johnson, and J. Paulus (1976); S.M. Goldfeld (1976); and R.D. Porter, T.D. Simpson, and E. Mauskopf (1979) is in the same spirit.

16. T.D. Simpson and R.D. Porter (1980) suggest that in light of financial innovations "and the inadequacy of standard money demand models, it is clear that further research is needed in the area of money demand." They also say that "one change in the specification suggested by the preceding discussion is the inclusion of a variable that captures the incentive to invest in money management techniques" (p. 172). Of course, this may be true when the quantity of money is solely demand determined. But when it is not, *what is needed is a new monetary framework*,—not simply a modification of the money-demand function. What is involved here is not simply "inadequacy of standard money demand models," but rather inadequacy of the existing monetary framework itself.

17. The reader who is interested in greater detail about the provisions of this act is referred to the *Federal Reserve Bulletin* (June 1980) and to the Federal Reserve Bank of Chicago, *Economic Perspectives* (September/ October 1980).

18. In practice, the Federal Reserve has widened the band of permissible interest-rate variability. But this range is not binding; rather, it is used by the Federal Open Market Committee only for "timely consultations." See *Federal Reserve Bulletin* (June 1981) pp. 500–01.

19. In Hadjimichalakis (1980b) and (1981b) it is shown that in the first year of the new operating procedures the Federal Reserve employed a "random walk" formula to forecast borrowings; and it is argued that this was a major contributing factor to the increased volatility of both the monetary aggregates and interest rates.

20. For a comparison of the roles of the discount-rate policy under the new operating procedures, see M.G. Hadjimichalakis (1981c, 1982).

21. See M.G. Hadjimichalakis (1981a, 1980a).

22. See K.G. Hadjimichalakis and M.G. Hadjimichalakis (1982).

Part II
The Financial Sector

3 The Current (and Disappearing) Monetary Regime

For the remainder of this book, we shall assume that the Federal Reserve pursues a reserves operating target, that is, that the Federal Reserve controls nonborrowed reserves, referred to here as the (nonborrowed) reserve base. Also, beginning with this chapter, we shall examine a financial sector model that consists of only three assets: (1) base money (that is, currency plus reserves), (2) demand deposits, and (3) earning assets, collectively called T-bills. Our choice of this model is based on two considerations: One is for simplicity and the other is the desire to use a model that is similar to the ones used by both the Federal Reserve and some of its critics. In particular, this three-asset model is a special case of the Tobin-Brainard framework;[1] it is consistent with the Federal Reserve's monthly model[2] and with the basic model that Brunner and Meltzer,[3] who are among the Federal Reserve's severest critics, have established and have been using for a long time.

In the next section we shall develop the financial model in abstraction from the real sector. The key assumption is that the nominal interest rate on demand deposits is fixed and is binding. This assumption, in turn, implies that the quantity of demand deposits is demand determined, which is true whether we rely on equilibrium of the deposit market, according to a perfectly elastic supply schedule, or we rely on disequilibrium of this market.

In the third section we shall determine the market-clearing interest rate (for earning assets, or T-bills). We shall then proceed to examine the effect on this interest rate of changes in various instruments of monetary control—the reserve base, the discount rate, the reserve requirement ratio—and the effect of various other deliberate or inadvertent shocks. The effects of the same changes on monetary aggregates, the quantity of demand deposits, borrowed reserves, and total reserves will be derived in the next two sections. And in the final section we shall examine the scope of shocks and, in particular, where they originate and where they are first felt.

The Development of the Model

The following notation will be used in the remainder of this book:

I = real planned investment per unit of capital.
S = real planned savings per unit of capital.

D^d = real planned demand for demand deposits per unit of capital.

D^s = real planned supply of demand deposits per unit of capital.

p = the price level.

r = the real rate of interest on earning asets, or bills.

ρ = the real rate of return on demand deposits.

i = nominal interest on earning assets.

ζ = nominal interest on demand deposits.

π = expected rate of inflation.

$\dfrac{\dot{p}}{p}$ = actual rate of inflation.

k = reserve-requirement ratio.

d = real discount rate.

$\bar{d}$ = nominal discount rate.

EDB = excess demand for bills, or earning assets.

EDR = excess demand for reserves.

EDD = excess demand for demand deposits.

EDG = excess demand for goods and services.

z_h = opportunity cost of holding demand deposits for households and nonfinancial firms.

z_f = net profit margin of financial institutions.

μ = shift parameter in the supply function for demand deposits.

β = shift parameter in the demand function for demand deposits.

α = shift parameter in the investment demand function.

R = real nonborrowed reserves, or real reserve base.

R_* = nominal nonborrowed reserves, or nominal reserve base.

R_R = real required reserves.

R_E = real excess reserves.

R_B = real borrowed reserves.

Throughout this book a dot over a symbol will denote the time derivative of that symbol. For example, $\dot{x} \equiv dx/dt$.

The financial sector consists of three assets: base money, T-bills, and demand deposits. The first is the demand debt of the government, and it is held only by financial institutions. In other words, we shall assume, for simplicity, that the public's holding of currency is fixed—say, at zero—so that base money is identical to reserves. The second asset, T-bills, is a portmanteau variable designed to include, collectively, all earning assets held by financial institutions. In the real world, of course, earning assets consist of the debt of the private sector as well as of the public sector. Finally, the third asset, demand deposits, is the debt of financial institutions, and it is held by nonfinancial firms and households. In the real world, however, we have demand deposits proper and other checkable deposits. Demand deposits proper yield a zero, explicit, pecuniary nominal interest rate, whereas other checkable deposits, consisting mainly of NOW and ATS accounts, yield a positive and fixed interest rate. In our analysis we shall lump all deposits together and assume that they yield a fixed, (nonzero) explicit, nominal deposit rate, $\bar{\zeta}$.

In general, with three assets we need to examine explicitly only two asset markets because the three excess demands in stocks are constrained by Walras' Law:

$$EDB + EDR + EDD = 0, \tag{3.1}$$

where EDJ is the excess demand for asset J: bills, reserves, and demand deposits. We choose to examine explicitly the market for reserves and the market for demand deposits. The most natural specification of the financial sector occurs, as in chapter 4, when the deposit rate is market determined. The model, then, is specified by the solution of 3.2 and 3.3 for the two interest rates, the bills rate, i, and the deposit rate, ζ:

$$EDR = 0 \tag{3.2}$$

$$EDD = 0. \tag{3.3}$$

On the other hand, for the case examined in this chapter—namely, when the interest rate on demand deposits is fixed by the Central Bank at $\bar{\zeta}$—the model is specified by

$$EDR = 0 \tag{3.2}$$

$$D = D^d(\cdot) \tag{3.4}$$

—that is, the amount of demand deposits is demand determined. This specification is consistent with two interpretations: One is based on disequilibrium and the other is based on infinite elasticity of the supply curve of demand deposits.

Under the disequilibrium specification, equation 3.4 is accompanied by the inequality 3.3'.

$$EDD < 0 \tag{3.3'}$$

$$D = D^d(\cdot) \tag{3.4}$$

That is, the Central Bank fixes the nominal deposit rate at a sufficiently low level—say, at $\bar{\zeta}$—so that there is excess supply of deposits, $EDD < 0$. With demand less than supply, the financial institutions are off their notional supply curve. Of course, this is not the end of the story. The excess supply of deposits creates pressures for a rise in the deposit rate. But because the nominal pecuniary deposit rate is fixed by the Central Bank, the increase in the true deposit rate must come exclusively from an increase in the nonpecuniary, in-kind payments. The interpretation based on 3.3' and 3.4 must, therefore, imply that movements in these nonpecuniary interest payments on deposits are so slow that they can be treated as constant.[4]

The description of the financial sector by 3.2 and 3.4 also permits an equilibrium explanation, that is, $EDD = 0$, as in 3.3. According to this explanation the nominal deposit rate, ζ, is fixed at such a level that the supply of demand deposits by financial institutions is perfectly elastic at this level. Whichever explanation we employ, we must emphasize that the model consisting of 3.2 and 3.4 assumes that demand deposits are demand determined.

Anticipating our specifications of the demand and supply functions for demand deposits, we can illustrate the disequilibrium and the equilibrium interpretations with figures 3–1 and 3–2, respectively. In figure 3–1 the demand for demand deposits is depicted as an increasing function of the deposit rate, ζ (as specified in 3.6). Also, the supply of demand deposits is a decreasing function of the deposit rate, as we shall prove in chapter 4. Furthermore, we note that the deposit rate is fixed at $\bar{\zeta}$, which is below its market-clearing level, ζ_*. At $\bar{\zeta}$ the quantity demanded, D^d, is less than the

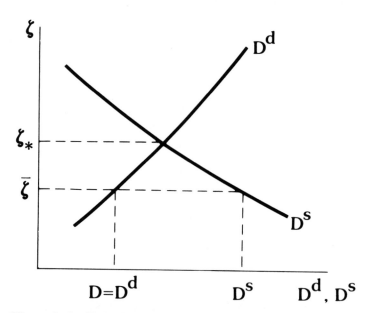

Figure 3–1. Fixed Deposit Rate: Disequilibrium Explanation

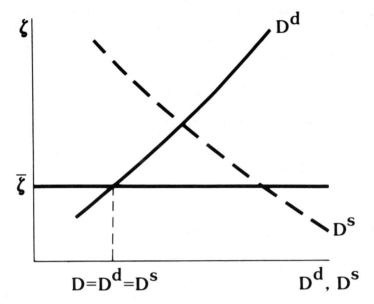

Figure 3–2. Fixed Deposit Rate: Equilibrium Explanation—Perfectly Elastic Supply

quantity supplied, D^s. The quantity demand deposits is the smaller of the two quantities—that is, $D = D^d < D^s$. In figure 3–2 the supply curve is perfectly elastic at the fixed deposit rate, $\bar{\zeta}$, and demand is equal to supply—that is, $D = D^d = D^s$.

To solve the financial-sector model represented by 3.2 and 3.4 we need to specify EDR and the behavioral relation, $D^d(\cdot)$. Beginning with the behavioral relation, we assume that the demand for demand deposits, D^d, is a decreasing function of the opportunity cost, z_h, of holding such deposits. This opportunity cost[5] is the difference between the real rate on T-bills, $r \equiv i - \pi$, and the real rate on demand deposits, $\rho \equiv \bar{\zeta} - \pi$. Hence we have $r - \rho = i - \pi - (\bar{\zeta} - \pi)$, or

$$z_h = r - \rho = i - \bar{\zeta}, \qquad (3.5)$$

and we can specify the demand function as

$$D = D^d(i - \bar{\zeta}), \frac{\partial D^d}{\partial z_h} < 0. \qquad (3.6')$$

Of course, a scale variable such as income or wealth also belongs in the demand function, but it will be omitted here because we shall examine cases for which income or wealth are held fixed. Later, we shall introduce a shock (shift) parameter, β, which reflects a positive shift in the demand function. In this case we shall use the specification

$$D = D^d(i - \bar{\zeta}; \beta), \frac{\partial D^d}{\partial z_h} < 0, \frac{\partial D^d}{\partial \beta} > 0. \qquad (3.6)$$

Next, we shall specify the excess demand for reserves, EDR. On the demand side are the required reserves, R_R, and excess reserves, R_E; on the supply side are the borrowed reserves, R_B, and the nonborrowed reserves, R, all in real terms. Hence,

$$EDR = R_R + R_E - R_B - R. \qquad (3.7)$$

Required reserves are equal to the product of the reserve requirement ratio, k, and demand deposits, D—that is,

$$R_R = k \cdot D. \qquad (3.8)$$

Real borrowed reserves, R_B, depend positively on the spread between the nominal rate on bills, i, and the nominal discount rate, $\bar{d}$, that is, on $i - \bar{d}$. This difference is also identical to the difference between the respective real rates, $r - d$, where d is the real discount rate. Again, a scale variable is suppressed, but a shift parameter, θ, which represents administration of the discount window by the Federal Reserve, is introduced. An increase in θ represents a loosening of discount window policy by the Federal Reserve whereas a decrease in θ represents a tightening of discount window policy:[6]

$$R_B = R_B(i - \bar{d}; \theta), \frac{\partial R_B}{\partial(i - \bar{d})} \equiv R'_B > 0, \frac{\partial R_B}{\partial \theta} > 0. \qquad (3.9)$$

Real excess reserves depend, similarly, on interest rates, but for simplicity—and without any loss of generality in our results—[7] we shall assume that they are fixed at $\bar{R}_E$:

$$R_E = \bar{R}_E. \qquad (3.10)$$

Now, substituting 3.6, 3.8, 3.9, and 3.10 into 3.7, we have the excess demand for real reserves:

$$EDR = k \cdot D^d(i - \bar{\zeta}; \beta) + \bar{R}_E - R_B(i - \bar{d}; \theta) - R. \qquad (3.11)$$

Of course, the Central Bank can control nominal, not real, reserves. Denoting nominal reserves by R_* and the price level by p, we have:

$$R = \frac{R_*}{p}.$$ (3.12)

Substituting 3.12 into 3.11, we get

$$EDR = k \cdot D^d(i - \bar{\zeta}; \beta) + \bar{R}_E + R_B(i - \bar{d}; \theta) - \frac{R_*}{p}.$$ (3.11′)

For compactness of terminology, nonborrowed reserves will be called the *reserve base*; nominal nonborrowed reserves, R_*, will be called the nominal reserve base; and real nonborrowed reserves, R, will be called the real reserve base.

We can now specify the dynamics of the interest-rate-adjustment process by appealing to the law of supply and demand:

$$\frac{di}{dt} \gtreqless 0 \text{ when } EDR \gtreqless 0.$$ (3.13)

In words, the interest rate rises when there is excess demand for reserves and falls when there is excess supply. It remains unchanged only when the reserves market is cleared. Of course, this is consistent with the omitted market. When there is excess demand for (supply of) reserves, there is excess supply of (demand for) T-bills, which accounts for the rising (falling) interest rate. The interest-rate-adjustment mechanism is captured by the following sign-preserving function:

$$\frac{di}{dt} = \delta \cdot EDR, \delta > 0$$ (3.14)

where δ—the speed of adjustment—is assumed constant, but only for simplicity.

The specification in 3.14 can be useful when the model is extended to incorporate the real sector. However, for our purposes in Part II of the book we need to examine only market clearance,

$$EDR = 0.$$ (3.2)

This clearance can be brought about when $di/dt = 0$, that is, when the interest rate does not change. Alternatively, we can assume that the speed of adjustment, δ, is infinite; that is, we can assume that the financial markets—represented collectively by 3.14—clear instantaneously:

$$\lim_{\delta \to \infty} \frac{di}{dt} \cdot \frac{1}{\delta} = EDR \to 0 \qquad (3.15)$$

—that is, that equation 3.2 always prevails. The assumption of an infinite speed of adjustment of financial markets is an idealization of the realistic assumption that the financial markets clear faster than the goods and services markets.

Monetary Policy and Stochastic Shocks: Effects on the Rate of Interest

Clearance of the entire financial sector is represented by setting EDR equal to zero in 3.11′; that is, clearance occurs when

$$k \cdot D^d(i - \bar{\zeta}; \beta) + \bar{R}_E - R_B(i - \bar{d}; \theta) - \frac{R_*}{p} = 0. \qquad (3.16)$$

Equation 3.16 is one equation in two endogenous variables, i and p, and the parameters R_*, $\bar{\zeta}$, $\bar{d}$, β, θ, and $\bar{R}_E$. We can solve this equation explicitly for i in terms of the endogenous variable, p, and the exogenous variables. We write this solution as

$$i = i_*(p; R_*, \bar{\zeta}, \bar{d}, \theta, \beta, \bar{R}_E, k). \qquad (3.17)$$

The partial derivatives of 3.17 can be derived by totally differentiating 3.16 and by solving for the appropriate differentials:

$$\left(k \frac{\partial D^d}{\partial z_h} - R'_B \right) di - k \frac{\partial D^d}{\partial z_h} d\bar{\zeta} + k \frac{\partial D^d}{\partial \beta} d\beta + d\bar{R}_E + D^d(\cdot)dk$$

$$+ R'_B d\bar{d} - \frac{\partial R_B}{\partial \theta} d\theta - \frac{1}{p} dR_* + \frac{R_*}{p^2} dp = 0. \qquad (3.18)$$

Now, defining

$$C = k \frac{\partial D^d}{\partial z_h} - R'_B < 0 \qquad (3.19)$$

and defining C^{-1} as the inverse of C, we get equations 3.20 through 3.27, which are the partial derivatives of 3.17:

$$\frac{\partial i_*}{\partial p} = -\frac{R_*}{p^2} \cdot C^{-1} > 0 \tag{3.20}$$

$$\frac{\partial i_*}{\partial R_*} = \frac{1}{p} \cdot C^{-1} < 0 \tag{3.21}$$

$$\frac{\partial i_*}{\partial \bar{\zeta}} = k \frac{\partial D^d}{\partial z_h} \cdot C^{-1} > 0 \tag{3.22}$$

$$\frac{\partial i_*}{\partial \bar{d}} = -R'_B \cdot C^{-1} > 0 \tag{3.23}$$

$$\frac{\partial i_*}{\partial \theta} = \frac{\partial R_B}{\partial \theta} \cdot C^{-1} < 0 \tag{3.24}$$

$$\frac{\partial i_*}{\partial \bar{R}_E} = -C^{-1} > 0 \tag{3.25}$$

$$\frac{\partial i_*}{\partial \beta} = -k \frac{\partial D^d}{\partial \beta} \cdot C^{-1} > 0 \tag{3.26}$$

$$\frac{\partial i_*}{\partial k} = -D^d(\cdot) \cdot C^{-1} > 0. \tag{3.27}$$

The interpretation of equations 3.20 through 3.27 is straightforward. These expressions denote the effect on the bills interest rate, i, when the respective variable changes *and* both financial markets are cleared. For example, an increase in the price level—while everything else remains the same—lowers the real reserve base, R_*/p. To eliminate the consequent excess demand for reserves the interest rate must rise. All this is expressed by equation 3.20. On the other hand, an increase in the nominal reserve base, R_*, with the price level and all other parameters remaining the same, causes excess supply of reserves, thereby lowering the interest rate, as in 3.21. Turning to 3.22, we see that an increase in the deposit rate, $\bar{\zeta}$, increases demand deposits (demanded and supplied), which increases required reserves, $k\,D$; this causes excess demand for reserves and, hence, an increase in the interest rate[8]. From 3.23 we see that an increase in the discount rate, $\bar{d}$, reduces the amount of borrowed reserves and, hence, the supply of reserves. The consequent excess demand for reserves puts pressure on the interest rate to rise. On the other hand, by 3.24, an increase in the shift parameter, θ, increases the amount of borrowed reserves, and the resulting excess supply of reserves causes the interest rate to fall. By 3.25, an exogenous increase in banks' demand for excess reserves creates excess demand for reserves, thereby raising the interest rate. In a similar fashion, excess demand for reserves and pressure for the interest rate to rise are created when there is a shift in the demand function for demand deposits, as in 3.26, or when there is an increase in the reserve requirement ratio, k, as in 3.27. The qualitative effects on the interest rate, i, are summarized in table 3–1.

If we use 3.11 rather than 3.11' and if we differentiate the resulting $EDR = 0$ equation, we get the same results as shown in 3.20 through 3.27, with modifications for 3.20 and 3.21. In place of 3.20 and 3.21, we have a single equation:

$$\frac{\partial i_*}{\partial R} = C^{-1} < 0. \tag{3.28}$$

An increase in the *real* reserve base, R, causes excess supply of real reserves, which lowers the interest rate. But an increase in the real reserve base can result either from an increase in the nominal reserve base, R_*, while the price level is constant, or from a fall in the price level, p, while the nominal reserve base, R_*, is fixed. This, of course, is consistent with 3.20 and 3.21. However, we can derive this from 3.28:

Table 3–1
Effects of Policy and Shocks on the (Bills) Interest Rate under a Fixed Deposit Rate

a_j	$\partial i_*/\partial a_j$
p	+
R_*	−
ζ	+
$\bar{d}$	+
θ	−
$\bar{R}_E$	+
β	+
k	+

$$\frac{\partial i_*}{\partial R_*} = \frac{\partial i_*}{\partial R} \frac{\partial R}{\partial R_*} = \frac{1}{p} C^{-1}$$

$$\frac{\partial i_*}{\partial p} = \frac{\partial i_*}{\partial R} \frac{\partial R}{\partial p} = -\frac{R_*}{p^2} C^{-1}.$$

Hence, an alternative way of expressing the solution to $EDR = 0$ is

$$i = i_*(R; R_*, \overline{\zeta}, \overline{d}, \theta, k, \beta, \overline{R}_E), \tag{3.29}$$

with partials, 3.28 and 3.21 through 3.27. This alternative will be useful when, in chapter 8, we examine the rate of inflation rather than the price level.

Effects on the Quantity of Demand Deposits

In this section we shall examine the effects of deliberate and inadvertent shocks on the quantity of demand deposits when, again, only the financial sector is in equilibrium.

Substituting 3.17 into 3.6 and defining the resulting function as D^*, we have:

$$D^* \equiv D^d\{i_*(p; R_*, \overline{d}, \overline{\zeta}, \theta, k, \beta, \overline{R}_E) - \overline{\zeta}; \beta\}. \tag{3.30}$$

The effects of a change in p and in the monetary parameters are found by taking the appropriate partial derivative of 3.30 and using 3.20 through 3.27:

$$\frac{\partial D^*}{\partial p} = \frac{\partial D^d}{\partial z_h} \frac{\partial i_*}{\partial p}$$

$$= -\frac{\dfrac{R_*}{p^2} \cdot \dfrac{\partial D^d}{\partial z_h}}{C} < 0. \tag{3.31}$$

As expected, an exogenous increase in the price level reduces the quantity of real demand deposits: The increase in the price level increases the interest rate on bills, i, which reduces the demand for demand deposits. Turning to the effect of an increase in the nominal reserve base, R_*, we get:

$$\frac{\partial D^*}{\partial R_*} = \frac{\partial D^d}{\partial z_h} \frac{\partial i_*}{\partial R_*},$$

or,

$$\frac{\partial D^*}{\partial R_*} = \frac{\dfrac{1}{p} \cdot \dfrac{\partial D^d}{\partial z_h}}{C} > 0. \tag{3.32}$$

As expected, an increase in the nominal reserve base lowers the interest rate, thereby increasing the demand for demand deposits.

An increase in the (fixed) deposit rate, ζ, has two effects: The direct effect, $-\partial D^d/\partial z_h$, is positive; but the indirect effect, $(\partial D^d/\partial z_h) \cdot (\partial i_*/\partial \bar{\zeta})$, is negative because the increase in $\bar{\zeta}$ increases the interest rate, i, which lowers the demand for demand deposits. The net result, however, is positive because the increase in i is less than the increase in $\bar{\zeta}$. (We should note that the last statement follows from 3.22.) At any rate, the end result is 3.33:

$$\frac{\partial D^*}{\partial \bar{\zeta}} = \frac{\dfrac{\partial D^d}{\partial z_h} \cdot R'_B}{C} > 0. \tag{3.33}$$

An increase in the discount rate, $\bar{d}$, has a negative effect on the amount of demand deposits, as expected:

$$\frac{\partial D^*}{\partial \bar{d}} = -\frac{R'_B \dfrac{\partial D^d}{\partial z_h}}{C} < 0. \tag{3.34}$$

On the other hand, a positive shift in the borrowings function—brought about, say, by a loosening in the administration of the discount window—increases the quantity of demand deposits:

$$\frac{\partial D^*}{\partial \theta} = \frac{\dfrac{\partial R_B}{\partial \theta} \dfrac{\partial D^d}{\partial z_h}}{C} > 0. \tag{3.35}$$

Similarly, an exogenous increase in the demand for excess reserves, $\bar{R}_E$, reduces the amount of demand deposits:

$$\frac{\partial D^*}{\partial \bar{R}_E} = -\frac{\dfrac{\partial D^d}{\partial z_h}}{C} < 0. \tag{3.36}$$

A positive shock in the demand function for demand deposits has a positive direct effect and a negative indirect effect, the negative effect caused by the consequent increase in the interest rate. However, the positive effect dominates:

$$\frac{\partial D^*}{\partial \beta} = \frac{\partial D^d}{\partial \beta} + \frac{\partial D^d}{\partial z_h} \frac{\partial i_*}{\partial \beta}$$

$$= -\frac{R'_B \dfrac{\partial D^d}{\partial \beta}}{C} > 0. \tag{3.37}$$

Finally, as expected, an increase in the reserve requirement ratio reduces the amount of demand deposits by raising the interest rate, i:

$$\frac{\partial D^*}{\partial k} = -\frac{D^d(\cdot) \dfrac{\partial D^d}{\partial z_h}}{C} < 0. \tag{3.38}$$

Again, we tabulate the qualitative effects on the quantity of demand deposits in table 3–2.

Comparing table 3–1 with table 3–2, we observe that in all cases but two the interest rate and the quantity of money serve equally well as indicators of expansion and contraction. For example, according to table 3–2 an exogenous increase in the price level is contractionary because the real quantity of demand deposits, or money, falls. According to table 3–1, the rise in the price level is also contractionary because it raises the interest rate. Similarly, an increase in the nominal reserve base is expansionary. In summary, we see

Table 3–2
Effects of Policy and Shocks on the Quantity of Demand Deposits under a Fixed Deposit Rate

a_j	$\partial D^*/\partial a_j$
p	$-$
R_*	$+$
$\overline{\zeta}$	$+$
$\overline{d}$	$-$
θ	$+$
$\overline{R}_E$	$-$
β	$+$
k	$-$

that the two indicators give the same signals for all shocks but two: first, in the case when the (fixed) deposit rate, $\bar{\zeta}$, is raised by the Central Bank; and second, when the demand for demand deposits rises (say, because of financial innovations).

According to table 3-1, such an increase in the deposit rate is contractionary because it raises the interest rate, i. In contrast, table 3-2 shows that such an increase in the deposit rate is expansionary because it increases the quantity of demand deposits. This increase in the deposit rate can come about by raising the ceiling on the interest payments on NOW accounts or even, as we have seen, by introducing NOW accounts nationwide, as occurred on December 31, 1980. In effect, introducing NOW accounts nationwide,[9] as opposed to only in the New England States, was tantamount to raising the fixed deposit rate, $\bar{\zeta}$.

We now turn to the case when the demand function for demand deposits shifts—that is, when the shift parameter, β, rises. According to table 3-1, the effect of this shock is contractionary, because the interest rate, i, rises. But according to table 3-2, the effect is expansionary, because the quantity of money (that is, of demand deposits) increases. This particular shock has been applied to the issue of financial innovations; in particular, it has been applied to cases in which a fall in β and, hence, a negative shift in money demand is the consequence of financial innovations that reduce the need for cash. The consequence of this shock is a quantity of demand deposits that is lower than expected. Also, financial innovations are the reason given for this overprediction of the quantity of money. Futhermore, because the interest rate also falls and because this fall by itself is expansionary, it is further argued that effective money growth is greater than observed, or actual growth.[10]

Effects on Borrowed and Total Reserves

Effects on Borrowed Reserves

The structural equation for borrowed reserves is 3.9, reproduced here as 3.39:

$$R_B = R_B(i - \bar{d}; \theta). \qquad (3.39)$$

Substituting the market solution for i—that is, 3.17 into 3.39—and defining the resulting function as R_B^*, we have:

$$R_B^* \equiv R_B|i_*(p,R_*,\bar{\zeta},\bar{d},\theta,\bar{R}_E, \beta,k) - \bar{d}; \theta|. \qquad (3.40)$$

We see that with the exception of the two shocks—$\bar{d}$ and θ—that originate in the function for borrowed reserves, the effect of deliberate and inadvertent shocks on borrowed reserves must come only indirectly through their effect on the interest rate. In particular, borrowed reserves will rise (fall) if and only if the shock increases (reduces) the interest rate. In the case of a change in the discount rate, $\bar{d}$, and in the shift parameter, θ, there is also a direct effect that is of the opposite sign to the indirect effect; the sign of the overall effect depends on which effect predominates.

First, we examine shocks that have only an indirect effect on borrowed reserves. Differentiating 3.40 partially with respect to p, we have:

$$\frac{\partial R_{B}^{*}}{\partial p} = R'_B \frac{\partial i_*}{\partial p} > 0. \tag{3.41}$$

This effect is positive by 3.20; that is, an increase in the price level raises the interest rate which, in turn, increases the quantity of real borrowed reserves because it widens the spread, $i-\bar{d}$. Similarly, differentiating partially with respect to the nominal reserve base, R_*, we have a negative effect by 3.21:

$$\frac{\partial R_{B}^{*}}{\partial R_*} = R'_B \frac{\partial i_*}{\partial R_*}. \tag{3.42}$$

That is, an increase in the nominal reserve base lowers the interest rate, narrows the spread, $i-\bar{d}$, and, hence, reduces borrowed reserves. We recall that this negative relation between borrowed and nonborrowed reserves was also established in chapter 2, where it was shown that such a relationship was central to explaining the variability in interest rates and in aggregates in 1980. Interpretation of the remaining effects is similar:

$$\frac{\partial R_{B}^{*}}{\partial \bar{\zeta}} = R'_B \frac{\partial i_*}{\partial \bar{\zeta}} > 0 \tag{3.43}$$

$$\frac{\partial R_{B}^{*}}{\partial \bar{R}_E} = R'_B \frac{\partial i_*}{\partial \bar{R}_E} > 0 \tag{3.44}$$

$$\frac{\partial R_{B}^{*}}{\partial \beta} = R'_B \frac{\partial i_*}{\partial \beta} > 0 \tag{3.45}$$

$$\frac{\partial R_{B}^{*}}{\partial k} = R'_B \frac{\partial i_*}{\partial k} > 0. \tag{3.46}$$

Next, we shall derive the effects of shocks originating in the function for borrowed reserves. A change in the discount rate, $\bar{d}$, has a direct effect and an indirect effect:

$$\frac{\partial R_{\tilde{B}}^{*}}{\partial \bar{d}} = -R_B' + R_B' \frac{\partial i_*}{\partial \bar{d}}.$$

(3.47)

The direct effect is negative, but the indirect effect is positive. Similarly, a positive shift in the function for borrowed reserves has a direct effect, which is positive, and an indirect effect, which is negative:

$$\frac{\partial R_{\tilde{B}}^{*}}{\partial \theta} = \frac{\partial R_B}{\partial \theta} + R_B' \frac{\partial i_*}{\partial \theta}.$$

(3.48)

Intuition suggests that the direct effect must outweigh the indirect effect, and this turns out to be so: Substituting 3.23 into 3.47, we find:

$$\frac{\partial R_{\tilde{B}}^{*}}{\partial \bar{d}} = -\frac{kR_B' \dfrac{\partial D^d}{\partial z_h}}{C} < 0,$$

(3.49)

which is negative, the same sign as $(-R_B')$. Similarly, substituting 3.24 into 3.48, we get

$$\frac{\partial R_{\tilde{B}}^{*}}{\partial \theta} = \frac{k \dfrac{\partial R_B}{\partial \theta} \dfrac{\partial D^d}{\partial z_h}}{C} > 0,$$

(3.50)

which has the same sign as $\partial R_B / \partial \theta$.

Effects on Total Reserves

The definition of real total reserves, R_T, is

$$R_T = \frac{R_*}{p} + R_B(i - \bar{d}; \theta).$$

(3.51)

Substituting 3.17 into 3.51 and defining the resulting function as $R_{\tilde{B}}^{*}$, we have:

$$R_T^{*} = \frac{R_*}{p} + R_{\tilde{B}}^{*}.$$

(3.52)

The effect of a change in a_j on R_T^{*} is given by $\partial R_T^{*} / \partial a_j$. We see that except for a change in either the nominal reserve base, R_*, or in the price level, p, it is obvious that the sign of $\partial R_T^* / \partial a_j$ is the same as $\partial R_B^* / \partial a_j$. Therefore, we shall examine separately only the effects of a change in these two variables. The effect of a change in the price level is

$$\frac{\partial R_T^*}{\partial p} = -\frac{R_*}{p^2} + \frac{\partial R_B}{\partial p} . \qquad (3.53)$$

That is, an increase in the price level has two effects: It reduces the nonborrowed real reserve base, R_*/p, but it increases borrowed reserves. To see which effect predominates, we substitute 3.41 and then 3.20 into 3.53 and find that

$$\frac{\partial R_T^*}{\partial p} = -\frac{k \dfrac{\partial D^d}{\partial z_h} \dfrac{R_*}{p^2}}{C} < 0; \qquad (3.54)$$

that is, we find that the first real-balance effect outweighs the second.

Next, we examine the effect of an increase in the nominal reserve base, R_*, on the total real reserves, given the price level:

$$\frac{\partial R_T^*}{\partial R_*} = \frac{1}{p} + \frac{\partial R_B^*}{\partial R_*} . \qquad (3.55)$$

An increase in the nominal nonborrowed reserve base has a positive direct effect but a negative indirect effect on borrowed reserves. However, substituting 3.42 and 3.21 into 3.55, we can prove that the effect on borrowed reserves is outweighed by the effect on the real nonborrowed reserve base. There will be an increase in real total reserves:

$$\frac{\partial R_T^*}{\partial R_*} = \frac{k \dfrac{\partial D^d}{\partial z_h}}{p \cdot C} > 0. \qquad (3.56)$$

The effects on both reserve aggregates are summarized in table 3–3.

Concluding Comments: The Scope of Shocks

We have devoted most of this chapter to the examination of the effects of shocks on the interest rate and on monetary and reserve aggregates. These shocks can be policy shocks, or shocks caused by innovations, or even true stochastic shocks. Whatever their source, we have examined these shocks in

Table 3–3
**Effects of Policy and Shocks on Borrowed and Total Reserves under a
Fixed Deposit Rate**

a_j	$\partial R_B^*/\partial a_j$	$\partial R_T^*/\partial a_j$
p	+	−
R_*	−	+
$\bar{\zeta}$	+	+
$\bar{d}$	−	−
θ	+	+
$\bar{R}_E$	+	+
β	+	+
k	+	+

isolation, that is, we have examined them without tying them explicitly to shocks in any other relationship. Of course, shocks in one market must be felt in at least one other market. We know from the seminal paper by Brainard and Tobin (1968) that when we do not specify which market absorbs the shock, this means that the effects of such a shock are absorbed by the "omitted" market. In our model this is the earning-assets market. With this in mind, we can check the plausibility of the shocks we have examined.

Starting with an examination of the positive shock (captured by an increase in the parameter β) in the demand for demand deposits, we see that an increase in the demand for demand deposits will immediately cause an increase in required reserves and, hence, will create excess demand for reserves. According to Walras' Law, this excess demand for reserves will be reflected as excess supply in the omitted equation, that is, an excess supply of earning assets (loan securities or bills). In other words, the increase in the demand by households and firms for demand deposits is at the expense of their demand for "earning assets." But is this plausible? The answer is yes, provided that the shock makes deposits more desirable, a case in which rational firms and households will substitute deposits for other assets.

A similar explanation applies to the shock representing an increase in the deposit rate, $\bar{\zeta}$. It raises the demand for demand deposits and, hence, increases required reserves. The consequent excess demand for reserves is reflected as excess supply of earning assets.

The shock of an increase in the nominal reserve base causes an immediate excess supply of reserves, which registers as excess demand for earning assets of an equal amount by virtue of the essence of open-market operations. The nominal reserve base increases only when earning assets are sold by the Federal Reserve; such a sale reduces the supply of earning assets, thereby creating excess demand for them.

Using a similar argument, we can establish that an increase in excess reserves held by banks must be at the expense of their demand for earning assets; the increase in excess reserves creates excess demand for reserves that registers as excess supply of (that is, as a shortfall in demand for) earning assets. Although this is a plausible bank practice, at the very least it needs confirmation from a micro theory of bank behavior, a task we undertake in the next chapter.

We shall now turn to the two shocks that originate in the borrowings function. A reduction in the discount rate registers as an excess demand for earning assets (that is, as an increase in credit) because the lower discount rate raises borrowed reserves and, hence, causes excess supply of reserves. And we see that a reduction in the discount rate is reflected in an increased supply of credit by banks, a result that relies on the behavior of both the banking firm and the administrator of the discount window. Ideally, then, we need a theory that describes the operation of the discount window. This need is even more pronounced when we examine the loosening of the administration of the discount window (that is, an increase in θ for a given discount rate, d). Such a shock is also reflected in excess demand for assets, that is, in greater provision of bank credit. This reaction by banks is understandable or plausible, but it may or may not be consistent with the aim of the discount-window administrator.

In the next chapter we shall derive the behavioral functions of the banking firm from a simple profit-maximizing model. In this setting, we shall confirm the wisdom of our implicit assumptions regarding these and other shocks.

Notes

1. For examples of the work done by J. Tobin, W.C. Brainard, and their associates of the "Yale school," see J. Tobin (1963b), J. Tobin and W.C. Brainard (1963), W.C. Brainard and J. Tobin (1968), J. Tobin (1969), and J. Tobin (1981). For an important work strongly influenced by and extending Tobin's work, see S.M. Goldfeld (1966).

2. For the most recent version, see H.T. Farr (1981).

3. For examples of the K. Brunner and A.H. Meltzer work, see K. Brunner and A.H. Meltzer (1964, 1966, 1967, and 1968).

4. In chapter 2 we noted that although the implicit rate has been binding, it has also been rising during the last twenty years. For references, see note 2 in chapter 2.

5. H. Rose (1973) derives the dependence of the demand for money on this opportunity cost from both a household-choice theory and a theory of the firm.

6. The borrowings function represented by 3.9 is in the spirit of the seminal paper by S.M. Goldfeld and E.J. Kane (1966). In chapter 4 we shall derive this relation from a simple profit-maximizing theory of the banking firm.

7. There is no loss of generality because borrowed reserves depend on i and $\bar{d}$. This guarantees that the amount of free reserves—$R_F \equiv R_E - R_B$—depends on i and $\bar{d}$.

8. The nationwide introduction of NOW accounts on December 31, 1980 was, in effect, an increase in the deposit rate from one fixed level to another fixed level. Relying on a more complicated model, we saw in chapter 2 that such an increase in the deposit rate raises all interest rates. For the actual effects of NOW accounts on interest rates, see M.G. Hadjimichalakis (1980a).

9. See M.G. Hadjimichalakis (1980a).

10. The earliest explanation along these lines—limited to explaining the reason for overpredicting the quantity of money—is found in J. Enzler, L. Johnson, and J. Paulus (1976). For the most extensive treatment of the same issue, see T.D. Simpson and R.D. Porter (1980). For a recent Congressional testimony on these issues by a member of the Board of Governors, see L.E. Gramley (1982).

4

The Emerging Regime: Market-Determined Interest on Demand Deposits

In this chapter we modify the model of chapter 3 to permit market determination of an additional interest rate, namely, the deposit rate, ζ. As we have seen in chapter 2, this is the direction toward which the money markets are inexorably driven. Both the financial innovations and the governmental deregulation of the last few years point toward a financial environment where all deposit rates will be market determined and where active liability management will become the norm.

In order to focus on the issue of monetary control in such an environment, we shall examine a situation in which financial institutions supply only one liability, which is managed actively. In other words, the supply of this liability is based on profit-maximizing decisions by the financial firm. We shall refer to this single financial liability as demand deposits. However, the framework can be extended to incorporate additional managed liabilities, such as negotiable certificates of deposit, which may be analyzed using the techniques introduced here for market-determined demand deposits.[1]

This chapter concentrates on development of the new financial model and on detailed examination of the market for demand deposits. This model is derived from microeconomic principles, that is, its behavioral, or structural, relations reflect profit-maximizing behavior of some firm. We shall introduce a very simple profit-maximizing theory of the financial, or banking, firm to derive the behavioral relations we use in the model—that is, the supply of demand deposits, the demand for borrowed reserves, and the demand for earning assets. Of course, the supply of demand deposits is the new ingredient of the model that is developed later in this chapter. In developing this model we shall focus on the key feature: that the deposit rate is determined in the market for demand deposits by supply as well as by demand.

In this new financial regime, the deposit rate and the quantity of demand deposits are market determined. This attribute confronts the researcher with a mathematical difficulty: Should the demand for or the supply of demand deposits be used to calculate required reserves? Of course, the answer is that *both* should be used. To resolve this difficulty we look to clearance of the deposit market to make the quantity demanded equal to the quantity supplied. For this reason in the final section we examine, in detail, deposit-market clearance, determination of the deposit rate, determination of the quantity of demand deposits, and the effect of changes in policy and of other shocks on these variables.

A Simple Theory of the Banking Firm

Before proceeding to develop, in the next section, the model at the market and at the aggregate level, we shall attempt to motivate the behavior of financial institutions. In particular, we shall use a very simple profit-maximizing theory of the *financial firm*, or *bank*, to derive the behavioral relations of such a firm—that is, the supply of demand deposits, the demand for borrowed reserves, and the demand for earning assets, or bills.[2]

We shall begin with the balance-sheet identity of the bank:

$$B + R_R + R_E = D^s + R_B \qquad (4.1)$$

where

B = earning assets, or bills.
R_R = required reserves.
R_E = excess reserves.
D^s = supply of demand deposits.
R_B = borrowed reserves.
R_F = free reserves.

Equation 4.1 states that the bank holds three assets—namely, bills, B, required reserves, R_R, and excess reserves, R_E. Their sum is exactly balanced by the sum of the two kinds of liabilities incurred by the bank—namely, the amount of demand deposits, which are supplied by the bank, D^s, and the amount of borrowed reserves, R_B. The balance sheet itself looks like table 4–1.

Because required reserves are equal to the reserve-requirement ratio, k, times the quantity of demand deposits—that is, $R_R = kD^s$—we can rewrite the balance-sheet identity as 4.2, which concentrates on *net* assets and liabilities.

$$(1 - k)D^s = B + (R_E - R_B). \qquad (4.2)$$

Of course, $R_E - R_B = R_F$, that is, free reserves. The balance sheet corresponding to 4.2 is illustrated in table 4–2.

Table 4–1
The Bank's Balance Sheet

Assets	Liabilities
B	D^s
R_R	R_B
R_E	

Table 4–2
The Bank's Net Balance Sheet

Assets	Liabilities
B	$(1 - k)D^s$
R_E	R_B

Because we want our results to be consistent with our earlier and following stipulation that the demand for excess reserves is fixed, we assume that R_E is fixed at $\bar{R}_E$:

$$R_E = \bar{R}_E. \tag{4.3}$$

Therefore, the balance-sheet identity can be written as 4.4, below:

$$(1 - k)D^s + R_B - \bar{R}_E - B = 0. \tag{4.4}$$

We want to determine D^s, R_B, and B, in such a way that they obey the balance-sheet identity (that is, 4.4) and in a way that is implied by profit maximization. To specify the profit, π, we must subtract the cost associated with incurring the liabilities described, D^s and R_B. Therefore, let us define f, the cost of servicing demand deposits:

$$f = f(D^s; \mu) \tag{4.5}$$

with properties:

$$\frac{\partial f}{\partial D^s} \equiv f'(D^s; \mu) > 0 \tag{4.5a}$$

$$\frac{\partial^2 f}{(\partial D^s)^2} \equiv f'' > 0 \tag{4.5b}$$

and

$$\frac{\partial f'(D^s; \mu)}{\partial \mu} < 0. \tag{4.5c}$$

Equation 4.5a states that the total cost of servicing demand deposits is an increasing function of their amount. Equation 4.5b states that the marginal cost of servicing demand deposits is increasing. Finally, 4.5c depicts a shift parameter, μ, whose increase denotes cost-reducing innovations: An increase in μ reduces the marginal cost of servicing demand deposits. This shift parameter will play an important role in our later analysis. Of course, we have an additional cost associated with demand deposits when interest on them is permitted. With ζ denoting the deposit rate, this cost is equal to $\zeta \cdot D^s$.

We now turn to borrowed reserves R_B. The explicit cost associated with borrowed reserves is the discount rate, $\bar{d}$, with overall payment, $\bar{d} \cdot R_B$. But there are additional costs associated with borrowed reserves. These are mostly implicit—say, "frowns," or "harrassment"—by the administrator of the discount window[3] We shall denote these implicit costs with $g(\cdot)$ in 4.6:

$$g = g(R_B; \theta) \qquad (4.6)$$

with properties

$$\frac{\partial g}{\partial R_B} \equiv g'(R_B; \theta) > 0 \qquad (4.6a)$$

$$\frac{\partial^2 g}{(\partial R_B)^2} \equiv g''(\cdot) > 0 \qquad (4.6b)$$

and

$$\frac{\partial g'(R_B; \theta)}{\partial \theta} < 0. \qquad (4.6c)$$

The implicit cost of borrowing is an increasing function of the amount of borrowed reserves, according to 4.6a. But according to 4.6b the marginal cost itself is increasing.[4] Finally, by 4.6c, θ is a shift parameter designed to denote "easing" in the administration of the discount window: An increase in θ reduces the marginal implicit cost of borrowing. Of course, we have encountered this specification in the preceding chapter, but here we shall derive it from profit-maximizing behavior.

To complete the definition of profit, π, we need to consider the revenue associated with the assets. Excess reserves yield zero explicit (and implicit here) return. This is the reason they are assumed fixed. On the other hand, the earning assets—that is, bills B— yield the interest rate, i. Hence total revenue from earning assets is $i \cdot B$. In summary, profit, π, is:

$$\pi = i \cdot B - \zeta \cdot D^s - f(D^s; \mu) - \bar{d} \cdot R_B - g(R_B; \theta). \qquad (4.7)$$

The financial firm's problem is to maximize profit, π, shown by 4.7, subject to the net balance-sheet constraint, 4.2, that is,

$$\underset{B,\, D^s,\, R_B}{\text{Max }} \pi = i \cdot B - \zeta \cdot D^s - f(D^s; \mu) - \bar{d} \cdot R_B - g(R_B; \theta)$$

$$\text{s.t. } (1 - k)D^s + R_B - \bar{R}_E - B = 0.$$

We shall use the Lagrangian expression, V:

$$V = i \cdot B - \zeta \cdot D^s - f(D^s; \mu) - \bar{d} \cdot R_B - g(R_B; \theta)$$

$$+ \lambda[(1 - k)D^s + R_B - \bar{R}_E - B]. \qquad (4.8)$$

And the first-order conditions are given by:

$$\frac{\partial V}{\partial B} = i - \lambda = 0 \qquad \text{or} \qquad i = \lambda \qquad (4.9)$$

$$\frac{\partial V}{\partial D^s} = -\zeta - f' + \lambda(1-k) = 0 \quad \text{or} \quad \lambda(1-k) - \zeta = f'(D^s; \mu) \qquad (4.10)$$

$$\frac{\partial V}{\partial R_B} = -\bar{d} - g' + \lambda = 0 \qquad \text{or} \qquad \lambda - \bar{d} = g'(R_B; \theta) \qquad (4.11)$$

$$\frac{\partial V}{\partial \lambda} = (1-k)D^s + R_B - \bar{R}_E - B = 0. \qquad (4.12)$$

Now, substituting 4.9 into 4.10 and 4.11, we get, respectively:

$$(1 - k)i - \zeta = f'(D^s; \mu) \qquad (4.13)$$

$$i - \bar{d} = g'(R_B; \theta). \qquad (4.14)$$

We can solve 4.13 explicitly for D^s as a function of $[(1-k)i - \zeta]$ and the shift parameter, μ. Of course, $[(1 - k)i - \zeta]$ is the financial firm's net profit margin for supplying one unit (say, one dollar) of demand deposits. We shall denote this profit margin as z_f:

$$z_f \equiv (1-k)i - \zeta. \tag{4.15}$$

[We note parenthetically that z_f is the *real* net-profit margin of supplying one real unit of demand deposits.] To see that it is the real profit margin, let us introduce expected inflation, π, and the distinction between real deposit rate, ρ, and nominal deposit rate, ζ, where

$$\rho = \zeta - \pi.$$

The nominal revenue is $(1-k)\cdot i$ and the real revenue is $[(1-k)\cdot i - \pi]$. Subtracting the two *real* yields, in order to find the true opportunity cost, or real profit margin, we get:

$$[(1-k)i - \pi] - \rho = (1-k)\cdot i - \pi - \zeta + \pi = (1-k)i - \zeta$$

which, by 4.15, is z_f].

Substituting 4.15 into 4.13 we get

$$z_f = f'(D^s; \mu). \tag{4.16}$$

Now, we can solve 4.16 for D^s:

$$D^s = D^s(z_f; \mu). \tag{4.17}$$

To find the partial derivatives of D^s we must differentiate 4.16 and get:

$$dz_f = f'' \, dD^s + \frac{\partial f'}{\partial \mu} \, d\mu. \tag{4.18}$$

Setting $d\mu = 0$ in 4.18 and solving, we get the partial derivative of D^s with respect to z_f:

$$\frac{\partial D^s}{\partial z_f} = \frac{1}{f''} > 0. \tag{4.19}$$

This partial derivative is positive because of increasing marginal cost—that is, because of $f'' > 0$. We have just established that the supply by banks of demand deposits increases when the profit margin increases. Now, setting dz_f in 4.18 and solving, we find the partial derivative with respect to the cost reducing shift factor, μ:

$$\frac{\partial D^s}{\partial \mu} = -\frac{\dfrac{\partial f'}{\partial \mu}}{f''} > 0. \qquad (4.20)$$

This partial is positive by 4.5a and 4.5b. It says that cost-reducing financial innovations induce the bank to increase its supply of demand deposits.

Similarly, we can solve 4.14 explicitly for R_B as a function of $(i - \bar{d})$ and the shift parameter, θ:

$$R_B = R_B (i - \bar{d}; \theta). \qquad (4.21)$$

Similarly, in order to find the partial derivatives of R_B we must differentiate 4.14 and get:

$$d(i - \bar{d}) = g'' \, dR_B + \frac{\partial g'}{\partial \theta} d\theta. \qquad (4.22)$$

Setting $d\theta = 0$ in 4.22, we find the partial derivatives of R_B with respect to the first argument:

$$\frac{\partial R_B}{\partial (i - \bar{d})} \equiv R'_B = \frac{1}{g''} > 0. \qquad (4.23)$$

This partial derivative is positive by the assumption of increasing marginal implicit cost, as specified in 4.6b; equation 4.23 says that an increase in the difference between the earning asset rate, i, and the explicit cost of borrowing (that is, the discount rate) induces banks to borrow more from a Federal Reserve Bank. Similarly, to find the partial derivative of R_B with respect to the second argument, θ, we set $d(i - \bar{d}) = 0$ in 4.22 and get the following:

$$\frac{\partial R_B}{\partial \theta} = -\frac{\dfrac{\partial g'}{\partial \theta}}{g''} > 0, \qquad (4.24)$$

which is positive by 4.6b and 4.6c. Equation 4.24 says that easing the administration of the discount window encourages more borrowing.

In summary, 4.19 and 4.20 are the partial derivatives of D^s, and 4.23 and 4.24 are the partial derivatives of R_B. We can specify and renumber these functions as 4.25 and 4.26:

$$D^s = D^s[(1 - k)i - \zeta; \mu]; \quad \frac{\partial D^s}{\partial z_f} > 0; \quad \frac{\partial D^s}{\partial \mu} > 0 \qquad (4.25)$$

$$R_B = R_B(i - \bar{d}, \theta); \quad R_B' \equiv \frac{\partial R_B}{\partial(i - \bar{d})} > 0; \quad \frac{\partial R_B}{\partial \theta} > 0. \qquad (4.26)$$

Of course, we have one more decision variable, namely, B, the amount of bills, or earning assets, that the financial firm wants to hold. To find the specification of this "demand for bills," denoted as B_f^d, we must use the rest of our first-order conditions, that is, the budget constraint of 4.12 or 4.2. To find B we must substitute 4.25 and 4.26 into 4.12 and solve for B_f^d. This simply means that according to its budget, or balance-sheet, constraint the financial firm, or bank, knows the amount of earning assets, or bills, it wants to have in its portfolio when it knows the following: the amount of demand deposits it supplies, the amount of borrowed reserves it borrows, and, of course, the fixed amount of excess reserves. Hence by 4.25, 4.26, and 4.12, and by the definition of $B = B_f^d$, we have:

$$B_f^d(\cdot) = (1 - k)D^s[z_f; \mu] + R_B(i - \bar{d}; \theta) - \bar{R}_E. \qquad (4.27)$$

By 4.27 we can specify the functional form of B_f^d:

$$B_f^d = B_f^d(z_f, i - \bar{d}; \mu, \theta, \bar{R}_E, k). \qquad (4.28)$$

Although the bills or earning-assets market is the one we chose to omit at the market level, equations 4.27 and 4.28, which were derived at the firm level, can help us understand some assumptions we have made and some we will make about where the shocks are absorbed. The most important of these assumptions is that the supply-side-shock, $\partial D^s/\partial \mu$, is absorbed initially and exclusively by the bills market. The shift parameter, μ, does not enter as an argument in the borrowings function, R_B, in 4.26, and, of course, it does not enter in $\bar{R}_E$. This result means that cost-reducing innovations that increase the bank's supply of demand deposits will also increase its demand for earning assets; in other words, it will also increase the bank's supply of credit:

$$\frac{\partial B_f^d}{\partial \mu} = (1 - k)\frac{\partial D^s}{\partial \mu} > 0. \qquad (4.29)$$

We can similarly derive the effects of the other shift parameters, $\theta, \bar{d}, \bar{R}_E$, and k, as well as the effects of a change in the profit rate, z_f, and its two components, i, and ζ. We simply record them as follows beginning with the latter effects:

$$\frac{\partial B_f^d}{\partial z_f} = (1 - k)\frac{\partial D^s}{\partial z_f} > 0 \qquad (4.30\text{a})$$

$$\frac{\partial B_f^d}{\partial i} = (1 - k)^2\frac{\partial D^s}{\partial z_f} > 0 \qquad (4.30\text{b})$$

$$\frac{\partial B_f^d}{\partial \zeta} = -(1 - k)\frac{\partial D^s}{\partial z_f} < 0 \qquad (4.30\text{c})$$

$$\frac{\partial B_f^d}{\partial \bar{d}} = -R_B' < 0 \qquad (4.30\text{d})$$

$$\frac{\partial B_f^d}{\partial \theta} = \frac{\partial R_B}{\partial \theta} > 0 \qquad (4.30\text{e})$$

$$\frac{\partial B_f^d}{\partial \bar{R}_E} = -1 < 0 \qquad (4.30\text{f})$$

$$\frac{\partial B_f^d}{\partial k} = -(1 - k)i\frac{\partial D^s}{\partial z_f} - D^s < 0. \qquad (4.30\text{g})$$

The interpretation of these effects is self-evident and will not be given here. At this point we are ready to build the financial model that reflects the new financial environment.

The Model

We remind the reader that in this chapter (and in the remainder of this book) we shall employ the notation introduced in chapter 3. Therefore, we shall not repeat the notation here. However, for the convenience of the reader, we shall allow the repetition inherent in building our new model *ab initio*.

As in the model of chapter 3, the financial sector consists of three financial assets, two of which are public-debt instruments. For simplicity, and without any loss of generality, we shall assume that one of these instruments—base money—is held only by financial institutions called banks. In other words, we shall assume that currency held by the public is fixed—say, at zero—so that base money is identical to reserves. The second public-debt instrument is available to both the financial and nonfinancial public, and it is called collectively bills or earning assets. The third financial asset is the debt of financial institutions, that is, demand deposits.

Equilibrium in the financial sector requires that the markets for these three assets are cleared, that is, that the excess demand for each of these assets is zero:

$$EDB = 0 \qquad \qquad \text{Bills Market}$$

$$EDR = 0 \qquad \qquad \text{Reserves Market}$$

$$EDD = 0 \qquad \qquad \text{Demand Deposits Market}$$

But the financial sector is constrained by Walras' Law for stocks:

$$EDB + EDR + EDD = 0. \qquad (4.31)$$

This equality holds whether or not the assets markets are cleared. We can, therefore, eliminate any one of the three assets markets. We shall choose to eliminate the market for earning assets or bills and, hence, to examine explicitly only the reserves and the demand-deposits markets. The equilibrium of the entire financial sector is, therefore, captured by:

$$EDD = 0 \qquad (4.32)$$

$$EDR = 0. \qquad (4.33)$$

System 4.32 through 4.33 must be contrasted to the case of a fixed deposit rate examined in the preceding chapter, where the financial sector was specified by:

$$EDR = 0 \qquad (4.33)$$

$$D = D^d(\cdot). \qquad (4.34)$$

In this chapter we are examining equilibrium of the financial sector alone, irrespective of what happens to the real sector. For this pursuit, we need only to develop and to use the model consisting of 4.32 and 4.33. However, because in later chapters we shall extend the model to include the real sector and because we shall then examine the consistency and stability of the equilibrium specification for the financial sector, ($EDD = 0$, $EDR = 0$ and, hence, $EDB = 0$), we must also spell out the dynamic adjustments by which this equilibrium is achieved. For these asset markets we rely on the law of supply and demand: The deposit rate rises with a speed of adjustment equal to λ if and only if there is excess supply of deposits; similarly, the bills or earning-assets rate rises with a speed of adjustment equal to δ if and only if there is excess demand for reserves, that is, excess supply of bills. These adjustment mechanisms are summarized by the differential equations that follow. (Recall that a dot over a symbol denotes the time derivative of that symbol.)

$$\dot{\zeta} = -\lambda\, EDD, \qquad \lambda > 0 \tag{4.35}$$

$$\frac{di}{dt} = \delta\, EDR, \qquad \delta > 0. \tag{4.36}$$

The only important difference between this model and the model examined in the previous chapter lies in 4.35. Here the deposit rate, ζ, varies according to the law of supply and demand, and it remains unchanged only when the deposit market and all other markets are cleared. In the model in chapter 3, ζ was fixed by the Central Bank at $\bar{\zeta}$, that is, $d\zeta/dt = 0$—always.

We can use the adjustment mechanisms in 4.35 and 4.36 to guarantee equilibrium of all three asset markets even if the remaining part of the entire economy—that is, the real sector—is not in equilibrium. All we need to assume is that both λ and δ are infinite. This assumption implies that all three asset markets are always in equilibrium:

$$-\lim_{\lambda \to \infty} \frac{1}{\lambda} \cdot \dot{\zeta} = EDD \to 0 \text{ or } EDD = 0 \tag{4.37}$$

$$\lim_{\delta \to \infty} \frac{1}{\delta} \frac{di}{dt} = EDR \to 0 \text{ or } EDR = 0. \tag{4.38}$$

This technique will be employed in a later chapter when we want to maintain continuous equilibrium in the financial sector while permitting disequilibrium in the real sector. In this chapter we shall examine the case when $EDD = 0$, $EDR = 0$, and, hence, $EDB = 0$, irrespective of how equilibrium is achieved—whether it is achieved because the entire system is in equilibrium or because the financial sector alone is in equilibrium (by means of $\lambda \to \infty$, $\delta \to \infty$).

To examine equilibrium of the financial sector, as described by equations 4.32 and 4.33, we need to specify first the components of excess demand for demand deposits and of excess demand for reserves. Excess demand for demand deposits, EDD, is the difference between the demand for demand deposits, $D^d(\cdot)$, and the supply of demand deposits, $D^s(\cdot)$:

$$EDD = D^d(\cdot) - D^s(\cdot). \qquad (4.39)$$

We have already stipulated in chapter 3 that the demand for demand deposits, $D^d(\cdot)$, depends negatively on the opportunity cost of holding demand deposits, z_h, and positively on a shift (shock) parameter, β; that is,

$$D^d = D^d(z_h; \beta), \frac{\partial D^d}{\partial z_h} < 0, \frac{\partial D^d}{\partial \beta} > 0. \qquad (4.40)$$

We suppress a scale variable—income or wealth—because this scale variable is assumed fixed for most of the chapters in this work. Now, the opportunity cost, z_h, that is relevant for households and for the nonfinancial public[5] is the difference between the real rate of return on bills, r, and the real rate of return on demand deposits, ρ. But since $r = i - \pi$, which is the difference between the nominal return on bills and expected inflation, and since $\rho = \zeta - \pi$, which is the difference between the nominal interest rate on demand deposits and expected inflation, it follows that

$$z_h = r - \rho = i - \pi - (\zeta - \pi) = i - \zeta. \qquad (4.41)$$

Hence the demand function is specified by

$$D^d = D^d(i - \zeta; \beta), \frac{\partial D^d}{\partial z_h} < 0, \frac{\partial D^d}{\partial \beta} > 0. \qquad (4.42)$$

As we have already seen in this chapter, the supply (by financial institutions) of demand deposits, D^s, depends positively on the real net profit margin of financial institutions, z_f, which is defined as

$$z_f = (1 - k)i - \pi - \rho. \qquad (4.43')$$

And since $\rho = \zeta - \pi$, z_f becomes

$$z_f = (1 - k)i - \zeta, \qquad (4.43)$$

which, of course, is the first argument in the supply function, D^s, derived in the previous discussion as 4.25. We saw there that the partial derivative of D^s with respect to z_f is positive; in other words, the supply of demand deposits by banks depends positively on the profit margin. Again, we must note that since we are assuming a fixed income and employment level, we shall not include this variable among the arguments of the demand and supply functions for demand deposits. Moreover, since we have inserted a shift parameter, β, in the demand function, we shall insert a shift parameter, μ, in the supply function. As we saw in the preceding section, this shift parameter captures among others cost-reducing financial innovations. For easy reference we shall record here and renumber as 4.44 and 4.45, the demand and supply functions:

$$D^d = D^d(1 - \zeta; \beta), \frac{\partial D^d}{\partial z_h} < 0, \frac{\partial D^d}{\partial \beta} > 0 \qquad (4.44)$$

$$D^s = D^s[(1 - k)i - \zeta; \mu], \frac{\partial D^s}{\partial z_f} > 0, \frac{\partial D^s}{\partial \mu} > 0. \qquad (4.45)$$

Substituting 4.44 and 4.45 into 4.39 and setting it equal to zero, we have the market clearance for demand deposits, $EDD = 0$:

$$EDD = D^d(i - \zeta; \beta) - D^s[(1 - k)i - \zeta; \mu] = 0. \qquad (4.46)$$

We see from 4.46 that $EDD = 0$ is an implicit function of the bill rate of interest, i, and the deposit rate, ζ, which are endogenous variables, and of β, μ, and k, which are true parameters. Our interest here is to determine the two interest rates—i and ζ—which are determined by the assets markets. We shall see that the second equation, $EDR = 0$, is also a function of i and ζ and of the remaining variables. Therefore, in principle we can solve the two equations $EDD = 0$ and $EDR = 0$, explicitly for i and ζ, in terms of the remaining variables. In fact, we can write these solutions as $i(p; \ldots)$ and $\zeta(p; \ldots)$, that is, as functions of the remaining endogenous variable, p, the price level, and the exogenous variables, some of which are true shocks and some of which are true policy instruments.

The mathematical difficulty arises in the market for reserves. As in chapter 3, EDR is specified as

$$EDR = R_R + \bar{R}_E - R_B - \frac{R_*}{p}.$$

Borrowed reserves, R_B, depend on the endogenous variable, i, and on the parameters, $\bar{d}$ and θ. Furthermore, we treat $\bar{R}_E$, R_*, and, at this stage, p as parameters. But required reserves are the product of the reserve requirement ratio, k, and the quantity of demand deposits, D:

$$R_R = k \cdot D.$$

But what is D? In chapter 3, where the deposit rate was fixed and the quantity of demand deposits was demand determined, D was simply demand, $D^d(\cdot)$. But now supply is on an equal footing with demand, and D must be both supply, D^s, and demand, D^d. To resolve the mathematical difficulty we must make the demand for demand deposits *identically* equal to the supply. This can happen only at the deposit rate that clears the demand-deposit market.

Our approach, introduced in the literature for the first time, is to solve the two equations, $EDD = 0$ and $EDR = 0$, sequentially, beginning with 4.46. In particular, we shall solve 4.46 explicitly for ζ as a function of all the remaining variables, including i. Of course, solving $EDD = 0$ for ζ makes economic sense: The level of ζ, so determined, is the one consistent with clearance of the demand-deposits market. Then we can find the effect on this deposit market-clearing deposit rate of changes in all the remaining variables, taken one at a time. We shall undertake this in the next section. And we shall examine clearance of the remaining markets, in addition to clearance of the deposit market, in chapter 5.

Determination of the Market-Clearing Deposit Rate

In this section we want to find the deposit rate, ζ, that clears the deposit market. This is the solution of 4.46 for ζ, which we write as:

$$\zeta = \hat{\zeta}(i; \beta, \mu, k). \tag{4.47}$$

This equation says that ζ is a function of the endogenous variable, i, and of the exogenous variables or parameters β, μ, k. To find the partial derivatives $\partial\hat{\zeta}/\partial i$, $\partial\hat{\zeta}/\partial\beta$, $\partial\hat{\zeta}/\partial\mu$ and $\partial\hat{\zeta}/\partial k$, which denote the comparative static effects of a change in the corresponding variables on ζ when the deposit market alone is cleared, we need to differentiate 4.46 totally:

$$\left[\frac{\partial D^d}{\partial z_h} - (1-k)\frac{\partial D^s}{\partial z_f}\right] di - \left(\frac{\partial D^d}{\partial z_h} - \frac{\partial D^s}{\partial z_f}\right) d\zeta$$

$$+ \frac{\partial D^d}{\partial\beta} d\beta - \frac{\partial D^s}{\partial\mu} d\mu + \frac{\partial D^s}{\partial z_f}\cdot idk = 0. \tag{4.48}$$

First we find the partial derivative of ζ with respect to the endogenous variable, i. Setting $d\beta = d\mu = dk = 0$ in 4.48 and solving, we get:

$$\frac{\partial \hat{\zeta}}{\partial i} = -\frac{(1-k)\dfrac{\partial D^s}{\partial z_f} - \dfrac{\partial D^d}{\partial z_h}}{\dfrac{\partial D^d}{\partial z_h} - \dfrac{\partial D^s}{\partial z_f}} > 0. \qquad (4.49)$$

Expression 4.49 states that an increase in the bill or earning-assets rate, i, while keeping all parameters fixed, necessitates an increase in the demand deposit rate, ζ, if clearance of the deposit market is to be maintained. The reason must be made clear. At the original equilibrium level of ζ an increase in i increases the opportunity cost of holding demand deposits ($z_h = i - \zeta$), thereby decreasing the demand for demand deposits; an increase in i also increases the profit margin of banks, $z_f = (1 - k)i - \zeta$, thereby causing an increase in the supply of demand deposits. The decreased demand and the increased supply mean excess supply of demand deposits. By the law of supply and demand, this excess supply is eliminated only if the banks offer a higher deposit rate, ζ.

Similarly, setting $di = d\mu = dk = 0$ in 4.48 and solving, we find the partial derivative of $\hat{\zeta}$ with respect to β:

$$\frac{\partial \hat{\zeta}}{\partial \beta} = \frac{\dfrac{\partial D^s}{\partial \beta}}{\dfrac{\partial D^d}{\partial z_h} - \dfrac{\partial D^s}{\partial z_f}} < 0. \qquad (4.50)$$

This partial derivative says that a positive shift in the demand function for demand deposits will *lower* the deposit rate, ζ. Although at first this result seems counterintuitive, the explanation is straightforward: At the original equilibrium level of the deposit rate, ζ, an increase in the demand for demand deposits causes excess demand, $EDD > 0$; this excess demand can be eliminated so that $EDD = 0$ can be reestablished only if the deposit rate falls. Because of the excess demand, the demanders will be satisfied with a lower rate of return on demand deposits.

On the other hand, a positive shift—for whatever reason, say, because of cost-reducing innovations—in the supply function of demand deposits causes excess supply, which is eliminated only if banks, or financial institutions, raise the interest rate paid on demand deposits. This result is derived by setting $di = d\beta = dk = 0$ in 4.48 and solving for $\partial \hat{\zeta}/\partial \mu$:

$$\frac{\partial \hat{\zeta}}{\partial \mu} = - \frac{\dfrac{\partial D^s}{\partial \mu}}{\dfrac{\partial D^d}{\partial z_h} - \dfrac{\partial D^s}{\partial z_f}} > 0. \qquad (4.51)$$

Finally, setting $di = d\beta = d\mu = 0$ and solving for $\partial \hat{\zeta}/\partial k$, we find:

$$\frac{\partial \hat{\zeta}}{\partial k} = \frac{i \cdot \dfrac{\partial D^s}{\partial z_f}}{\dfrac{\partial D^d}{\partial z_h} - \dfrac{\partial D^s}{\partial z_f}} < 0. \qquad (4.52)$$

That is, the increase in the reserve-requirement ratio, k, reduces the profit margin of banks, $z_f = (1 - k)i - \zeta$, thereby reducing the supply of demand deposits offered by banks. This reduction in supply causes excess demand for demand deposits, which can be eliminated by a fall in the deposit rate, ζ.

In summary, clearance of the market for demand deposits, $EDD = 0$—that is, equation 4.46 can be replaced by the solution 4.47 and its characteristics, equations 4.49 through 4.52.

We now come to a key step. Substituting 4.47—and its characteristics—into D^d (equation 4.44) and D^s (equation 4.45), we get the *identity*:

$$D^d[i - \hat{\zeta}(i; k, \beta, \mu); \beta] \equiv D^s[(1 - k)i - \hat{\zeta}(i; k, \beta, \mu); \mu]. \qquad (4.53)$$

Therefore, we can define as follows:

$$\hat{D} = D(i; k, \beta, \mu) \equiv D^d[i - \hat{\zeta}(i; k, \beta, \mu); \beta] \qquad (4.54)$$

and

$$\hat{D} = D(i; k, \beta, \mu) \equiv D^s[(1 - k)i - \hat{\zeta}(i; k, \beta, \mu); \mu]. \qquad (4.55)$$

Therefore, the partial derivatives, $\partial \hat{D}/\partial i$, $\partial \hat{D}/\partial k$, $\partial \hat{D}/\partial \beta$, and $\partial \hat{D}/\partial \mu$ will be the same whether they are derived by using 4.54 or by using 4.55. In fact, we can use this property as a test for arithmetical correctness. As an illustration, let us find $\partial \hat{D}/\partial i$. First, using 4.55, we get:

$$\frac{\partial \hat{D}}{\partial i} = \frac{\partial D^s}{\partial z_f} \left[(1 - k) - \frac{\partial \hat{\zeta}}{\partial i} \right] \qquad \text{by 4.55}$$

$$= \frac{\partial D^s}{\partial z_f} \cdot \left\{ (1 - k) - \frac{\dfrac{\partial D^d}{\partial z_h} - (1 - k)\dfrac{\partial D^s}{\partial z_f}}{\dfrac{\partial D^d}{\partial z_h} - \dfrac{\partial D^s}{\partial z_f}} \right\} \qquad \text{by 4.49}$$

$$= \frac{\partial D^s}{\partial z_f} \cdot \frac{(1 - k)\dfrac{\partial D^d}{\partial z_h} - (1 - k)\dfrac{\partial D^s}{\partial z_f} - \dfrac{\partial D^d}{\partial z_h} + (1 - k)\dfrac{\partial D^s}{\partial z_f}}{\dfrac{\partial D^d}{\partial z_h} - \dfrac{\partial D^s}{\partial z_f}}$$

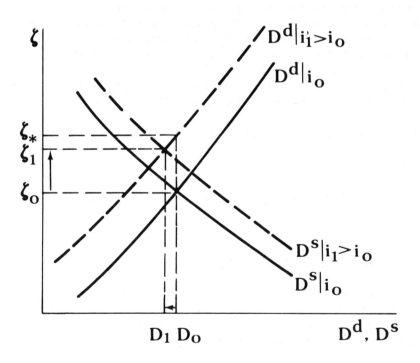

Figure 4–1. The Deposit Market: $\dfrac{\partial \hat{\zeta}}{\partial i} > 0,\ \dfrac{\partial \hat{D}}{\partial i} < 0$

or

$$\frac{\partial \hat{D}}{\partial i} = - \frac{k \dfrac{\partial D^s}{\partial z_f} \cdot \dfrac{\partial D^d}{\partial z_h}}{\dfrac{\partial D^d}{\partial z_h} - \dfrac{\partial D^s}{\partial z_f}} < 0. \qquad (4.56)$$

Now, using 4.54 we get:

$$\frac{\partial \hat{D}}{\partial i} = \frac{\partial D^d}{\partial z_h} \left(1 - \frac{\partial \hat{\zeta}}{\partial i} \right).$$

Substituting 4.49 for $\partial \hat{\zeta}/\partial i$, we get expression 4.56; according to 4.56, an increase in the bills interest rate, i, reduces the quantity of market-determined demand deposits. This is not as obvious as it seems, because the increase in i has opposite effects on the two sides of the deposit market, as we shall illustrate in figure 4–1.

Using either 4.54 or 4.55, we can find the effect of a change in the parameters, β, μ, k. These are given by 4.57 through 4.59.

$$\frac{\partial \hat{D}}{\partial \beta} = - \frac{\dfrac{\partial D^d}{\partial \beta} \cdot \dfrac{\partial D^s}{\partial z_f}}{\dfrac{\partial D^d}{\partial z_h} - \dfrac{\partial D^s}{\partial z_f}} > 0 \qquad (4.57)$$

$$\frac{\partial \hat{D}}{\partial \mu} \quad \frac{\dfrac{\partial D^d}{\partial z_h} \cdot \dfrac{\partial D^s}{\partial \mu}}{\dfrac{\partial D^d}{\partial z_h} - \dfrac{\partial D^s}{\partial z_f}} \qquad (4.58)$$

$$\frac{\partial \hat{D}}{\partial k} = - \frac{i \cdot \dfrac{\partial D^s}{\partial z_f} \cdot \dfrac{\partial D^d}{\partial z_h}}{\dfrac{\partial D^d}{\partial z_h} - \dfrac{\partial D^s}{\partial z_f}} < 0. \qquad (4.59)$$

As expected, a positive shift in the demand schedule for demand deposits increases the market-determined quantity of demand deposits—as does a positive shift in the supply function of demand deposits. Finally, we see that an increase in the reserve-requirement ratio, k, reduces the quantity of market-determined demand deposits.

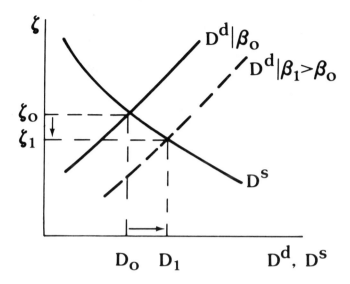

Figure 4–2. The Deposit Market: $\dfrac{\partial \hat{\zeta}}{\partial \beta} < 0, \dfrac{\partial \hat{D}}{\partial \beta} > 0$

However, we should emphasize that the results depicted by equations 4.56 through 4.59 are the effects on the quantity of demand deposits when there is a corresponding change in i, β, μ, or k and when the demand-deposit market alone is cleared.

Figures 4–1 to 4–4 illustrate and explain the results embodied in equations 4.49 through 4.52 and in 4.56 through 4.59. Figure 4–1 explains the pair of results in 4.49 and 4.56—that is, the effect of an exogenous increase in i on the deposit rate and on the quantity of demand deposits. For a given level of i—say, i_0—the pair (ζ_0, D_0) depicts the market-clearing deposit rate and the market-clearing level of demand deposits. When the interest rate is at i_1, greater than i_0, the demand schedule, $D^d(\cdot)$, shifts to the left and the supply schedule, $D^s(\cdot)$, shifts to the right. This by itself is sufficient to guarantee that the deposit rate will rise (to ζ_1), as expression 4.49 suggests. Anytime there is a shift of this kind ζ will rise. On the other hand, the result of 4.56, that D will fall (to D_1), appears to depend entirely on the way figure 4–1 is drawn; that is, on the stipulation that the increase in i (to i_1) shifts the demand curve $D^d(\cdot)$ vertically upward by more than it shifts the supply curve $D^s(\cdot)$.

The question, then, boils down to this: Will an increase in i always shift the D^d curve by more than it shifts the D^s curve? The answer is yes, and the

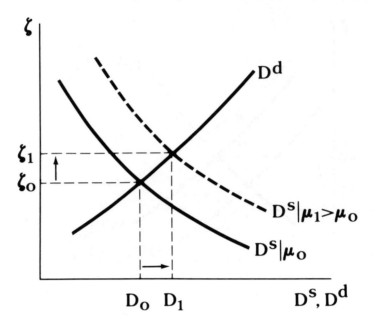

Figure 4–3. The Deposit Market: $\dfrac{\partial \hat{\zeta}}{\partial \mu} > 0, \ \dfrac{\partial \hat{D}}{\partial \mu} > 0$

reason is the following: Suppose that the interest rate rises from i_0 to i_1 and that we want the quantity of demand deposits to remain at D_0. The only way this will happen is if the opportunity cost of holding demand deposits— $z_h = i - \zeta$—remains unchanged. This requires that the percentage change in ζ—namely, $\zeta_* - \zeta_0$—equal the percentage change in i, $i_1 - i_0$. Now, let us pose the same question for the quantity supplied. The quantity supplied— D^s—will remain at D_0 only if the net profit margin of banks, $z_f = (1 - k)i - \zeta$, remains unchanged. This requires that ζ rises by only $(1 - k)$ times the change in i, which, of course, is less than the change in i. Hence, the vertical shift in the supply curve is less than the vertical shift in the demand curve.[6]

Next, illustrating the results of 4.50 and 4.57 is simple. In figure 4–2 the positive shock, $\partial D^d/\partial \beta$, shifts the demand schedule to the right with the clearcut effects of a lower deposit rate and a larger quantity of demand deposits. Similarly, figure 4–3 illustrates the results of 4.51 and 4.58. The increase in the supply function of demand deposits shifts the D^s curve to the right (and upward), raising both the deposit rate and the quantity of demand deposits. Finally, the results of 4.52 and 4.59 are shown in figure 4–4 with a

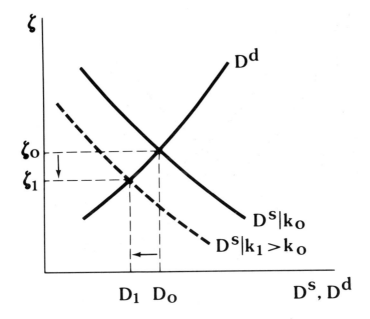

Figure 4–4. The Deposit Market: $\dfrac{\partial \hat{\zeta}}{\partial k} < 0, \dfrac{\partial \hat{D}}{\partial k} < 0$

leftward shift in the D^s curve that results in a reduction in ζ and a reduction in D.

Concluding Comments

Having specified the entire new financial structure, we have examined the market for demand deposits in isolation, and we have determined the market-clearing deposit rate and the quantity of demand deposits. We have further determined the effects of monetary policy and of other monetary shocks on the deposit rate and on the quantity of demand deposits when the deposit market alone is required to clear.

These results will be useful in the next chapter when we examine the clearance of all financial markets. The market-determined quantity of demand deposits will be the relevant variable for specifying required reserves and, hence, for examining reserves-market clearance. Finally, we should point out that in the next chapter we shall derive the effects of monetary policy and of other shocks on the deposit rate and on the quantity of demand deposits when *all* financial markets are cleared.

Notes

1. See K. G. Hadjimichalakis and M. G. Hadjimichalakis (1982).

2. In the literature of the *banking firm*, several contributions stand out: A. J. Meigs (1962); S. M. Goldfeld (1966), S. M. Goldfeld and E. J. Kane (1966); M. A. Klein (1972); and B. Klein (1974). The appendix in D. E. Lindsey (1977) also has a theory of the banking firm. However, none of these specifications fit our specifications exactly. For this reason we introduce a theory that is tailored to the needs of our study.

3. See S. M. Goldfeld and E. J. Kane (1966).

4. This assumption captures the spirit of the administration of the discount window; the more—and the more frequently—a financial institution borrows from a Federal Reserve Bank, the more difficult it becomes to borrow further. My understanding of discount-window borrowings has benefited from discussions with John Spitzer, who until March 1982 was the senior economist in charge of the Discount Function, Federal Reserve Board.

5. See H. Rose (1973).

6. A corollary to this is the result that the equilibrium increase in ζ is less than the increase in i. In figure 4–1 we have $\zeta_1 - \zeta_0 < i_1 - i_0$. In expression 4.49 the numerator is less than the denominator; hence, $0 < \partial \hat{\zeta}/\partial i < 1$.

5

The Emerging Regime: Effects of Policy and Other Shocks on Interest Rates and on Aggregates in Full Financial Equilibrium

In this chapter we shall examine the determination of interest rates and of aggregates when all financial markets—those for reserves, for T-bills, and for demand deposits—are cleared. And we shall proceed to find the effects of changes in instruments of monetary control and the effects of shocks on the two interest rates and on monetary and reserves aggregates.

We shall first show that by exploiting the technique introduced in the previous chapter we can reduce the full equilibrium of the entire financial system to one qualitatively indistinguishable from the equilibrium of the fixed-deposit-rate regime.[1] Then we shall proceed to determine the effects of monetary policy and of shocks on the bills interest rate when all financial markets are cleared. It is interesting to note here that the interest rate rises whether there is an increase in the demand function for or in the supply function of demand deposits.

Our result—that the bill rate rises when there is a positive shift in the demand for demand deposits—is expected; in fact, it is standard in the literature. What is unexpected and, in fact, what exemplifies the fundamental difference between the two regimes is the following result: An increase in the supply of demand deposits (that is, an increase in the supply of "money") will *increase* the bill rate. That is, an increase in the supply of money is, in this case, contractionary. The reason for this drastic departure in results is simple: A positive shift (an increase) in the supply function of demand deposits causes excess supply (of demand deposits), which is eliminated only when the (variable) deposit rate rises. This rise shifts wealth away from other earning assets (away from bills) causing excess supply of bills, which, in turn, is eliminated only if the bill rate rises.

In the third section, we shall inquire whether the effects of policy and of other monetary shocks on the deposit rate will change when all asset markets—not merely the deposit market as in chapter 4—are required to equilibrate. We shall see that the key difference occurs when we consider the effect of an increase in the demand function for demand deposits. When the demand-deposit market alone is required to clear, the positive shift in the demand function lowers the deposit rate; but when all financial markets are required to clear, this negative effect may or may not prevail. However, we shall specify the conditions for either case. (And in chapter 6 we shall see that variability of interest rates and aggregates depends on these same conditions.)

In the rest of this chapter, we shall examine the effects of the same deliberate and inadvertent shocks on monetary and reserves aggregates, namely, on the quantity of market-determined demand deposits and on the quantities of borrowed and total reserves, in full financial equilibrium. The effects on demand deposits (money) are important, especially if the Central Bank follows the procedure of intermediate targeting, as is currently the case in the United States. Knowledge of the effects of changes in monetary instruments and of shocks on the quantity of demand deposits is obviously necessary for monetary control. This knowledge is also important to those who try to interpret the actions of the Central Bank—the Fed watchers—by deciphering the releases of monetary data. And furthermore, knowledge of the effects on the reserves aggregates are useful for similar purposes.

In the section Effects on Demand Deposits, we shall concentrate on the effects on the quantity of demand deposits. Particularly interesting is the result that positive shifts in either the demand function or the supply function of demand deposits will lead to an increase in the quantity of demand deposits. Since, as noted above, these same shocks also increase the interest rates, there is a conflict between the signals provided by interest rates and by monetary aggregates as indicators of economic activity. While the supply of money increases in these two cases, it is contractionary.

Next, we shall examine the effects of the same shocks on borrowed and on total reserves. And in the final section, we shall apply our analysis of demand and supply shocks to the issue of financial innovations.

Full Financial Equilibrium: Effects of Policy and Shocks on the (Bills) Interest Rate

We are now ready to specify the excess demand for reserves (EDR), and to determine both the bills rate and the deposit rate when all asset markets are cleared. We shall also examine the effects of monetary policy and of shocks on these interest rates—again, when all asset markets are cleared.

As stipulated in chapter 3, there are two components on the supply side of the reserves market: real borrowed reserves, R_B, and real nonborrowed reserves, R. The amount of real borrowed reserves is an endogenous variable depending primarily on the spread $(r - d)$. The wider the spread between the real bills interest rate and the real discount rate, the higher the amount borrowed by financial institutions from the Central Bank. But the spread between the two *real* rates is identical to the spread between the nominal rates: $r - d = i - \pi - (\bar{d} - \pi) = i - \bar{d}$. Hence, we can specify the behavioral relation,

$$R_B = R_B(i - \bar{d};\ \theta),\quad \frac{\partial R_B}{\partial(i - \bar{d})} \equiv R'_B > 0,\quad \frac{\partial R_B}{\partial \theta} > 0, \quad (5.1)$$

where θ is a shift parameter. Of course, this is the relation we have derived in chapter 4 from the profit-maximizing decisions of the banking firm.

Turning to the second component of the supply of real reserves, we observe that real nonborrowed reserves—R—which we shall hereafter call the real reserve base, are defined as the ratio of nonborrowed nominal reserves, or the nominal reserve base, and the price level, p:

$$R \equiv \frac{R_*}{p}. \qquad (5.2)$$

The demand side also has two components: required (real) reserves and excess (real) reserves. Excess (real) reserves depend on competing rates of return, since they—as well as "free reserves" of which they are a component—are the result of the rational behavior of financial institutions. However, for simplicity we shall assume at this point that excess reserves are constant. Moreover, since we assume that borrowed reserves—the other component of free reserves—depend on competing rates, the results remain qualitatively unchanged. Hence, we assume that

$$R_E = \bar{R}_E. \qquad (5.3)$$

Now we shall turn to the second component of the demand for reserves—namely, required reserves, R_R. These are the product of the reserve-requirement ratio, k, and demand deposits. Demand deposits are the result of the market system—that is, of D—which is the equality of demand for and supply of demand deposits.

$$R_R = k \cdot D. \qquad (5.4)$$

In summary, we see that EDR is

$$EDR = k \cdot D + \bar{R}_E - R_B(i - \bar{d};\ \theta) - \frac{R_*}{p}. \qquad (5.5)$$

Now we can see the mathematical difficulty noted in the preceding chapter: Required reserves are the product of the reserve-requirement ratio, k, and the quantity of demand deposits, D. But what is D? In chapter 3, because the quantity of demand deposits was demand determined, we used the demand for demand deposits, that is,

$$D = D^d(\,\cdot\,).$$

But now both supply and demand are on an equal footing. Is it D^d or D^s? In fact, it is both, and this is captured by

$$D = \hat{D}(i; k, \beta, \mu). \qquad (5.6)$$

Hence, required reserves are given by

$$R_R = k\hat{D}(i; k, \beta, \mu),$$

where $\hat{D}$ is inserted for D in 5.4. Market clearance for reserves implies that

$$EDR = k \cdot \hat{D}(i; k, \beta, \mu) + \bar{R}_E - R_B(i - \bar{d}; \theta) - \frac{R_*}{p} = 0. \qquad (5.7)$$

Thus we have reduced equilibrium of the entire financial sector of the emerging regime to one equation, 5.7. Comparing this equation with the corresponding equation for the fixed-deposit-rate regime (that is, equation 3.16), we see that they are qualitatively equivalent.

Following the earlier technique we can solve 5.7 for i as a function of the endogenous variable, p, and the remaining policy and shock parameters. The effects of these variables and parameters on i can be found by differentiating 5.7 totally:

$$\left(k\frac{\partial \hat{D}}{\partial i} - R'_B \right) di + \left[\hat{D}(\,\cdot\,) + k\frac{\partial \hat{D}}{\partial k} \right] dk + d\bar{R}_E + \frac{R_*}{p^2} dp$$

$$- \frac{\partial R_B}{\partial \theta} d\theta - \frac{dR_*}{p} + R'_B d\bar{d} + k\frac{\partial \hat{D}}{\partial \beta} d\beta + k\frac{\partial \hat{D}}{\partial \mu} d\mu = 0. \quad (5.8)$$

And the solution of 5.7 for i is represented by 5.9,

$$i = i(p; R_*, k, \bar{R}_E, \mu, \beta, \theta). \qquad (5.9)$$

We want to derive the partials of i, as given by 5.9. These are the comparative static effects on i when one of the parameters is changed while the other parameters are fixed and when all assets markets are cleared. We have seen that the problem of clearance of all three assets markets is reduced to the clearance of the reserves market of equation 5.7. If we are interested only in the signs of the effects on i, we can derive them informally and simply, directly from 5.7.

First, let us suppose that there is an exogenous increase in the price level. This increase reduces the real reserve base, thereby causing excess demand for reserves (which registers as excess supply of bills). But the excess demand for reserves and, hence, the excess supply of bills is eliminated only if the interest rate, i, rises. Therefore, we have demonstrated that an exogenous increase in the price level raises the interest rate on bills, i. This corresponds to the familiar leftward shift of the LM curve when the price level rises. (Equivalently, it corresponds to the Wicksell effect.) We expect, then, to prove formally that $\partial i/\partial p > 0$.

On the other hand, we can reverse the argument and show that an increase in the nominal reserve base lowers the interest rate, that is, that $\partial i/\partial R_* < 0$. The increase in the nominal reserve base actually increases the real reserve base, given the price level, thereby causing excess supply of reserves (that is, excess demand for bills), which necessitates a fall in the interest rate if clearance of these markets is to be maintained. Similarly, an increase in the discount rate, $\bar{d}$, reduces borrowed reserves which, in turn, causes excess demand for reserves (that is, excess supply of bills). Equilibrium is reestablished only if the interest rate rises—that is, if $\partial i/\partial\bar{d} > 0$. We have the opposite effect on i when there is a positive shift in the borrowings function. Now let us suppose that for some reason—at the initiative of either the Central Bank or of financial institutions—borrowed reserves rise. This causes excess supply of reserves (excess demand for bills), which reduces the interest rate; that is, $\partial i/\partial\theta < 0$.

Next, an increase in excess reserves, $\bar{R}_E$, will cause excess demand for reserves (excess supply of bills), thereby raising the interest rate—that is, $\partial i/\partial\bar{R}_E > 0$. A positive shock in the demand for demand deposits will also increase the bills interest rate, i. The reason, of course, lies in the increase in the quantity of demand deposits—that is, in the result $\partial\hat{D}/\partial\beta > 0$. This, in turn, increases required reserves, causing excess demand for reserves; as a result, the interest rate rises, $\partial i/\partial\beta > 0$. For precisely the same reason—that is, because the quantity of deposits is increased—a positive shock in the supply of demand deposits raises the interest rate, $\partial i/\partial\mu > 0$.

All these comparative statics results are derived from equation 5.8. For example, setting all differentials except di and dp equal to zero and solving, we get:

$$\frac{\partial i}{\partial p} = -\frac{\dfrac{R_*}{p^2}}{k\dfrac{\partial\hat{D}}{\partial i} - R'_B} > 0. \tag{5.10}$$

Similarly, we get the remaining results:

$$\frac{\partial i}{\partial R_*} = \frac{\dfrac{1}{p}}{k\dfrac{\partial \hat{D}}{\partial i} - R'_B} < 0 \qquad (5.11)$$

$$\frac{\partial i}{\partial \bar{d}} = -\frac{R'_B}{k\dfrac{\partial \hat{D}}{\partial i} - R'_B} > 0 \qquad (5.12)$$

$$\frac{\partial i}{\partial \theta} = \frac{\dfrac{\partial R_B}{\partial \theta}}{k\dfrac{\partial \hat{D}}{\partial i} - R'_B} < 0 \qquad (5.13)$$

$$\frac{\partial i}{\partial \bar{R}_E} = -\frac{1}{k\dfrac{\partial \hat{D}}{\partial i} - R'_B} > 0 \qquad (5.14)$$

$$\frac{\partial i}{\partial \beta} = -\frac{k\dfrac{\partial \hat{D}}{\partial \beta}}{k\dfrac{\partial \hat{D}}{\partial i} - R'_B} > 0 \qquad (5.15)$$

$$\frac{\partial i}{\partial \mu} = -\frac{k\dfrac{\partial \hat{D}}{\partial \mu}}{k\dfrac{\partial \hat{D}}{\partial i} - R'_B} > 0 \qquad (5.16)$$

The final comparative-statics result that we must examine is a change in the reserve-requirement ratio, k. It is clear from 5.7 that an increase in k has two opposite effects. First, for the same amount of deposits, $\hat{D}$, an increase in k increases required reserves, which creates excess demand for reserves. On the other hand, the amount of demand deposits will, in fact, fall because $\partial \hat{D}/\partial i < 0$; this fall, in turn, contributes to a fall in required reserves. Whether the interest rate rises or falls depends on which effect predominates. Formally, from 5.8 we get:

$$\frac{\partial i}{\partial k} = -\frac{\hat{D}(\cdot) + k \dfrac{\partial \hat{D}}{\partial k}}{k \dfrac{\partial \hat{D}}{\partial i} - R_B'}. \qquad (5.17)$$

We shall postpone the derivation of conditions that sign $\partial i/\partial k$ until we derive formulas for $\partial i/\partial p$, $\partial i/\partial R_*, \ldots, \partial i/\partial k$, which incorporate only ultimate behavioral parameters. Our expressions 5.10 through 5.17 are partly in terms of market relations, reflected in $\partial \hat{D}/\partial i$, $\partial \hat{D}/\partial \beta$, $\partial \hat{D}/\partial \mu$, and $\partial \hat{D}/\partial k$. Therefore, we need to substitute into 5.10 through 5.17 expressions 4.27 through 4.30 from chapter 4—renumbered here as 5.18 through 5.21—which rely entirely on behavioral coefficients.

$$\frac{\partial \hat{D}}{\partial i} = -\frac{k \dfrac{\partial D^s}{\partial z_f} \cdot \dfrac{\partial D^d}{\partial z_h}}{\dfrac{\partial D^d}{\partial z_h} - \dfrac{\partial D^s}{\partial z_f}} < 0 \qquad (5.18)$$

$$\frac{\partial \hat{D}}{\partial \beta} = -\frac{\dfrac{\partial D^d}{\partial \beta} \cdot \dfrac{\partial D^s}{\partial z_f}}{\dfrac{\partial D^d}{\partial z_h} - \dfrac{\partial D^s}{\partial z_f}} > 0 \qquad (5.19)$$

$$\frac{\partial \hat{D}}{\partial \mu} = \frac{\dfrac{\partial D^d}{\partial z_h} \cdot \dfrac{\partial D^s}{\partial \mu}}{\dfrac{\partial D^d}{\partial z_h} - \dfrac{\partial D^s}{\partial z_f}} > 0 \qquad (5.20)$$

$$\frac{\partial \hat{D}}{\partial k} = - \frac{i \cdot \dfrac{\partial D^s}{\partial z_f} \cdot \dfrac{\partial D^d}{\partial z_h}}{\dfrac{\partial D^d}{\partial z_h} - \dfrac{\partial D^s}{\partial z_f}} < 0. \qquad (5.21)$$

Substituting 5.18 into 5.10 through 5.14, we get, respectively:

$$\frac{\partial i}{\partial p} = \frac{\dfrac{R_*}{p^2} \left(\dfrac{\partial D^d}{\partial z_h} - \dfrac{\partial D^s}{\partial z_f} \right)}{Q} > 0 \qquad (5.22)$$

$$\frac{\partial i}{\partial R_*} = - \frac{\dfrac{1}{p} \left(\dfrac{\partial D^d}{\partial z_h} - \dfrac{\partial D^s}{\partial z_f} \right)}{Q} < 0 \qquad (5.23)$$

$$\frac{\partial i}{\partial \bar{d}} = \frac{R_B' \left(\dfrac{\partial D^d}{\partial z_h} - \dfrac{\partial D^s}{\partial z_f} \right)}{Q} > 0 \qquad (5.24)$$

$$\frac{\partial i}{\partial \theta} = - \frac{\dfrac{\partial R_B}{\partial \theta} \left(\dfrac{\partial D^d}{\partial z_h} - \dfrac{\partial D^s}{\partial z_f} \right)}{Q} < 0 \qquad (5.25)$$

$$\frac{\partial i}{\partial \bar{R}_E} = \frac{\left(\dfrac{\partial D^d}{\partial z_h} - \dfrac{\partial D^s}{\partial z_f} \right)}{Q} > 0 \qquad (5.26)$$

And substituting equations 5.19 through 5.21, in addition to 5.18, into 5.15 through 5.17, we get 5.27 through 5.29:

$$\frac{\partial i}{\partial \beta} = - \frac{k \dfrac{\partial D^d}{\partial \beta} \cdot \dfrac{\partial D^s}{\partial z_f}}{Q} > 0 \qquad (5.27)$$

$$\frac{\partial i}{\partial \mu} = \frac{k \dfrac{\partial D^d}{\partial z_h} \cdot \dfrac{\partial D^s}{\partial \mu}}{Q} > 0 \qquad (5.28)$$

$$\frac{\partial i}{\partial k} = \frac{\hat{D} \cdot \left(\dfrac{\partial D^d}{\partial z_h} - \dfrac{\partial D^s}{\partial z_f} \right) - ik \dfrac{\partial D^s}{\partial z_f} \cdot \dfrac{\partial D^d}{\partial z_h}}{Q} \gtreqless 0, \qquad (5.29)$$

where

$$Q = k^2 \frac{\partial D^s}{\partial z_f} \frac{\partial D^d}{\partial z_h} + R'_B \left(\frac{\partial D^d}{\partial z_h} - \frac{\partial D^s}{\partial z_f} \right) < 0 \qquad (5.30)$$

Now, we are ready to derive plausible conditions that guarantee that an increase in the reserve-requirement ratio, k, will increase the bills rate, i— that is, $\partial i / \partial k > 0$. Since $Q < 0$, we see from 5.29 that a sufficient condition for $\partial i / \partial k > 0$ is 5.I, as follows:

$$ik \frac{\partial D^d}{\partial z_h} + D^d > 0. \qquad (5.I)$$

Defining the absolute interest elasticity, ε^d, of the demand for demand deposits,

$$\varepsilon^d \equiv - \frac{\partial D^d}{\partial z_h} \cdot \frac{i - \zeta}{D^d},$$

we can rewrite the sufficient condition in 5.I as 5.II:

$$i(1 - k \, \varepsilon^d) - \zeta > 0. \qquad (5.II)$$

We note immediately that when $\varepsilon^d = 1$, this sufficient condition becomes $(1 - k)i - \zeta > 0$, which is satisfied for our profit-maximizing firm. On the other hand, when $\varepsilon^d < 1$, condition 5.II is again satisfied.

We have shown that a sufficient condition for $\partial i/\partial k > 0$ is $\varepsilon^d \leqq 1$. But all empirical estimates of this elasticity are 0.5 or lower, and, hence, satisfaction of the condition is guaranteed. Moreover, in our model the term *demand deposits* is all-inclusive, which implies that the elasticity will be even smaller because in a model like ours there are fewer and more remote substitutes for demand deposits than in the existing model.

Effects on the Deposit Rate

So far in this chapter we have determined the effects of monetary policy and of inadvertent shocks on the bills interest rate when all financial markets are cleared. In this section we determine the corresponding effects on the deposit rate.

Recall that in chapter 4 we derived the effects of changes in the parameters β, μ, and k on the deposit rate when the deposit market *alone* is cleared; these effects were denoted by $\partial\zeta/\partial\beta$, $\partial\hat\zeta/\partial\mu$ and $\partial\hat\zeta/\partial k$. In this section we derive the effects of deliberate and inadvertent shocks on the deposit rate when all markets are cleared. There are two additional facets to this problem: The effects of previously examined shocks are more complex because there are feedback effects from the other markets to consider; also, there are additional shocks—namely, those emanating from the remaining markets—to examine.

We begin our analysis with the solution for ζ when the deposit market alone is cleared, that is when $EDD = 0$. This solution is represented by equation 4.18; 4.18 is renumbered here as 5.31:

$$\zeta = \hat\zeta\,(i;\, \beta,\, \mu,\, k). \tag{5.31}$$

Next we substitute the solution for i when all financial markets are cleared into 5.31; that is, we substitute 5.9 and its partials, depicted by 5.22 through 5.29, into 5.31. The result is

$$\zeta = \hat\zeta[i(p;R_*,\, \bar d,\, \theta,\, \bar R_E,\, \beta,\, \mu,\, k);\, \beta,\, \mu,\, k]. \tag{5.32}$$

In summary, expression 5.31 represents the solution for ζ when the demands-deposit market alone clears, whereas expression 5.32 represents the solution for ζ when all financial markets clear.

We shall denote the "total" effect of shock a_j on ζ—that is, the effect of shock a_j on the deposit rate when all markets are cleared—by $\Delta\zeta/\Delta a_j$. Total differentiation of 5.32 yields, in compact form:

$$\frac{\Delta\zeta}{\Delta a_j} = \frac{\partial\hat{\zeta}}{\partial a_j} + \frac{\partial\hat{\zeta}}{\partial i}\frac{\partial i}{\partial a_j}, \tag{5.33}$$

where

$$a_j = p, R_*, \bar{d}, \theta, \bar{R}_E, \beta, \mu, \text{ or } k.$$

We see, then, that for the three shocks, β, μ, k, the total effect on the deposit rate consists of a "direct" effect and an indirect effect. The direct effect—$\partial\hat{\zeta}/\partial a_j$—operates through the deposit market in isolation. The indirect effect operates through all financial markets and is incorporated into the effect on the bills rate, i, and through this, into the deposit rate; this is the meaning of the component $(\partial\hat{\zeta}/\partial i)/(\partial i/\partial a_j)$. For the remaining shocks, p, R_*, $\bar{d}$, θ, and $\bar{R}_E$, only the indirect effect is operative.

Explicitly, these effects are

$$\frac{\Delta\zeta}{\Delta p} = \frac{\partial\hat{\zeta}}{\partial i}\frac{\partial i}{\partial p} > 0 \tag{5.34}$$

$$\frac{\Delta\zeta}{\Delta R_*} = \frac{\partial\hat{\zeta}}{\partial i}\frac{\partial i}{\partial R_*} < 0 \tag{5.35}$$

$$\frac{\Delta\zeta}{\Delta\bar{d}} = \frac{\partial\hat{\zeta}}{\partial i}\frac{\partial i}{\partial\bar{d}} > 0 \tag{5.36}$$

$$\frac{\Delta\zeta}{\Delta\theta} = \frac{\partial\hat{\zeta}}{\partial i}\frac{\partial i}{\partial\theta} < 0 \tag{5.37}$$

$$\frac{\Delta\zeta}{\Delta\bar{R}_E} = \frac{\partial\hat{\zeta}}{\partial i}\frac{\partial i}{\partial\bar{R}_E} > 0 \tag{5.38}$$

$$\frac{\Delta \zeta}{\Delta \beta} = \frac{\partial \hat{\zeta}}{\partial \beta} + \frac{\partial \hat{\zeta}}{\partial i} \frac{\partial i}{\partial \beta} \tag{5.39}$$

$$\frac{\Delta \zeta}{\Delta \mu} = \frac{\partial \hat{\zeta}}{\partial \mu} + \frac{\partial \hat{\zeta}}{\partial i} \frac{\partial i}{\partial \mu} > 0 \tag{5.40}$$

$$\frac{\Delta \zeta}{\Delta k} = \frac{\partial \hat{\zeta}}{\partial k} + \frac{\partial \hat{\zeta}}{\partial i} \frac{\partial i}{\partial k}. \tag{5.41}$$

As we see from expressions 5.34 through 5.41, the signs of some of these total effects on the deposits rate can readily be ascertained. The cases in which only the indirect effects are present fall into this category. These cases are represented by expressions 5.34 through 5.38. In the case of 5.34, an increase in the price level will raise the bills interest rate, which, in turn, raises the deposit rate. However, the opposite forces are in operation in the case of 5.35; an increase in the nominal reserve base, R_*, lowers the interest rate, which, in turn, pulls down the deposit rate. In 5.36 we see that an increase in the discount rate raises the interest rate, i, which, in turn, raises the deposit rate, ζ. By 5.37 we see that the positive shock in the borrowed-reserves function—say, because of a more liberalized operation of the discount window—reduces the interest rate, i, which, in turn, lowers the deposit rate. On the other hand, an increase in the holdings of excess reserves by the financial institutions will raise the bills interest rate, i, and, hence, the deposit rate.

The key to all these explanations is the positive relation between ζ and i, captured by $\partial \zeta / \partial i$. This is the result of substitution between assets. When, in 5.36, for example, the increased discount rate raises the interest on bills, households and firms shift from demand deposits to bills, thereby causing an excess supply of demand deposits, and, hence, causing pressure on banks to raise their deposit rate. Similar explanations apply to all other expressions of 5.34 through 5.38.

Thus we have covered the cases when the indirect effect on the deposit rate is zero. But in 5.40 we can sign outright the effect even in the presence of a direct effect. Of course, the reason is obvious; both the direct and the indirect effects are of the same sign, namely, positive. An increase in the supply function of demand deposits requires an increase in the deposit rate if the deposit market is to be cleared. But it also raises the interest rate on bills, which pushes the deposit rate even higher.

However, in the case of a positive shift in the demand for demand deposits, the two effects pull in opposite directions. The direct effect is negative whereas the indirect effect is positive. It is imperative, therefore, that we examine whether the direct effect dominates or whether the indirect effect wins out, thereby raising the deposit rate. Finally, in the typical case when an increase in the reserve-requirement ratio increases the bills interest rate, again the direct and indirect effects are of opposite signs.

To see which effect dominates we must resort to expressions that rely exclusively on behavioral coefficients. Such equivalent expressions for the remaining formulas, 5.34 through 5.38 and 5.39, are necessary if we want to undertake comparison of effects between the two regimes. We proceed, therefore, to derive the total effects on ζ—that is, all $\Delta\zeta/\Delta a_j$, in terms of behavioral relations.

Substituting 4.20 through 4.23 and 5.22 through 5.29 into 5.34 through 5.41, we get, after tedious manipulations:

$$\frac{\Delta\zeta}{\Delta p} = -\frac{\dfrac{R_*}{p^2}}{Q} \cdot \left\{(1-k)\frac{\partial D^s}{\partial z_f} - \frac{\partial D^d}{\partial z_h}\right\} > 0 \qquad (5.42)$$

$$\frac{\Delta\zeta}{\Delta R_*} = \frac{1}{pQ} \cdot \left\{(1-k)\frac{\partial D^s}{\partial z_f} - \frac{\partial D^d}{\partial z_h}\right\} < 0 \qquad (5.43)$$

$$\frac{\Delta\zeta}{\Delta\bar{d}} = -\frac{R_B'}{Q} \cdot \left\{(1-k)\frac{\partial D^s}{\partial z_f} - \frac{\partial D^d}{\partial z_h}\right\} > 0 \qquad (5.44)$$

$$\frac{\Delta\zeta}{\Delta\theta} = \frac{\dfrac{\partial R_B}{\partial\theta}}{Q} \cdot \left\{(1-k)\frac{\partial D^s}{\partial z_f} - \frac{\partial D^d}{\partial z_h}\right\} < 0 \qquad (5.45)$$

$$\frac{\Delta \zeta}{\Delta \bar{R}_E} = -\frac{1}{Q} \cdot \left\{ (1-k)\frac{\partial D^s}{\partial z_f} - \frac{\partial D^d}{\partial z_h} \right\} > 0 \qquad (5.46)$$

$$\frac{\Delta \zeta}{\Delta \beta} = \frac{\dfrac{\partial D^d}{\partial \beta}}{Q} \cdot \left\{ k(k-1)\frac{\partial D^s}{\partial z_f} + R'_B \right\} \gtreqless 0 \qquad (5.47)$$

$$\frac{\Delta \zeta}{\Delta \mu} = \frac{\dfrac{\partial D^s}{\partial \mu}}{Q} \cdot \left\{ k\frac{\partial D^d}{\partial z_h} - R'_B \right\} > 0 \qquad (5.48)$$

$$\frac{\Delta \zeta}{\Delta k} =$$

$$-\left\{ \frac{iR'_B \dfrac{\partial D^s}{\partial z_f} + \left(\dfrac{\partial D^d}{\partial z_h} - \dfrac{\partial D^s}{\partial z_f} \right) \cdot \hat{D}(\cdot) - ik\dfrac{\partial D^s}{\partial z_f}\dfrac{\partial D^d}{\partial z_h} + k\dfrac{\partial D^s}{\partial z_f} \cdot \hat{D}(\cdot)}{Q} \right\}$$

$$(5.49)$$

As expected, the overall effect of a change in the reserve-requirement ratio on the deposit rate is indeterminate without additional assumptions. However, the most important of the results listed is the indeterminancy of $\Delta\zeta/\Delta\beta$. Under some conditions the sign is negative, but under some other plausible conditions the sign becomes positive. When the sign becomes positive, it means that the indirect effect must outweigh the direct effect. Let us recall that the direct effect—$\partial\hat{\zeta}/\partial\beta$—says that an increase (shift) in the demand for demand deposits lowers the deposit-market-clearing deposit rate. But the market-determined quantity of demand deposits rises, which, in turn, raises the (bills) interest rate. Of course, when the indirect effect predominates, this rise is sufficient to increase ζ, to the point where it negates the original fall.

We can write the conditions for signing the term $\Delta\zeta/\Delta\beta$ as

$$\frac{\Delta\zeta}{\Delta\beta} \underset{>}{\overset{<}{=}} 0 \text{ when } \left\{ k(k-1)\frac{\partial D^s}{\partial z_f} + R'_B \right\} \underset{<}{\overset{\geq}{=}} 0. \qquad (5.50)$$

We note immediately some special cases: First, when the amount of borrowed reserves does not depend on the spread, $i - \bar{d}$—that is, when R'_B is zero—the term in braces is negative and the deposit rate rises when the demand function rises. Schematically,

$$R'_B = 0 \text{ implies } \frac{\Delta\zeta}{\Delta\beta} > 0. \qquad (5.51)$$

Second, when the supply of demand deposits is horizontal—that is, when $\partial D^s/\partial z_f$ is infinite—again the deposit rate rises. That is,

$$\frac{\partial D^s}{\partial z_f} \to \infty \text{ implies } \frac{\Delta\zeta}{\Delta\beta} > 0. \qquad (5.52)$$

Of course, neither 5.51 nor 5.52 is likely to apply in the real world. The former brings us back in time to the pre-Tobin, "old view" of a mechanical money multiplier.[2] On the other hand, condition $\partial D^s/\partial z_f \to \infty$ is tantamount to a condition of perfect competition and interest arbitrage. Although this condition may hold under some plausible circumstances, under existing institutional arrangements financial markets are characterized by limited entry, which precludes infinite elasticity of the supply of demand deposits.

We shall now turn to some conditions that guarantee a fall in the deposit rate when the demand for demand deposits rises—and, of course, all the asset markets clear. We see from 5.50 that when the reserve-requirement ratio, k, is zero, the deposit rate will fall. Surprisingly, we get the same result in the other polar case, namely, when $k = 1$. We can record these results as follows:

$$k = 0 \text{ implies } \frac{\Delta\zeta}{\Delta\beta} < 0 \qquad (5.53)$$

$$k = 1 \text{ implies } \frac{\Delta\zeta}{\Delta\beta} < 0. \qquad (5.54)$$

In general, the deposit rate will fall when there is a positive shift in the demand for demand deposits if and only if

$$k(k-1)\frac{\partial D^s}{\partial z_f} + R'_B > 0. \qquad (5.55)$$

This condition will have profound implications when we compare the magnitudes of interest-rate sensitivity and demand-deposit sensitivity to shocks in the demand for demand deposits under a flexible and under a fixed-deposit-rate regime.

The qualitative effects, $\partial\zeta/\partial a_j$, $\Delta\zeta/\Delta a_j$, and $\Delta i/\Delta a_j = \partial i/\partial a_j$, are summarized in table 5–1.

Effects on Demand Deposits

In the remainder of this chapter we shall examine the effects of deliberate and inadvertent shocks on monetary aggregates—in particular, on the quantity of demand deposits and on the quantity of borrowed and total reserves. The effects on deposits are especially interesting if the Central Bank uses intermediate targeting, as is currently the case in the United States. Deriving these effects may shed light on some problems facing policymakers in their attempt to achieve preannounced targets for money growth. Achieving announced (or unannounced but specified) targets for growth in money—say,

Table 5–1
Effects of Policy and Shocks on Interest Rates under a Flexible Deposit Rate

Change in Parameter a_j	Change in Interest Rates		
	$\dfrac{\partial\hat\zeta}{\partial a_j}$	$\dfrac{\Delta\zeta}{\Delta a_j}$	$\dfrac{\Delta i}{\Delta a_j}=\dfrac{\partial i}{\partial a_j}$
$a_1 = p$	N.A.[a]	+	+
$a_2 = R_*$	N.A.[a]	−	−
$a_3 = \bar d$	N.A.[a]	+	+
$a_4 = \theta$	N.A.[a]	−	−
$a_5 = \bar R_E$	N.A.[a]	+	+
$a_6 = \beta$	−	−,0,+	+
$a_7 = \mu$	+	+	+
$a_8 = k$	−	$\oplus$[b]	$\oplus$[b]

[a]N.A. means not applicable.

[b]A circle around a sign indicates that the sign is indeterminate but that an appropriate assumption can produce the indicated sign.

M1—is the goal of monetary control. In this sense, monetary control is a narrow version of monetary policy, which is concerned with the effects of monetary instruments on final targets—usually inflation and employment. In both the broad and narrow versions of monetary policy, the influence of monetary instruments on other endogenous variables, such as borrowed reserves, must be examined because these influences can be good indicators of monetary policy.

We shall first examine the effects of deliberate and inadvertent shocks on the quantity of *real* demand deposits, that is, on nominal demand deposits deflated by the price level. To derive these effects we must use equation 5.6, renumbered here as 5.56:

$$D = \hat{D}(i; \beta, \mu, k).$$ (5.56)

Substituting $i(p; R_*, \bar{d}, \theta, \bar{R}_E, \mu, \beta, k)$ and redefining, we get

$$D(p; R_*, \bar{d}, \theta, \bar{R}_E, \mu, \beta, k)$$

$$= \hat{D}[i(p; R_*, \bar{d}, \theta, \bar{R}_E, \mu, \beta, k); \beta, \mu, k]$$ (5.57)

Although expression 5.56 represents the solution for D when the demand deposits market alone is cleared, expression 5.57 represents the solution for D when all markets are cleared.

Differentiation 5.57 totally, we can derive the effects of the relevant shocks. The compact expression for these effects is given by 5.58, where, as with the total effects on the deposit rate, we use the symbol Δ to denote the total effects on demand deposits:

$$\frac{\Delta D}{\Delta a_j} = \frac{\partial \hat{D}}{\partial a_j} + \frac{\partial \hat{D}}{\partial i} \frac{\partial i}{\partial a_j},$$ (5.58)

where $a_j = p, R_*, \bar{d}, \theta, \bar{R}_E, \beta, \mu$, and k.

Expression 5.58 reveals that a change in a monetary parameter will have two effects on demand deposits—one direct and the other indirect. The former operates through the deposits market alone. For example, an increase, that is, shift, in the supply function for demand deposits will increase deposits directly, $\partial \hat{D}/\partial \mu > 0$. But there is also an indirect effect; the increase in the supply function will increase the deposit rate, ζ, which, in turn, will pull the bills rate, i, upward (that is, $\partial i/\partial \mu > 0$) and this, in turn, will lower the quantity of demand deposits. In such a case, therefore, we need to see which effect predominates.

Substituting into 5.58, we see that some of these effects consist of only indirect effects and that they can be signed immediately. We see from 5.10

that an increase in the price level will reduce the quantity of real demand deposits when all asset markets are cleared. This increase in the price level diminishes the real reserve base, R_*/p, and raises the bills interest rate which, in turn, reduces the quantity of real demand deposits:

$$\frac{\Delta D}{\Delta p} = \frac{\partial \hat{D}}{\partial i} \; \frac{\partial i}{\partial p} < 0. \qquad (5.59)$$

On the other hand, by 5.11, an increase in the nominal reserve base, R_*, given the price level, will increase the quantity of real demand deposits. This increase in the real reserve base lowers the interest rate which, in turn, increases the quantity of real demand deposits:

$$\frac{\Delta D}{\Delta R_*} = \frac{\partial \hat{D}}{\partial i} \; \frac{\partial i}{\partial R_*} > 0. \qquad (5.60)$$

Next, we see from 5.61 that when the discount rate changes there is, once again, only an indirect effect. An increase in the discount rate raises the bills rate, which lowers the amount of deposits:

$$\frac{\Delta D}{\Delta \bar{d}} = \frac{\partial \hat{D}}{\partial i} \; \frac{\partial i}{\partial \bar{d}} < 0. \qquad (5.61)$$

As expected, a positive shift in the borrowed-reserves function increases the quantity of demand deposits by lowering the bills interest rate:

$$\frac{\Delta D}{\Delta \theta} = \frac{\partial \hat{D}}{\partial i} \; \frac{\partial i}{\partial \theta} > 0. \qquad (5.62)$$

We see from 5.63 that an exogenous increase in excess reserves will lower the quantity of demand deposits; it will raise the bills or earning-assets rate by putting pressure on the market for reserves, which will, in turn, lower demand deposits:

$$\frac{\Delta D}{\Delta \bar{R}_E} = \frac{\partial \hat{D}}{\partial i} \; \frac{\partial i}{\partial \bar{R}_E} < 0. \qquad (5.63)$$

The remaining three effects—$\Delta D/\Delta \beta$, $\Delta D/\Delta \mu$, and $\Delta D/\Delta k$—seem at first to be indeterminate in sign. For $\Delta D/\Delta \beta$ and $\Delta D/\Delta \mu$, the indirect effect is opposite in sign to the direct effect. In the case of $\Delta D/\Delta k$, the indirect effect is itself indeterminate—in the absence of additional assumptions:

$$\frac{\Delta D}{\Delta \beta} = \frac{\partial \hat{D}}{\partial \beta} + \frac{\partial \hat{D}}{\partial i} \quad \frac{\partial i}{\partial \beta} \tag{5.64}$$

$$\frac{\Delta D}{\Delta \mu} = \frac{\partial \hat{D}}{\partial \mu} + \frac{\partial \hat{D}}{\partial i} \quad \frac{\partial i}{\partial \mu} \tag{5.65}$$

$$\frac{\Delta D}{\partial k} = \frac{\partial \hat{D}}{\partial k} + \frac{\partial \hat{D}}{\partial i} \quad \frac{\partial i}{\partial k}. \tag{5.66}$$

However, we can show that the direct effect of the first two shocks—β and μ—negate their respective indirect effects and, hence, that their total effects are positive. On the other hand, the total effect of a change in the reserve-requirement ratio, k, has the sign of the direct effect.

To show these results we must express the effects in terms of behavioral (structural) coefficients alone. In fact, we shall express the effects of all shocks entirely in terms of behavioral coefficients since such expressions are necessary for quantitative comparisons of the two regimes. Substituting 5.18 through 5.21 and 5.22 through 5.29 into 5.59 through 5.66, we get:

$$\frac{\Delta D}{\Delta p} = - \frac{k \dfrac{R_*}{p^2} \dfrac{\partial D^s}{\partial z_f} \dfrac{\partial D^d}{\partial z_h}}{Q} < 0 \tag{5.67}$$

$$\frac{\Delta D}{\Delta R_*} = \frac{\left(\dfrac{1}{p}\right) k \dfrac{\partial D^s}{\partial z_f} \cdot \dfrac{\partial D^d}{\partial z_h}}{Q} > 0 \tag{5.68}$$

$$\frac{\Delta D}{\Delta \bar{d}} = - \frac{k R'_B \dfrac{\partial D^d}{\partial z_h} \dfrac{\partial D^s}{\partial z_f}}{Q} < 0 \tag{5.69}$$

$$\frac{\Delta D}{\Delta \theta} = \frac{k \dfrac{\partial R_B}{\partial \theta} \dfrac{\partial D^s}{\partial z_f} \dfrac{\partial D^d}{\partial z_h}}{Q} > 0 \qquad (5.70)$$

$$\frac{\Delta D}{\Delta \bar{R}_E} = - \frac{k \dfrac{\partial D^s}{\partial z_f} \cdot \dfrac{\partial D^d}{\partial z_h}}{Q} < 0 \qquad (5.71)$$

$$\frac{\Delta D}{\Delta \mu} = \frac{R'_B \dfrac{\partial D^s}{\partial \mu} \cdot \dfrac{\partial D^d}{\partial z_h}}{Q} > 0 \qquad (5.72)$$

$$\frac{\Delta D}{\Delta \beta} = - \frac{R'_B \dfrac{\partial D^d}{\partial \beta} \cdot \dfrac{\partial D^s}{\partial z_f}}{Q} > 0 \qquad (5.73)$$

$$\frac{\Delta D}{\Delta k} = - \frac{\{i \cdot R'_B + k D\} \dfrac{\partial D^d}{\partial z_h} \cdot \dfrac{\partial D^s}{\partial z_f}}{Q} < 0. \qquad (5.74)$$

A Special Case: The Old View of Banking

At this point it is interesting to inquire about the implications of the assumption that borrowed reserves are independent of the spread, $i - \bar{d}$, or, in general, that they are independent of the (bills) interest rate, i.

The most striking result concerns the implications of this assumption for shocks in the demand for demand deposits and in the supply of demand deposits. Setting $R'_B \equiv 0$ in 5.72 and 5.73, we see immediately that $\Delta D/\Delta \beta = 0$ and $\Delta D/\Delta \mu = 0$; that is, neither a shift in the demand for demand deposits nor a shift in the supply of demand deposits will affect the quantity of demand deposits. Since profit-maximizing financial institutions *do* react positively to a change in the spread between the rate on earning assets and the discount rate, the importance of these results hinges on revealing the errors that will be made when model builders or when policymakers adopt the assumption that $R'_B = 0$; Errors in the form of "unexpected" changes in the quantity of demand deposits—attributed to shifts in either the demand for or the supply of demand deposits—will result.

Another important implication of setting $R'_B \equiv 0$ is the reduction of our model to one that gives the result associated with the so-called old view in banking. Note that since we already assumed that the demand for excess reserves is fixed at $\bar{R}_E$, independent of the interest rate, the assumption that borrowed reserves are also independent of the interest rate is tantamount to assuming that *free reserves*—$R_F = R_E - R_B$—are independent of the interest rate. This is the old view of banking, which mechanically applies the money multiplier—$1/k$—to any change in reserves in order to find the quantity of demand deposits. We see that we can reenact the results of the old view when $R'_B \equiv 0$.

We recall that by 5.30 we have

$$Q = k^2 \frac{\partial D^s}{\partial z_f} \frac{\partial D^d}{\partial z_h} + R'_B \left(\frac{\partial D^d}{\partial z_h} - \frac{\partial D^s}{\partial z_f} \right) < 0 \qquad (5.75)$$

and that by setting $R'_B = 0$ in both 5.30 and in 5.68, we have the following:

$$\frac{\Delta D}{\Delta R_*} = \frac{\left(\dfrac{1}{p}\right) k \dfrac{\partial D^s}{\partial z_f} \dfrac{\partial D^d}{\partial z_h}}{k^2 \dfrac{\partial D^s}{\partial z_f} \dfrac{\partial D^d}{\partial z_h}} = \frac{1}{k} \cdot \frac{1}{p}.$$

Alternatively, since p is assumed fixed in this exercise, we can write the expression as:

$$\frac{\Delta p D}{\Delta R_*} = \frac{1}{k}. \qquad (5.76)$$

In other words, we see that the increase in the amount of *nominal* demand deposits caused by an increase in the nominal base is equal to the multiplier—$1/k$—or that the increase in the quantity of nominal demand deposits is equal to the fixed multiplier—$1/k$—times the change in the nominal reserve base, ΔR_*. Next, substituting Q and $R'_B \equiv 0$ in 5.67, we find the effect of an increase in the price level on the quantity of real demand deposits:

$$\frac{\Delta D}{\Delta p} = -\frac{1}{k} \cdot \frac{R_*}{p^2}. \qquad (5.77)$$

That is, real demand deposits shrink by the amount— $- R_*/p^2$—that the real reserve base shrinks, times the fixed multiplier—$1/k$.

Similarly, substituting in 5.69, we see that the reduction in the quantity of real demand deposits is equal to the decrease—$(-R'_B \Delta \bar{d})$—in real reserves caused by the rise in the discount rate, times the multiplier, $1/k$:

$$\Delta D = -\frac{1}{k}(R'_B \Delta \bar{d}). \qquad (5.78)$$

Similar interpretations can be used for the changes in real demand deposits caused by shifts in the borrowed-reserves function, R_B, induced by a change in θ and by shifts in the excess reserves function, $\bar{R}_E$:

$$\Delta D = \frac{1}{k} \cdot \left(\frac{\partial R_B}{\partial \theta} \Delta \theta \right) \qquad (5.79)$$

$$\Delta D = -\frac{1}{k} \cdot \Delta \bar{R}_E. \qquad (5.80)$$

Finally, the percentage decrease in the quantity of demand deposits is equal to the percentage increase in the reserve-requirement ratio, as the fixed multiplier implies.

$$\frac{\Delta D}{\Delta k} = -\frac{D}{k},$$

or,

$$\frac{\Delta D}{D} = -\frac{\Delta k}{k}. \qquad (5.81)$$

Effects on Borrowed and on Total Reserves

Effects on Borrowed Reserves

We now turn briefly to the derivation of the effects on the remaining aggregates—namely, the quantity of borrowed reserves, R_B, and the quantity of total reserves, R_T. Total reserves are defined as the sum of the nonborrowed reserves base and the quantity of borrowed reserves, that is, $R_T \equiv R_*/p + R_B$. Of course, with the exception of a shock in the price level, p, and a shock in the nominal reserve base, R_*, knowledge of the effect of a shock on borrowed reserves immediately permits us to determine the effect on total reserves; this is the implication of treating the nominal reserve base as a parameter. We shall, therefore, begin by examining the effects of various shocks on borrowed reserves. Also, we shall repeat the function for borrowed reserves, renumbered here as 5.82:

$$R_B = R_B(i - \bar{d}; \theta). \tag{5.82}$$

To find the effect of a particular shock we need to differentiate totally 5.82 with respect to the shock. In general, we have:

$$\frac{\Delta R_B}{\Delta a_j} = R'_B \frac{\partial i}{\partial a_j} \tag{5.83}$$

for $a_j = p$, R_*, $\bar{R}_E$, β, μ, and k.
For d and θ, we have, respectively,

$$\frac{\Delta R_B}{\Delta \bar{d}} = -R'_B + R'_B \frac{\partial i}{\partial \bar{d}} \tag{5.84}$$

$$\frac{\Delta R_B}{\Delta \theta} = \frac{\partial R_B}{\partial \theta} + R'_B \frac{\partial i}{\partial \theta}. \tag{5.85}$$

Substituting 5.24 into 5.84 and manipulating, we get:

$$\frac{\Delta R_B}{\Delta \bar{d}} = -\frac{k R'_B \frac{\partial \hat{D}}{\partial i}}{k \frac{\partial \hat{D}}{\partial i} - R'_B} < 0. \tag{5.86}$$

That is, an increase in the discount rate, d, has a negative direct effect by initially reducing the spread—$i - \bar{d}$—and a positive indirect effect by subsequently increasing the spread as the interest rate—i—rises). However, the indirect positive effect is not strong enough to outweigh the negative effect. Therefore, the end result is negative.

Similarly, substituting 5.25 into 5.85, we see that the positive direct effect of a positive shock in the function for borrowed reserves—$\partial R_B/\partial \theta$—outweighs the negative indirect effect—$R'_B \partial i/\partial \theta$—and that the end result is positive:

$$\frac{\Delta R_B}{\Delta \theta} = \frac{k^2 \dfrac{\partial R_B}{\partial \theta} \dfrac{\partial D^s}{\partial z_f} \dfrac{\partial D^d}{\partial z_h}}{Q} > 0. \qquad (5.87)$$

(We should note that when $R'_B \equiv 0$, this effect reduces to

$$\frac{\Delta R_B}{\Delta \theta} = \frac{\partial R_B}{\partial \theta};$$

that is, the total effect is merely the partial effect.)

Now let us examine the remaining shocks, which have only an indirect effect:

$$\frac{\Delta R_B}{\Delta p} = R'_B \frac{\partial i}{\partial p} > 0. \qquad (5.88)$$

In words, an increase in the price level raises the interest rate which, in turn, increases the spread—$i - \bar{d}$—thereby increasing the amount of real borrowed reserves. On the other hand, an increase in the nominal reserve base, R_*, given the price level, lowers the interest rate, lowers the spread, and therefore reduces the amount of borrowed reserves:[3]

$$\frac{\Delta R_B}{\Delta R_*} = R'_B \frac{\partial i}{\partial R_*} < 0. \qquad (5.89)$$

Now, we note that an increase in excess reserves, $\bar{R}_E$, will increase borrowed reserves:

$$\frac{\Delta R_B}{\Delta \bar{R}_E} = R'_B \frac{\partial i}{\partial \bar{R}_E} > 0. \qquad (5.90)$$

Because the interest rate will rise, borrowed reserves will also rise when the demand for demand deposits increases:

$$\frac{\Delta R_B}{\Delta \beta} = R'_B \frac{\partial i}{\partial \beta} > 0, \qquad (5.91)$$

or, when the supply of demand deposits increases,

$$\frac{\Delta R_B}{\Delta \mu} = R'_B \frac{\partial i}{\partial \mu} > 0. \qquad (5.92)$$

Finally, assuming that the interest rate will rise, an increase in the reseve-requirement ratio will also increase borrowed reserves:

$$\frac{\Delta R_B}{\Delta k} = R'_B \frac{\partial i}{\partial k} > 0. \qquad (5.93)$$

Effects on Total Reserves

The quantity of real total reserves is the sum of real nonborrowed reserves and real borrowed reserves:

$$R_T = \frac{R_*}{p} + R_B.$$

Differentiating totally, we can see that, with the exception of a change in R_* or in p, the sign of $\Delta R_T / \Delta a_j$ is the same as the sign of $\Delta R_B / \Delta a_j$. A shock in either R_* or in p, however, has an effect on the real-reserve base and an effect on the real amount of borrowed reserves. These effects are opposite in sign. Let us now consider, first, the effect of an exogenous change in p:

$$\frac{\Delta R_T}{\Delta p} = -\frac{R_*}{p^2} + \frac{\Delta R_B}{\Delta p}.$$

The increase in the price level increases real borrowed reserves, but it shrinks the real nonborrowed reserve base. Substituting, we find that the net effect is negative:

$$\frac{\Delta R_T}{\Delta p} = -\frac{\dfrac{R_*}{p^2}}{Q} \cdot k^2 \frac{\partial D^s}{\partial z_f} \quad \frac{\partial D^d}{\partial z_h} < 0.$$

On the other hand, an increase in the nominal reserve base, given the price level, increases the real reserve base, but it reduces real borrowed reserves:

$$\frac{\Delta R_T}{\Delta R_*} = \frac{1}{p} + \frac{\Delta R_B}{\Delta R_*}.$$

Substituting, we find that the end result is positive:

$$\frac{\Delta R_T}{\Delta R_*} = \frac{1}{pQ} \cdot k^2 \frac{\partial D^s}{\partial z_f} \quad \frac{\partial D^d}{\partial z_h} > 0.$$

The pattern of signs of the effects of various shocks on the three aggregates is given in table 5–2, where we see that with the exception of the effects in a change in k, the sign pattern of the effects on demand deposits is the same as the sign pattern of total reserves. In other words, the money (that is, deposit) multipliers do not change signs. However, we shall see in the next chapter that there are quantitative differences as we move from the fixed-deposit-rate regime to a market-determined deposit rate regime. Returning to a change in the reserve-requirement ratio, k—that is, to the last row—the

Table 5–2
Effects of Policy and Shocks on Monetary and Reserves Aggregates under a Flexible Deposit Rate

Shock	Demand Deposits, D	Borrowed Reserves, R_B	Total Reserves, R_T
	Endogenous Monetary Aggregate		
p	−	+	−
R_*	+	−	+
$\bar{d}$	−	−	−
θ	+	+	+
$\bar{R}_E$	−	+	+
β	+	+	+
μ	+	+	+
k	−	+	+

results are also expected. An increase in the reserve-requirement ratio may increase the amount of borrowed and, hence, of total, reserves by raising the interest rate, but it reduces the amount of demand deposits that can be created because more reserves are needed.

We can combine some columns of table 5–1 and 5–2 and touch on the topic of indicators of contraction or expansion. In table 5–3 we compare the effects of shocks on the interest rate, i, and on the monetary aggregate—demand deposits—D. Some economists consider the money stock—in our case, the quantity of demand deposits—as the sole indicator of expansion or contraction. In particular, they argue that a shock is expansionary when it causes an increase in the quantity of money (that is, deposits) and that it is contractionary when it causes a reduction in the quantity of money. Other economists consider the change in the *real* rate of interest as the only indicator of expansion or contraction. They argue that because aggregate demand for goods and services depends negatively on the real rate of interest, a shock that decreases the interest rate is expansionary and a shock that increases the interest rate is contractionary. (We should note that since one-shot-changes in shocks do not affect expected inflation, a change in the nominal interest rate is also a change in the real rate.)

We note in table 5–3 that two key genuine shocks—the shift in the demand for demand deposits and the shift in the supply of demand deposits—give conflicting signals to policymakers. With the interest rate as the indicator, both shocks are contractionary because they increase the interest rate. On the other hand, with monetary aggregates as the indicator, the shocks are expansionary because money (that is, demand deposits) rises.

Table 5–3
Indicators of Expansion or Contraction under a Flexible Deposit Rate

| Shock | Indicators | |
	Interest Rate, i	Demand Deposits
p	−	−
$\bar{R}_*$	+	+
$\bar{d}$	−	−
θ	+	+
$\bar{R}_E$	−	−
β	−	+
μ	−	+
k	−	−

+ = Expansionary.
− = Contractionary.

Concluding Comments: Financial Innovations

Although there are many ways in which the results of this chapter can be applied, we shall now limit the application of our analysis of demand and supply shocks to the issue of financial innovations. As we stated in chapter 2, financial innovations that reduce the need for cash directly or that induce holders to economize on cash shift the demand for demand deposits inward. This is the standard treatment of financial innovations found in the literature—which assumes, of course, a fixed deposit rate. Under a variable-deposit-rate regime, the effects of these types of financial innovations on the two interest rates are captured by

$$- \frac{\partial i}{\partial \beta} < 0, - \frac{\Delta \zeta}{\Delta \beta} \gtrless 0.$$

The effects on the real quantity of demand deposits, on borrowed reserves, and on total reserves are as follows:

$$- \frac{\Delta D}{\Delta \beta} < 0, - \frac{\Delta R_B}{\Delta \beta} < 0, - \frac{\Delta R_T}{\Delta \beta} < 0.$$

That is, financial innovations that affect negatively the demand for demand deposits decrease the quantity of all monetary and reserves aggregates. They also reduce the bills interest rate. But the effect on the deposit rate can be positive or negative, depending on additional empirical assumptions.

These results are consistent with the standard interpretation of financial innovations in a fixed-deposit-rate regime. In fact, financial innovations have been cited as the main reason for overpredictions in the quantity of money (that is, demand deposits) in the middle and late 1970s and in part of 1980 and 1981. Moreover, because, *ceteris paribus*, such financial innovations reduce the interest rate on bills, which in itself is expansionary, the reduction in the quantity of money is not considered conractionary. Rather, it suggests that the effective rate of growth of money is greater than the realized or observed rate.[4]. Under these circumstances, the original target paths will be more expansionary (that is, inflationary) than the policymaker originally intended. Hence, there is reason to revise downward the original target paths. There is an immediate corollary to this result: When we have demand-reducing innovations, both the old and the new frameworks give the same implications.

When financial innovations are of the cost-reducing variety and, therefore, affect positively the supply of demand deposits, the effects on interest rates and on aggregates are reversed; so are the implications for monetary policy. The positive shift in the supply of demand deposits raises both the bills interest rate and the deposit rate:

$$\frac{\partial i}{\partial \mu} > 0, \; \frac{\Delta \zeta}{\Delta \mu} > 0.$$

This shift also increases the quantity of money (that is, the quantity of demand deposits), borrowed reserves, and total reserves:

$$\frac{\Delta D}{\Delta \mu} > 0, \; \frac{\Delta R_B}{\partial \mu} > 0, \; \frac{\Delta R_T}{\Delta \mu} > 0.$$

These results suggest that in the presence of cost-reducing financial innovations, the effective rate of growth of money is lower than the observed rate. Because, in this case, the original target paths will be more contractionary than originally intended, they should be revised upward.[5]

In summary, we see that financial innovations that reduce the need for cash are associated with a lower or falling interest rate on bills and with lower or falling monetary and reserve aggregates. On the other hand, cost-reducing—that is, supply-enhancing—financial innovations are associated with a higher, increasing interest rate on bills and with greater monetary and reserves aggregates. From these results, we see that whether the policymaker should revise the target paths for money growth upward or downward depends on whether financial innovations on the demand side or on the supply side predominate.

The richness of our new monetary framework has therefore been revealed: It has permitted us to uncover this important result. However, a more detailed comparison of the two monetary frameworks will be undertaken in the next chapter.

Notes

1. D.E. Lindsey (1977) examines the implications of a market-determined deposit rate for some aspects of monetary control. Even though his work consists of the same number of assets as ours, the models are different. His primary objective is to describe the disequilibrium aspects of the deposit market. However, his framework is such that it does not permit formal treatment of this issue. More important, the techniques available to him could not permit him to solve even for the equilibrium values of the model. The issue of paying interest on demand deposits is also examined in a study by the staff of the Board of Governors of the Federal Reserve System

(1977). Finally, the implications of a financial system without Regulation Q are examined by B.B. White (1982).

2. The term *new view* was introduced in J. Tobin (1963*a*).

3. We must recall that this negative relation between borrowed and non-borrowed reserves, derived in a more complicated setting in chapter 2, played a key role in our explanation of the observed volatility in aggregates in 1980.

4. Such an explanation is found in T.D. Simpson and R.D. Porter (1980), who also use the terms *effective* and actual money growth (p. 187).

5. This is not the conclusion reached by J.P. Judd and J. L. Scadding (1981) but only because in their model, supply is not on an equal footing with demand.

6 Comparison of Regimes: Relative Variability in Interest Rates and Aggregates

At this point in our analysis we must ask the following questions: Are there any qualitative differences in the effects of shocks on the interest rate when the deposit rate is market determined as opposed to when the deposit rate is fixed by the Central Bank? In the absence of qualitative differences, are there any quantitative differences? Similar questions can be posed for the monetary aggregates: Are there any qualitative or quantitative differences in the effects of shocks on monetary aggregates—that is, on demand deposits and on borrowed reserves? These questions, which we shall consider in this chapter, are central to the conduct of monetary policy.

The sensitivity of monetary aggregates to monetary shocks is crucial to a Central Bank committed to achieving targets expressed in monetary aggregates. The sensitivity of interest rates is crucial to those who consider changes in interest rates as the key indicator of the state of the entire economy. Similarly, the effects of shocks on interest rates are crucial to portfolio holders or to consultants to portfolio holders.

In the next section, we shall compare interest-rate responses to (deliberate and inadvertent) shocks when the deposit rate is fixed and when it is market determined. The comparison is qualitative and, more important, quantitative. We shall see that when a comparison is legitimate, the two regimes give the same qualitative results; that is, the direction of change in the interest rate, because of shocks, is the same with fixed and with flexible deposit rates. However, the responses differ quantitatively. In particular— with one important possible exception—interest rates are more responsive to shocks when the deposit rate is flexible than when it is fixed. The possible exception refers to responsiveness of the interest rate to demand-side (for demand deposits) shocks. The relative responsiveness of the interest rate to demand-side shocks depends on the sign of the overall effect of demand-side shocks on the deposit rate when the latter is flexible. If a positive shift in money demand lowers (raises) the deposit rate, the interest rate responsiveness to this shock is lower (greater) under a flexible deposit rate than under a fixed deposit rate. And we shall specify the conditions that permit each of these results.

Another difference occurs in the effects of a positive shift in the supply of demand deposits. This difference occurs by default. Under a fixed deposit rate the supply side does not matter. Hence, an increase in supply will leave the interest rate unchanged (when the deposit rate is kept fixed). But under a

117

flexible deposit rate the increase in supply will raise both rates and, in particular, it will raise the (bills) interest rate.

In the section Demand Deposit Variability we shall compare the responses of the quantity of demand deposits to the same shocks. As expected, there is a smaller response (variability) in this quantity when the deposit rate is market determined than when it is fixed—with one definite and one possible exception. The exceptions aside, this result establishes a tradeoff between variability (volatility) in interest rates and variability in the quantity of money (demand deposits). In this sense, the move toward a market-determined deposit rate strengthens the precision of control of monetary aggregates, at the price of greater volatility in interest rates.

The exceptions concern genuine shocks in demand and in supply. A positive shock in the supply of demand deposits increases the quantity of demand deposits under a flexible deposit rate but leaves demand deposits unchanged under a fixed deposit rate. Hence, under a flexible deposit rate there will be greater response of monetary aggregates to shifts in the supply of demand deposits. Combining this result with the corresponding greater interest-rate response to the same shock, we can say that if the economy is prone to (financial) supply-side shocks, the move to a market-determined deposit rate will increase the variability of both aggregates and interest rates.

As in the preceding section, the consequences of a (positive) shift in the demand for demand deposits are not as clear-cut. The response of the quantity of demand deposits to demand-side shocks may increase or decrease when we move to the market-determined deposit rate regime. However, the response of this aggregate will increase when the response of the interest rate increases; and the response of this aggregate will be reduced when the response of the interest rate is reduced. Furthermore, we know from the preceding section that the relative interest-rate response hinges on whether the deposit rate falls or rises when the demand for demand deposits rises. That is, those conditions that guarantee a reduction (increase) in the deposit rate with a positive shift in the demand function also guarantee a smaller (larger) increase in both the interest rate and in the quantity of demand deposits with such a shift.

Next, we shall compare variability in the reserves aggregates under the two regimes. Because the quantity of borrowed reserves depends on the interest rate, the greater variability in the interest rate under a flexible deposit rate also manifests itself as a greater variability in borrowed reserves—again, with some exceptions. Of course, the case of demand shocks is obvious: The variability of borrowed reserves will imitate the variability of the interest rate—greater or smaller. The true exceptions occur in shocks that originate in the borrowings function itself. In particular, borrowings variability caused by a change in the discount rate is smaller under a flexible deposit rate than under a fixed deposit rate. And so is the variability caused by a change in the administration of the discount window. Finally, we compare the variability in total reserves, and we find that its pattern coincides with that of demand deposits.

Comparison of Interest-Rate Responses

We shall first compare the effects of shocks on the rate of interest when the deposit rate is fixed with the corresponding effects when the deposit rate is market determined. We have seen that when the deposit rate is fixed, the functional relation between the interest rate and shocks is given by equation 3.17, reproduced here as 6.1:

$$i = i_*(p; R_*, \bar{d}, \bar{\zeta}, \theta, \bar{R}_E, \beta, k). \tag{6.1}$$

The effects of policy and of shocks are given by the partial derivatives of 6.1. More precisely, the partial derivatives of $i_*(\cdot)$ depict separately the effects on the interest rate of a change in each of the variables that are arguments in $i_*(\cdot)$ when all financial markets are cleared. These effects, found by differentiating 6.1, are

$$\frac{\partial i_*}{\partial p} = -\frac{R_*}{p^2} \cdot C^{-1} > 0 \tag{6.2}$$

$$\frac{\partial i_*}{\partial R_*} = \frac{1}{p} \cdot C^{-1} < 0 \tag{6.3}$$

$$\frac{\partial i_*}{\partial \bar{d}} = -R'_B \cdot C^{-1} > 0 \tag{6.4}$$

$$\frac{\partial i_*}{\partial \bar{\zeta}} = k \frac{\partial D^d}{\partial z_h} \cdot C^{-1} > 0 \tag{6.5}$$

$$\frac{\partial i_*}{\partial \theta} = \frac{\partial R_B}{\partial \theta} \cdot C^{-1} < 0 \tag{6.6}$$

$$\frac{\partial i_*}{\partial \bar{R}_E} = -C^{-1} > 0 \tag{6.7}$$

$$\frac{\partial i_*}{\partial \beta} = - k \frac{\partial D^d}{\partial \beta} \cdot C^{-1} > 0 \qquad (6.8)$$

$$\frac{\partial i_*}{\partial k} = - D^d(\cdot) \cdot C^{-1} > 0, \qquad (6.9)$$

where

$$C = k \frac{\partial D^d}{\partial z_h} - R'_B < 0 \qquad (6.10)$$

and C^{-1} is the inverse of C.

Under the emerging regime of a flexible, market-determined deposit rate, the relation between the equilibrium interest rate and shocks is given by:

$$i = i(p, R_*, \bar{d}, \theta, \bar{R}_E, \beta, \mu, k), \qquad (6.11)$$

whose partials, as follows, are the effects of monetary policy and shocks:

$$\frac{\partial i}{\partial p} = \frac{\dfrac{R_*}{p^2} \left(\dfrac{\partial D^d}{\partial z_h} - \dfrac{\partial D^s}{\partial z_f} \right)}{Q} > 0 \qquad (6.12)$$

$$\frac{\partial i}{\partial R_*} = - \frac{\dfrac{1}{p} \left(\dfrac{\partial D^d}{\partial z_h} - \dfrac{\partial D^s}{\partial z_f} \right)}{Q} < 0 \qquad (6.13)$$

$$\frac{\partial i}{\partial \bar{d}} = \frac{R'_B \left(\dfrac{\partial D^d}{\partial z_h} - \dfrac{\partial D^s}{\partial z_f} \right)}{Q} > 0 \qquad (6.14)$$

$$\frac{\partial i}{\partial \theta} = - \frac{\dfrac{\partial R_B}{\partial \theta} \left(\dfrac{\partial D^d}{\partial z_h} - \dfrac{\partial D^s}{\partial z_f} \right)}{Q} < 0 \qquad (6.15)$$

$$\frac{\partial i}{\partial \bar{R}_E} = \frac{\left(\dfrac{\partial D^d}{\partial z_h} - \dfrac{\partial D^s}{\partial z_f} \right)}{Q} > 0 \qquad (6.16)$$

$$\frac{\partial i}{\partial \beta} = -\frac{k\dfrac{\partial D^d}{\partial \beta} \cdot \dfrac{\partial D^s}{\partial z_f}}{Q} > 0 \qquad (6.17)$$

$$\frac{\partial i}{\partial \mu} = \frac{k\dfrac{\partial D^d}{\partial z_h} \cdot \dfrac{\partial D^s}{\partial \mu}}{Q} > 0 \qquad (6.18)$$

$$\frac{\partial i}{\partial k} = \frac{\hat{D} \cdot \left(\dfrac{\partial D^d}{\partial z_h} - \dfrac{\partial D^s}{\partial z_f}\right) - ik\dfrac{\partial D^s}{\partial z_f} \cdot \dfrac{\partial D^d}{\partial z_h}}{Q} \gtreqless 0. \quad (6.19)$$

where

$$Q = k^2 \frac{\partial D^s}{\partial z_f}\frac{\partial D^d}{\partial z_h} + R'_B\left(\frac{\partial D^d}{\partial z_h} - \frac{\partial D^s}{\partial z_f}\right) < 0. \qquad (6.20)$$

With the possible exception of the effect of a change in the reserve-requirement ratio, k, we see that the qualitative effects of comparable shocks are indistinguishable between monetary regimes. Even the possible difference in the direction of the effect of a change in k is more apparent than real: With the deposit-rate market determined, we do expect the interest rate to rise when k rises.

Visual comparison of the qualitative effects is aided by using table 6–1, where we see that for all comparable shocks the effects are qualitatively the

Table 6–1
Qualitative Comparison of the Effects of Policy and Shocks on the (Bills) Interest Rate

Shocks	Effects on Interest Rate, i, with a Fixed Deposit Rate, ζ: $\partial i_*/\partial a_j$	Effects on Interest Rate, i, with a Market-Determined Deposit Rate, ζ: $\partial i/\partial a_j$
Price level, p	+	+
Reserve base, R_*	−	−
Discount rate, d	+	+
Borrowings shock, θ	−	−
Excess reserves, R_E	+	+
Demand function, β	+	+
Supply function, μ	0	+
Deposit rate, ζ	+	N.A. (+)
Reserve-requirement ratio, k	+	+

N.A. means not applicable.

same: An increase in the nominal reserve base, R_*, lowers the interest rate, with both fixed and flexible deposit rates; however, under both a fixed- and a flexible-deposit-rate regime an increase in the price level will raise the interest rate. So does an increase in the discount rate. On the other hand, a positive shock, θ, in the borrowed-reserves function—say, a more liberal administration of the discount window—will lower the interest rate under both regimes. An increase in either the excess-reserves function or in the demand for demand deposits will raise the interest rate under both regimes. Because the supply of demand deposits plays only a passive role under a fixed-deposit-rate regime, it is obvious that a positive shift will leave the interest rate unaffected. To this we must contrast the increase in the interest rate under a market-determined deposit-rate regime, an increase that will come as a surprise to some. On the other hand, strictly speaking, the effect of an increase in the deposit rate on the interest rate is not applicable under a flexible, market-determined deposit-rate regime because the deposit rate is not a parameter; nevertheless, there is a positive relation between the two rates.

Quantitative Comparisons

We shall now embark upon a quantitative comparison of the effects on the interest rate, i. We shall begin with the real reserve (that is, real balance) effect of a change in the price level on the interest rate, i. We know that both are positive. Substituting 6.2 and 6.12, we have:

$$\frac{\partial i_*}{\partial p} - \frac{\partial i}{\partial p} = -\frac{\dfrac{R_*}{p^2}}{C} - \frac{\dfrac{R_*}{p^2}\left(\dfrac{\partial D^d}{\partial z_h} - \dfrac{\partial D^s}{\partial z_f}\right)}{Q},$$

which, after tedious manipulation, is reduced to 6.21:

$$\frac{\partial i_*}{\partial p} - \frac{\partial i}{\partial p} = \frac{k\,R_*\dfrac{\partial D^d}{\partial z_h}}{p^2 \cdot C \cdot Q} \cdot \left\{(1-k)\frac{\partial D^s}{\partial z_f} - \frac{\partial D^d}{\partial z_h}\right\} < 0 \quad (6.21)$$

It must be noted here that the positive term in braces,

$$(1-k)\frac{\partial D^s}{\partial z_f} - \frac{\partial D^d}{\partial z_h} > 0,$$

which will appear repeatedly in this discussion, is the effect of a rise in the interest rate on the excess *supply* of demand deposits—that is, $-\partial EDD/\partial i$. Thus we have proved 6.22:

$$\frac{\partial i}{\partial p} > \frac{\partial i_*}{\partial p} > 0, \tag{6.22}$$

that is, we have proved that an increase in the price level raises the bills interest rate more when the deposit rate is market determined than when it is fixed by the Central Bank.

We shall now turn to the effects of a change in the nominal reserve base, R_*. By 6.3 and 6.13, these effects are negative. Comparing the two and using 6.3 and 6.13, we find:

$$\frac{\partial i}{\partial R_*} - \frac{\partial i_*}{\partial R_*} = -\frac{\frac{1}{p}\left(\frac{\partial D^d}{\partial z_h} - \frac{\partial D^s}{\partial z_f}\right)}{Q} - \frac{\frac{1}{p}}{C},$$

which is reduced to 6.23:

$$\frac{\partial i}{\partial R_*} - \frac{\partial i_*}{\partial R_*} = \frac{k\frac{\partial D^d}{\partial z_h}}{p \cdot C \cdot Q} \cdot \left\{ (1-k)\frac{\partial D^s}{\partial z_f} - \frac{\partial D^d}{\partial z_h} \right\} < 0. \tag{6.23}$$

That is, we find that

$$\frac{\partial i}{\partial R_*} < \frac{\partial i_*}{\partial R_*} < 0. \tag{6.24}$$

An increase in the nominal reserve base lowers the interest rate by more when the deposit rate is variable than when it is fixed. Since this interest rate, i, is an important (if not the sole) determinant of aggregate demand for goods and services, we see that monetary policy is more potent when the deposit rate is market determined than when it is fixed by the Central Bank.

Now we can combine the result in 6.24 with the result in 6.22 and end up with a fundamental difference between the two regimes, namely that *under a market-determined deposit rate the economy moves faster from one full equilibrium to another than it does under a fixed deposit rate.* Let us see why.

Full equilibrium, of course, is characterized by equilibrium in both the financial sector and the real sector; that is, equilibrium in all asset markets and in the goods and services market. At the new full equilibrium—whether the deposit rate is fixed or market determined—a one-shot increase in the nominal reserve base, R_*, will raise the price level by the same percentage, so that the interest rate, i, is unaffected. But an equal increase in the reserve base will initially lower the interest rate by more if the deposit rate is market determined than if it is fixed (this is the meaning of 6.24); hence, there will be greater initial excess demand for goods and services under a market-determined deposit rate than under a fixed deposit rate. This greater excess demand will raise the price level by more than it would be raised under a fixed deposit rate. But the result in 6.22 says that even with the same increase in the price level the interest rate will rise by more under a market-determined deposit rate than under a fixed-deposit rate. *A fortiori*, then, the price level will rise faster, and the interest rate—after its greater initial fall—will move faster to the new common equilibrium. We shall formally prove this result in chapter 10, when we extend the model to incorporate the real sector.

Turning to the effect of supplemental instruments of monetary control, we shall compare the effects of a change in the discount rate on the interest rate. By 6.4 and 6.14, an increase in the discount rate raises the interest rate, i. But comparing the two effects, we find that

$$\frac{\partial i}{\partial \bar{d}} - \frac{\partial i_*}{\partial \bar{d}} = \frac{R'_B \left(\dfrac{\partial D^d}{\partial z_h} - \dfrac{\partial D^s}{\partial z_f} \right)}{Q} + \frac{R'_B}{C}$$

and that after tedious manipulations, we have:

$$\frac{\partial i}{\partial \bar{d}} - \frac{\partial i_*}{\partial \bar{d}} = -\frac{k\, R'_B \dfrac{\partial D^d}{\partial z_h}}{C \cdot Q} \cdot \left\{ (1-k)\frac{\partial D^s}{\partial z_f} - \frac{\partial D^d}{\partial z_h} \right\} > 0. \quad (6.25)$$

In words, we find that an increase in the discount rate raises the bills interest rate, i, by more when the interest rate on demand deposits is market determined than when it is fixed. This, of course, means that the discount rate is a more potent instrument of monetary control under a market-determined deposit rate than under a fixed deposit rate.

Let us now turn to genuine shocks. We expect to show that for the same reason that the two instruments of monetary policy are more potent with a market-determined deposit rate than with a fixed deposit rate, the economy will be more vulnerable to shocks.[1] In particular, we expect to show that the response and, hence, the volatility, of the interest rate to outside monetary shocks will be greater with a flexible rather than with a fixed deposit rate.

We shall first compare the interest sensitivity to a shock emanating from the function for borrowed reserves—say, a loosening in the administration of the discount window. We know from 6.6 and 6.15 that the interest rate falls whether the deposit rate is fixed or market determined. Comparing the two, we have:

$$\frac{\partial i}{\partial \theta} - \frac{\partial i_*}{\partial \theta} = \frac{k \dfrac{\partial R_B}{\partial \theta} \dfrac{\partial D^d}{\partial z_h}}{C \cdot Q} \cdot \left\{ (1 - k) \frac{\partial D^s}{\partial z_f} - \frac{\partial D^d}{\partial z_h} \right\} < 0,$$

(6.26)

that is,

$$\frac{\partial i}{\partial \theta} < \frac{\partial i_*}{\partial \theta} < 0.$$

(6.27)

In words, we see that an increase in the borrowed-reserves function lowers the interest rate by more when the deposit rate is flexible than when it is fixed.

When the demand for excess reserves increases exogenously, the interest rate rises in both models. But comparing 6.7 and 6.16, we can see that the interest rate rises by more when the deposit rate is variable than when it is fixed:

$$\frac{\partial i}{\partial \bar{R}_E} - \frac{\partial i_*}{\partial \bar{R}_E} = - \frac{k \dfrac{\partial D^d}{\partial z_h}}{C \cdot Q} \cdot \left\{ (1 - k) \frac{\partial D^s}{\partial z_f} - \frac{\partial D^d}{\partial z_h} \right\} > 0,$$

(6.28)

that is,

$$\frac{\partial i}{\partial \bar{R}_E} > \frac{\partial i_*}{\partial \bar{R}_E} > 0.$$

(6.29)

In all of our comparisons so far, we have found that the (bills) interest rate is more responsive—both in the upward and in the downward direction—when the deposit rate is market determined than when it is fixed by fiat. There may be an exception, however, when there is a shift in the demand function for demand deposits. In such a case the interest rate on bills may rise by less when the deposit rate is market determined than when it is fixed. By 6.8 and 6.17, we get:

$$\frac{\partial i}{\partial \beta} - \frac{\partial i_*}{\partial \beta} = \frac{k \dfrac{\partial D^d}{\partial \beta} \dfrac{\partial D^d}{\partial z_h}}{C \cdot Q} \left\{ k(k-1) \frac{\partial D^s}{\partial z_f} + R_B' \right\} \gtreqless 0,$$

$$(6.30)$$

from which we derive the result that

$$0 < \frac{\partial i}{\partial \beta} < \frac{\partial i_*}{\partial \beta}$$

if and only if

$$k(k-1) \frac{\partial D^s}{\partial z_f} + R_B' > 0. \qquad (6.31)$$

We must recall that we encountered condition 6.31 in chapter 5, where we saw that when condition 6.31 holds, a positive shift in the demand for demand deposits will result in a lower deposit rate even when all asset markets clear. (Of course, we also know that a positive shift in the demand for demand deposits will cause a fall in the deposit rate when the demand deposits market alone clears.) If the inequality $\partial i/\partial \beta < \partial i_*/\partial \beta$, holds, it is this reduction in the deposit rate that is responsible. We can see this in the following way: With a fixed deposit rate, that is, with $\Delta \zeta \equiv 0$, the shift in the demand for demand deposits increases the bills interest rate by $(\partial i_*/\partial \beta) \, d\beta$. However, with a variable deposit rate, when condition 6.31 holds, the deposit rate falls—$\Delta \zeta/\Delta \beta < 0$. And since there is a positive relation between i and ζ, *ceteris paribus*, i must fall. That is, i will not increase by as much as when $\Delta \zeta \equiv 0$; in other words, the increase in i will be less than $(\partial i_*/\partial \beta) \, d\beta$. Thus we have completed our proof and explanation.

The possibility that the interest rate may be less responsive to demand-side shocks under the emerging regime of a market-determined deposit rate is very important and, hence, needs further examination. Under what conditions can this happen? That is, under what conditions can requirement 6.31 be satisfied? We see that this condition can be satisfied in the special case when the reserve-requirement ratio, k, is equal to one. Condition 6.31, then, is reduced to R_B', which *is* positive. The difference in the interest rate effects, by 6.30, can be reduced to

$$\frac{\partial i}{\partial \beta} - \frac{\partial i_*}{\partial \beta} = \frac{\dfrac{\partial D^d}{\partial \beta} \dfrac{\partial D^d}{\partial z_h} R_B'}{C \cdot Q} < 0$$

—that is,

$$0 < \frac{\partial i}{\partial \beta} < \frac{\partial i_*}{\partial \beta}.$$

Of course, when the reserve requirement is eliminated—that is, when $k = 0$—

$$\frac{\partial i}{\partial \beta} - \frac{\partial i_*}{\partial \beta} = 0.$$

The interest-rate sensitivity remains the same as we move into the regime of paying interest on demand deposits.

In general, condition 6.31 will be satisfied if the supply function of demand deposits is relatively less sensitive to the profit margin, z_f—that is, when $\partial D^s/\partial z_f$ is relatively small—and, simultaneously, the sensitivity of borrowed reserves to the spread, $i - \bar{d}$—that is, R'_B, is relatively great.

We shall now turn to circumstances that may prevent satisfying condition 6.31: The first case is when R'_B is zero; the second case is when the supply function is infinitely elastic at the existing profit margin—that is, when $\partial D^s/\partial z_f \to \infty$. This can be the consequence of free and rapid entry into the banking system, which makes it purely competitive. In both cases the shock in demand will raise the interest rate by more with a variable deposit rate than with a fixed deposit rate.

We shall now turn to the problem of supply-side shocks. In the fixed - deposit regime, such shocks leave the interest rate unchanged because the supply side always plays only a passive role:

$$\frac{\partial i_*}{\partial \mu} = 0.$$

But under a market-determined deposit rate, the interest rate rises when there is a shift in the supply function for demand deposits, as we know from 6.18. It follows, then, that

$$\frac{\partial i}{\partial \mu} > \frac{\partial i_*}{\partial \mu} = 0. \tag{6.32}$$

To the extent that the economy is prone to such supply shocks, as in the case of ongoing innovations in the financial industry, this greater interest variability is a shortcoming of the model with a market-determined interest rate.

By 6.19, the effect of a change in the reserve-requirement ratio on the interest rate cannot be signed without additional assumptions when the deposit rate is market determined; by 6.9, with a fixed deposit rate, the effect is positive. It is not surprising, then, that we cannot tell which effect is stonger.

$$\frac{\partial i}{\partial k} - \frac{\partial i_*}{\partial k} \gtreqless 0. \qquad (6.33)$$

The comparison of interest-rate sensitivity is aided visually in table 6–2, where we take the difference in the absolute value of the effects. This approach normalizes the effects, thereby permitting us to talk about variability without stating whether the interest rate rises or falls.

Comparison of Demand-Deposit Variability

In this section we shall compare the effects of deliberate and inadvertent shocks on the quantity of demand deposits when the deposit rate is market determined as opposed to being fixed. Our comparison will be both qualitative and quantitative.

We shall first summarize the effects of deliberate and inadvertent shocks—effects we derived in chapters 3 and 5. When the deposit rate is fixed, the relation between the quantity of real demand deposits and the shocks is given by:

Table 6–2
Quantitative Comparison of the Effects of Policy and Shocks on the (Bills) Interest Rate

Shocks	$\left\vert \dfrac{\partial i}{\partial a_j} \right\vert - \left\vert \dfrac{\partial i_*}{\partial a_j} \right\vert$
p	$+$
$\bar{R}_*$	$+$
$\bar{d}$	$+$
θ	$+$
$\bar{R}_E$	$+$
β	$+,0,-$
μ	$+$
k	$\oplus^a$

[a] A circle around a sign indicates that the sign is indeterminate but that an appropriate assumption can produce the indicated sign.

$$D \equiv D^*(p; R_*, \bar{d}, \theta, \bar{R}_E, \mu, \beta, k). \qquad (6.34)$$

The individual effects, beginning with the price level, are:

$$\frac{\partial D^*}{\partial p} = -\frac{\dfrac{R_*}{p^2} \cdot \dfrac{\partial D^d}{\partial z_h}}{C} < 0. \qquad (6.35)$$

That is, an exogenous increase in the price level reduces the quantity of real demand deposits.

On the other hand, an increase in the nominal reserve base, given the price level, increases the quantity of real demand deposits:

$$\frac{\partial D^*}{\partial R_*} = \frac{\dfrac{1}{p} \cdot \dfrac{\partial D^d}{\partial z_h}}{C} > 0. \qquad (6.36)$$

An increase in the discount rate, $\bar{d}$, has a negative effect on the amount of demand deposits, as expected.

$$\frac{\partial D^*}{\partial \bar{d}} = -\frac{R'_B \dfrac{\partial D^d}{\partial z_h}}{C} < 0. \qquad (6.37)$$

On the other hand, a positive shift in the borrowings function increases the quantity of demand deposits:

$$\frac{\partial D^*}{\partial \theta} = \frac{\dfrac{\partial R_B}{\partial \theta} \dfrac{\partial D^d}{\partial z_h}}{C} > 0. \qquad (6.38)$$

Furthermore, an exogenous increase in the demand for excess reserves, $\bar{R}_E$, reduces the amount of demand deposits:

$$\frac{\partial D^*}{\partial \bar{R}_E} = -\frac{\dfrac{\partial D^d}{\partial z_h}}{C} < 0. \qquad (6.39)$$

A positive shock in the demand for demand deposits increases their quantity:

$$\frac{\partial D^*}{\partial \beta} = -\frac{R'_B \dfrac{\partial D^d}{\partial \beta}}{C} > 0. \qquad (6.40)$$

Of course, with demand deposits being demand determined, a positive shift in the supply of demand deposits has no effect:

$$\frac{\partial D^*}{\partial \mu} \equiv 0. \qquad (6.41)$$

Finally, as expected, an increase in the reserve-requirement ratio reduces the amount of demand deposits by raising the interest rate, i:

$$\frac{\partial D^*}{\partial k} = -\frac{D^d(\cdot) \dfrac{\partial D^d}{\partial z_h}}{C} < 0. \qquad (6.42)$$

The effects of the same shocks on the quantity of demand deposits when the deposit rate is market determined are depicted by the partial derivatives of 6.43. Recall that we use the symbol, Δ, for these derivatives.

$$D = D(p; R_*, \bar{d}, \theta, \bar{R}_E, \beta, \mu, k). \qquad (6.43)$$

The effect of an exogenous increase in the price level is negative:

$$\frac{\Delta D}{\Delta p} = -\frac{k \dfrac{R_*}{p^2} \dfrac{\partial D^s}{\partial z_f} \dfrac{\partial D^d}{\partial z_h}}{Q} < 0, \qquad (6.44)$$

while the effect of an increase in the nominal reserve base, given p, is positive:

$$\frac{\Delta D}{\Delta R_*} = \frac{\left(\dfrac{1}{p}\right) k \dfrac{\partial D^s}{\partial z_f} \cdot \dfrac{\partial D^d}{\partial z_h}}{Q} > 0. \qquad (6.45)$$

The effect of an increase in the discount rate is, as expected, negative:

$$\frac{\Delta D}{\Delta \bar{d}} = -\frac{k R'_B \dfrac{\partial D^d}{\partial z_h} \dfrac{\partial D^s}{\partial z_f}}{Q} < 0. \qquad (6.46)$$

The effects of the remaining shocks have the expected signs, and we shall simply record them as follows:

$$\frac{\Delta D}{\Delta \theta} = \frac{k \dfrac{\partial R_B}{\partial \theta} \dfrac{\partial D^s}{\partial z_f} \dfrac{\partial D^d}{\partial z_h}}{Q} > 0 \qquad (6.47)$$

$$\frac{\Delta D}{\Delta \bar{R}_E} = -\frac{k \dfrac{\partial D^s}{\partial z_f} \cdot \dfrac{\partial D^d}{\partial z_h}}{Q} < 0 \qquad (6.48)$$

$$\frac{\Delta D}{\Delta \mu} = \frac{R_B' \dfrac{\partial D^s}{\partial \mu} \dfrac{\partial D^d}{\partial z_h}}{Q} > 0 \qquad (6.49)$$

$$\frac{\Delta D}{\Delta \beta} = -\frac{R_B' \dfrac{\partial D^d}{\partial \beta} \cdot \dfrac{\partial D^s}{\partial z_f}}{Q} > 0 \qquad (6.50)$$

$$\frac{\Delta D}{\Delta k} = -\frac{(i \cdot R_B' + k D) \dfrac{\partial D^d}{\partial z_h} \dfrac{\partial D^s}{\partial z_f}}{Q} < 0 \qquad (6.51)$$

Qualitative Comparisons

Comparing equations 6.43 through 6.51 with equations 6.35 through 6.42, we see that—ignoring the effect of a shift in the supply function—the

Table 6–3
Qualitative Comparison of the Effects of Policy and Shocks on Demand Deposits

a_j	$\partial D^*/\partial a_j$	$\Delta D/\Delta a_j$
p	−	−
R_*	+	+
$\bar{d}$	−	−
θ	+	+
$\bar{R}_E$	−	−
β	+	+
μ	0	+
k	−	−

qualitative effects of shocks are indistinguishable. That is, the signs coincide. Visual comparison is aided by table 6–3.

Quantitative Comparison of Effects

We shall begin by comparing the respective effects of the most important and deliberate shock—namely, an increase in the nominal reserve base, R_*. By 6.36 and 6.45, we get:

$$\frac{\partial D^*}{\partial R_*} - \frac{\Delta D}{\Delta R_*} = \frac{\dfrac{1}{p} \cdot \dfrac{\partial D^d}{\partial z_h}}{C} - \frac{\dfrac{1}{p} k \dfrac{\partial D^s}{\partial z_f} \dfrac{\partial D^d}{\partial z_h}}{Q}$$

Omitting the manipulations, we record:

$$\frac{\partial D^*}{\partial R_*} - \frac{\Delta D}{\Delta R_*} = - \frac{R'_B \dfrac{\partial D^d}{\partial z_h}}{p \cdot C \cdot Q} \cdot \left\{ (1-k)\frac{\partial D^s}{\partial z_f} - \frac{\partial D^d}{\partial z_h} \right\} > 0. \quad (6.52)$$

That is, we have proved this result:

$$\frac{\partial D^*}{\partial R_*} > \frac{\Delta D}{\Delta R_*} > 0. \quad (6.53)$$

The deposit-creating power of the nominal reserve base is greater under a fixed-deposit regime than under a regime with a market-determined deposit rate. Yet another way of stating this result is the following: The deposit multiplier is lower under a market-determined deposit rate than under a fixed deposit rate.

Next, we shall compare the effects of an exogenous increase in the price level. By 6.35 and 6.44, after the necessary manipulations, we have:

$$\frac{\partial D^*}{\partial p} - \frac{\Delta D}{\Delta p} = - \frac{R'_B \dfrac{R_*}{p^2} \dfrac{\partial D^d}{\partial z_h}}{C \cdot Q} \cdot \left\{ (1-k)\frac{\partial D^s}{\partial z_f} - \frac{\partial D^d}{\partial z_h} \right\} < 0. \quad (6.54)$$

That is, the decrease in real demand deposits is greater with a fixed deposit rate than with a market-determined deposit rate:

$$\frac{\partial D^*}{\partial p} < \frac{\Delta D}{\Delta p} < 0. \qquad (6.55)$$

Turning to the primary supplemental instrument of monetary control, the discount rate, $\bar{d}$, the comparison is again clear-cut. By 6.37 and 6.46, we get:

$$\frac{\partial D^*}{\partial \bar{d}} - \frac{\Delta D}{\Delta \bar{d}} = \frac{R'_B \dfrac{\partial D^d}{\partial z_h}}{C \cdot Q} \cdot \left\{ (1-k) \frac{\partial D^s}{\partial z_f} - \frac{\partial D^d}{\partial z_h} \right\} < 0. \quad (6.56)$$

Therefore, we have proved that

$$\frac{\partial D^*}{\partial \bar{d}} < \frac{\Delta D}{\Delta \bar{d}} < 0. \qquad (6.57)$$

That is, under a fixed deposit rate, an increase in the discount rate lowers demand deposits by more than they are lowered under a market-determined deposit rate.

Comparing the effects of a shock in the function for borrowed reserves, we find that

$$\frac{\partial D^*}{\partial \theta} - \frac{\Delta D}{\Delta \theta} = -\frac{R'_B \dfrac{\partial R_B}{\partial \theta} \dfrac{\partial D^d}{\partial z_h}}{C \cdot Q} \cdot \left\{ (1-k) \frac{\partial D^s}{\partial z_f} - \frac{\partial D^d}{\partial z_h} \right\} > 0$$

$$\qquad (6.58)$$

$$\frac{\partial D^*}{\partial \theta} > \frac{\Delta D}{\Delta \theta} > 0. \qquad (6.59)$$

In words, we see that the positive shift in the borrowings function increases the quantity of demand deposits by more when the deposit rate is fixed than when it is market determined. On the other hand, an exogenous shift (that is, an increase) in excess reserves, $\bar{R}_E$, reduces the quantity of demand deposits by more under a fixed deposit rate than under a market-determined deposit rate. By 6.39 and 6.48, we have:

$$\frac{\partial D^*}{\partial \bar{R}_E} - \frac{\Delta D}{\Delta \bar{R}_E} = -\frac{R'_B \dfrac{\partial D^d}{\partial z_h}}{C \cdot Q} \cdot \left\{ (1-k) \frac{\partial D^s}{\partial z_f} - \frac{\partial D^d}{\partial z_h} \right\} < 0, \quad (6.60)$$

or,

$$\frac{\partial D^*}{\partial \bar{R}_E} < \frac{\Delta D}{\Delta \bar{R}_E} < 0. \tag{6.61}$$

Of the two genuine shocks, one gives a clear-cut comparison by default. A positive shock in the supply function for demand deposits increases the quantity of demand deposits—$\Delta D/\Delta \mu > 0$—by 6.49. But a supply shift is irrelevant when the quantity of demand deposits is demand determined—that is, $\partial D^*/\partial \mu \equiv 0$, as in 6.41. Hence, we have:

$$\frac{\Delta D}{\Delta \mu} > \frac{\partial D^*}{\partial \mu} \equiv 0. \tag{6.62}$$

However, there is no such clear-cut result in the case of a demand-side shock. This positive shift in the demand function for demand deposits increases the quantity of demand deposits under either regime, by 6.40 and 6.50. Comparing the two effects, we get:

$$\frac{\partial D^*}{\partial \beta} - \frac{\Delta D}{\Delta \beta} = - \frac{R'_B \dfrac{\partial D^d}{\partial \beta} \dfrac{\partial D^d}{\partial z_h}}{C \cdot Q} \cdot \left\{ k(k-1)\frac{\partial D^s}{\partial z_f} + R'_B \right\} \gtrless 0. \tag{6.63}$$

It follows, then, that

$$\frac{\Delta D}{\Delta \beta} \lesseqgtr \frac{\partial D^*}{\partial \beta} \quad \text{when} \quad \left\{ k(k-1)\frac{\partial D^s}{\partial z_f} + R'_B \right\} \gtreqless 0. \tag{6.64}$$

In particular, we see that the positive shift in the demand for demand deposits increases the quantity of demand deposits by less under a variable deposit rate than under a fixed deposit rate when the expression in braces,

$$k(k-1)\frac{\partial D^s}{\partial z_f} + R'_B, \tag{6.65}$$

is positive. This is the same condition that guarantees that the interest variability, caused by a shift in demand, is lower with a market-determined deposit rate than with a fixed deposit rate. This is also the same condition that guarantees that the market-determined deposit rate falls when the demand function for demand deposits increases.

We have therefore established this interesting and verifiable result: A positive shift in the demand for demand deposits causes less variability in both the interest rate and in the quantity of demand deposits under a variable deposit rate than under a fixed deposit rate if and only if a positive shift in demand ultimately reduces the market-determined deposit rate. And, of course, the converse is true. But even more important is the following result: If the economy exhibits less variability in interest rates, it will also exhibit less variability in aggregates. If it exhibits greater variability in interest, it will also exhibit greater variability in aggregates (that is, demand deposits). In other words, there is no trade-off in variability.

It is interesting to inquire about the conditions under which expression 6.65 is positive and, hence, the conditions under which both the interest rate and the aggregates will vary less when the financial system moves to a market-determined deposit rate. The increase in demand deposits is greater under a fixed deposit rate than under a market-determined deposit rate in the special cases where either $k = 0$ or $k \equiv 1$. Also, in the general case, when k is greater than zero and less than one, but when the demand for borrowed reserves is very responsive to changes in the spread—that is, when R'_B is large—one would expect the inequality, $k(k - 1)\,(\partial D/\partial z_f) + R'_B > 0$. In this case, again, the quantity of demand deposits increases by more under a fixed deposit rate than under a market-determined deposit rate. On the other hand, if the supply of demand deposits is very elastic with respect to the profit margin, expression 6.65 will be negative; under these circumstances an increase in the demand function will increase both interest and demand deposits by more when the deposit rate is market determined than when it is fixed.

It is also interesting to note from 6.63 that when borrowed reserves do not depend on the interest rate, that is, when $R'_B \equiv 0$, the increase in the quantity of demand deposits will be the same:

$$\frac{\partial D^*}{\partial \beta} = \frac{\Delta D}{\Delta \beta}. \qquad (6.66)$$

Finally, it is not surprising that we cannot sign the difference between the effects of a change in the reserve-requirement ratio, k, without making additional assumptions:

$$\frac{\partial D^*}{\partial k} - \frac{\Delta D}{\Delta k} = -\frac{R'_B}{C \cdot Q} \cdot \left\{ D^d(\cdot)\frac{\partial D^d}{\partial z_h}\frac{\partial D^d}{\partial z_h} - \frac{\partial D^s}{\partial z_f} \right.$$

$$\left. - ik\left(\frac{\partial D^d}{\partial z_h}\right)^2\frac{\partial D^s}{\partial z_f} + iR'_B\frac{\partial D^d}{\partial z_h}\frac{\partial D^s}{\partial z_f} + k\,D(\cdot)\frac{\partial D^d}{\partial z_h}\frac{\partial D^s}{\partial z_f} \right\}. \qquad (6.67)$$

The relative variability of demand deposits is summarized in table 6–4.

Table 6–4
Quantitative Comparison of the Effects of Policy and Shocks on Demand Deposits

a_j	$\left\| \dfrac{\Delta D}{\Delta a_j} \right\| - \left\| \dfrac{\partial D^*}{\partial a_j} \right\|$
p	$-$
R_*	$-$
$\bar{d}$	$-$
θ	$-$
$\bar{R}_E$	$-$
μ	$+$
β	$+,0,-$
k	$\ominus^a$

[a]A circle around a sign indicates that this sign is indeterminate but that an appropriate assumption can produce the indicated sign.

Comparison of Variability in Borrowed and Total Reserves

We shall now compare the variability in borrowed and total reserves that results from shocks when the deposit rate is market determined as opposed to being fixed by the Central Bank. Examination of the respective variability is interesting in itself, but more important, it also provides insight into the variability of the other aggregate, demand deposits.

Borrowed Reserves

We begin by comparing the effects on borrowed reserves. We denote the effect of a change in parameter a_j on borrowed reserves when the deposit rate is fixed by $\partial R_B^*/\partial a_j$, and we denote the effect of the same parameter change on borrowed reserves when the deposit rate is market determined by $\Delta R_b/\Delta a_j$.

First we compare the effects of an exogenous change in the price level. The respective effects are:

$$\frac{\partial R_B^*}{\partial p} = R_B' \frac{\partial i_*}{\partial p} > 0$$

$$\frac{\Delta R_B}{\Delta p} = R_B' \frac{\partial i}{\partial p} > 0.$$

Subtracting the second from the first, we find that

$$\frac{\partial R_B^*}{\partial p} - \frac{\Delta R_B}{\Delta p} = R_B' \left(\frac{\partial i_*}{\partial p} - \frac{\partial i}{\partial p} \right) < 0, \qquad (6.68)$$

which is negative by 6.21. Thus we have proved that

$$\frac{\Delta R_B}{\Delta p} > \frac{\partial R_B^*}{\partial p} > 0 \qquad (6.69)$$

—that is, when the price level rises, borrowed reserves rise by more with a variable deposit rate than with a fixed deposit rate.

The effects of a change in the nominal reserve base, R_*, are

$$\frac{\partial R_B^*}{\partial R_*} = R_B' \frac{\partial i_*}{\partial R_*} < 0$$

$$\frac{\Delta R_B}{\Delta R_*} = R_B' \frac{\partial i}{\partial R_*} < 0.$$

Subtracting, we get

$$\frac{\partial R_B^*}{\partial R_*} - \frac{\Delta R_B}{\Delta R_*} = R_B' \left(\frac{\partial i_*}{\partial R_*} - \frac{\partial i}{\partial R_*} \right) > 0, \qquad (6.70)$$

which is positive by 6.23. That is,

$$\frac{\Delta R_B}{\Delta R_*} < \frac{\partial R_B^*}{\partial R_*} < 0. \qquad (6.71)$$

In words, we see that an increase in the nominal reserve base reduces real borrowed reserves by more when the deposit rate is variable than when it is fixed.

As compared with the other aggregate—demand deposits—we see that more variability in borrowed reserves is associated with changes in the price level and in the nominal reserve base under a flexible than under a fixed deposit rate. Indeed, it is this greater variability of borrowed reserves under a flexible deposit rate that allows for a smaller variability in demand deposits by providing a buffer.

Now we come to two shocks that create less variability under a variable deposit rate and that are associated with the borrowed-reserves function itself. To begin, we note that an increase in the discount rate has these positive effects:

$$\frac{\partial R_B^*}{\partial \bar{d}} = R_B' \frac{\partial i_*}{\partial \bar{d}} - R_B' > 0$$

$$\frac{\Delta R_B}{\Delta \bar{d}} = R_B' \frac{\partial i}{\partial \bar{d}} - R_B' > 0.$$

Subtracting, we get

$$\frac{\partial R_B^*}{\partial \bar{d}} - \frac{\Delta R_B}{\Delta \bar{d}} = R_B' \left(\frac{\partial i_*}{\partial \bar{d}} - \frac{\partial i}{\partial \bar{d}} \right) - R_B' + R_B'$$

or

$$\frac{\partial R_B^*}{\partial \bar{d}} - \frac{\Delta R_B}{\Delta \bar{d}} = R_B' \left(\frac{\partial i_*}{\partial \bar{d}} - \frac{\partial i}{\partial \bar{d}} \right) < 0, \qquad (6.72)$$

which is negative by 6.25. Therefore, we have proved that

$$\frac{\partial R_B^*}{\partial \bar{d}} < \frac{\Delta R_B}{\Delta \bar{d}} < 0. \qquad (6.73)$$

That is, when the discount rate is increased, borrowed reserves fall by *less* when the deposit rate is market determined. Similar smaller variability is observed when the borrowed-reseves function is shocked positively:

$$\frac{\partial R_B^*}{\partial \theta} = \frac{\partial R_B}{\partial \theta} + R_B' \frac{\partial i_*}{\partial \theta}$$

$$\frac{\Delta R_B}{\Delta \theta} = \frac{\partial R_B}{\partial \theta} + R_B' \frac{\partial i}{\partial \theta}.$$

Substituting and canceling common terms, we get:

$$\frac{\partial R_B^*}{\partial \theta} - \frac{\Delta R_B}{\Delta \theta} = R_B' \left(\frac{\partial i_*}{\partial \theta} - \frac{\partial i}{\partial \theta} \right), \qquad (6.74)$$

which is positive by 6.26. We have, therefore, proved that

$$\frac{\partial R_B^*}{\partial \theta} > \frac{\Delta R_B}{\Delta \theta} > 0. \tag{6.75}$$

In words, we note that the amount of real borrowed reserves rises by *less* when the deposit rate is market determined than when it is fixed. These two results—6.73 and 6.75—indicate a smaller variability in borrowed reserves under a flexible-deposit-rate regime because the direct effects of the shock are the same in each regime and they cancel out; only indirect effects based on interest rates are then left, and the higher variability in those reduces the variability in borrowed reserves in precisely the same manner that the higher variability of interest rates reduces the variability of demand deposits—with the one exception noted earlier.

Next we compare the effects of an exogenous increase in excess reserves that are

$$\frac{\partial R_B^*}{\partial \bar{R}_E} = R_B' \frac{\partial i_*}{\partial \bar{R}_E}$$

$$\frac{\Delta R_B}{\Delta \bar{R}_E} + R_B' \frac{\partial i}{\partial \bar{R}_E}.$$

Subtracting, we have

$$\frac{\partial R_B^*}{\partial \bar{R}_E} - \frac{\Delta R_B}{\Delta \bar{R}_E} = R_B' \left(\frac{\partial i_*}{\partial \bar{R}_E} - \frac{\partial i}{\partial \bar{R}_E} \right) < 0, \tag{6.76}$$

which is negative by 6.28. Hence, we get:

$$\frac{\Delta R_B}{\Delta \bar{R}_E} > \frac{\partial R_B^*}{\partial \bar{R}_E} > 0. \tag{6.77}$$

Again, borrowed reserves rise by more when the deposit rate is variable. The same result prevails, by default, when there is a positive shift in the supply of demand deposits:

$$\frac{\partial R_B^*}{\partial \mu} = R_B' \frac{\partial i_*}{\partial \mu} = 0$$

$$\frac{\Delta R_B}{\Delta \mu} = R_B' \frac{\partial i}{\partial \mu} > 0.$$

Hence,

$$\frac{\Delta R_B}{\Delta \mu} > \frac{\partial R_B^*}{\partial \mu} = 0 \qquad (6.78)$$

We now turn to a shock in the demand for demand deposits. The separate effects are

$$\frac{\partial R_B^*}{\partial \beta} = R_B' \frac{\partial i_*}{\partial \beta} > 0$$

$$\frac{\Delta R_B}{\Delta \beta} = R_B' \frac{\partial i}{\partial \beta} > 0.$$

And the difference is

$$\frac{\partial R_B^*}{\partial \beta} - \frac{\Delta R_B}{\Delta \beta} = R_B' \left(\frac{\partial i_*}{\partial \beta} - \frac{\partial i}{\partial \beta} \right) \gtreqless 0. \qquad (6.79)$$

Recalling the early indeterminancy of $(\partial i_*/\partial \beta - \partial i/\partial \beta)$, we see that the sign depends on

$$k(k - 1) \frac{\partial D^s}{\partial z_f} + R_B'. \qquad (6.80)$$

If it is positive, $(\partial i_*/\partial \beta - \partial i/\partial \beta) < 0$, by 6.31, and, hence,

$$\frac{\partial R_B^*}{\partial \beta} > \frac{\Delta R_B}{\Delta \beta} > 0 \qquad (6.81)$$

—that is, borrowed reserves, as with the other aggregate, demand deposits, will rise by *less* when the deposit rate is market determined. On the other hand, if 6.80 is negative, the opposite result will hold. Of course, if $R_B' \equiv 0$, there will be no change in borrowed reserves under either regime.

Finally, we compare the effects of a change in the reserve-requirement ratio and find that

$$\frac{\partial R_B^*}{\partial k} - \frac{\Delta R_B}{\Delta k} = R_B' \left(\frac{\partial i_*}{\partial k} - \frac{\partial i}{\partial k} \right) \gtreqless 0, \qquad (6.82)$$

with the presumption that $\partial i_*/\partial k - \partial i/\partial k < 0$ and, hence, that

$$\frac{\Delta R_B}{\Delta k} > \frac{\partial R_B^*}{\partial k} > 0. \qquad (6.83)$$

The variability in borrowed reserves is summarized in table 6–5. Comparison of the relative variability in the interest rate, in the monetary aggregate (that is, demand deposits), and in the reserve aggregate (borrowed reserves) is condensed in table 6–6, which consolidates table 6–2, 6–4, and 6–5.

Total Reserves

Comparison of the relative response of total reserves to shocks is easy because the quantity of total reserves consists of the real reserve base plus borrowed reserves:

$$R_T = \frac{R_*}{p} + R_B(\cdot).$$

Hence, with the exception of a change in either the nominal reserve base, R_*, or in the price level, p, the relative variability of total reserves is that of borrowed reserves,

$$\frac{\partial R_B^*}{\partial a_j} - \frac{\Delta R_T}{\Delta a_j} = \frac{\partial R_B^*}{\partial a_j} - \frac{\Delta R_B}{\Delta a_j};$$

and we have already established this variability.

Table 6–5
Quantitative Comparison of the Effects of Policy and Shocks on Borrowed Reserves

a_j	$\left\lvert \dfrac{\Delta R_B}{\Delta a_j} \right\rvert - \left\lvert \dfrac{\partial R_B^*}{\partial a_j} \right\rvert$
p	+
R_*	+
$\bar{d}$	−
θ	−
$\bar{R}_E$	+
μ	+
β	+,0,−
k	$\oplus^a$

[a]A circle around a sign indicates that this sign is indeterminate but that an appropriate assumption can produce the indicated sign.

Table 6–6
Relative Variability in Interest Rates, Demand Deposits, and Borrowed Reserves

a_j	$\left\|\dfrac{\partial i}{\partial a_j}\right\| - \left\|\dfrac{\partial i_*}{\partial a_j}\right\|$	$\left\|\dfrac{\Delta D}{\Delta a_j}\right\| - \left\|\dfrac{\partial D^*}{\partial a_j}\right\|$	$\left\|\dfrac{\Delta R_B}{\Delta a_j}\right\| - \left\|\dfrac{\partial R_B^*}{\partial a_j}\right\|$
p	+	−	+
R_*	+	−	+
$\bar{d}$	+	−	−
θ	+	−	−
$\bar{R}_E$	+	−	+
μ	+	+	+
β	±	±	±
k	$\oplus$ a	$\ominus$ a	$\oplus$ a

a A circle around a sign indicates that this sign is indeterminate but that an appropriate assumption can produce the indicated sign.

Therefore, we need to examine explicitly only the relative variability of total reserves for the shocks of a change in the nominal reserve base and in the price level. For a change in the price level, we have the following for the case of a fixed deposit rate:

$$\frac{\partial R_T^*}{\partial p} = -\frac{R_*}{p^2} + \frac{\partial R_B^*}{\partial p} < 0;$$

and for the case of a flexible deposit rate:

$$\frac{\Delta R_T}{\Delta p} = -\frac{R_*}{p^2} + \frac{\Delta R_B}{\Delta p} < 0.$$

Subtracting, we have

$$\frac{\partial R_T^*}{\partial p} - \frac{\Delta R_T}{\Delta p} = -\frac{R_*}{p^2} + \frac{R_*}{p^2} + \frac{\partial R_B^*}{\partial p} - \frac{\Delta R_B^*}{\Delta p} = \frac{\partial R_B}{\partial p} - \frac{\Delta R_B}{\Delta p} < 0,$$

which is negative by 6.68. Hence,

$$\frac{\partial R_T^*}{\partial p} < \frac{\Delta R_T}{\Delta p} < 0.$$

Turning to an increase in the nominal reserve base, R_*, we have the following for the fixed and for the flexible rates, respectively:

$$\frac{\partial R_T^*}{\partial R_*} = \frac{1}{p} + \frac{\partial R_B^*}{\partial R_*} > 0$$

$$\frac{\Delta R_T}{\Delta R_*} = \frac{1}{p} + \frac{\Delta R_B}{\Delta R_*} > 0.$$

Subtracting, we have:

$$\frac{\partial R_T^*}{\partial R_*} - \frac{\Delta R_T}{\Delta R_*} = \frac{\partial R_B^*}{\partial R_*} - \frac{\Delta R_B}{\Delta R_*} > 0.$$

Hence, we have:

$$\frac{\partial R_T^*}{\partial R_*} > \frac{\Delta R_T}{\Delta R_*} > 0$$

—that is, an increase in the nominal reserve base increases total reserves by less under a flexible deposit rate than under a fixed deposit rate.

The relative variability of total reserves is summarized in table 6–7, in which the relative variability of demand deposits is also incorporated in order to show that they coincide.

Table 6–7
Relative Variability in Demand Deposits and in Total Reserves

a_j	$\left\|\dfrac{\Delta R_T}{\Delta a_j}\right\| - \left\|\dfrac{\partial R_T^*}{\partial a_j}\right\|$	$\left\|\dfrac{\Delta D}{\Delta a_j}\right\| - \left\|\dfrac{\partial D^*}{\partial a_j}\right\|$
p	−	−
R_*	−	−
d	−	−
θ	−	−
$\bar{R}_E$	−	−
μ	+	+
β	±	±
k	⊖[a]	⊖[a]

[a]A circle around a sign indicates that this sign is indeterminate but that an appropriate assumption can produce the indicated sign.

Note

1. The originator of this idea is, of course, W.C. Brainard (1964), pp. 450–462. W.C. Brainard (1967) formally extended the analysis to include uncertainty. In such a stochastic setting, variability in interest rates and in aggregates due to stochastic shocks is identified with the resulting standard deviations. W. Poole (1970) applied this idea to the choice of instruments problem in a simple IS-LM macromodel. Our analysis can be easily extended to follow that approach. In fact, in chapter 7, a linear example of the analysis and results of chapters 3 to 6 is introduced partly as an aid to the interested reader who wants to introduce stochastic techniques. However, in this work we have not followed those stochastic techniques for two reasons. First, we want to examine a more general comparative statics problem, of which stochastic shocks are only one example. Second, the comparison undertaken in chapter 10 of the entire models representing the two regimes is an alternative to the choice-of-instruments problem.

7 A Simple Linear Model

In this chapter we shall examine an example based on the analysis of the preceding four chapters. We shall use a linear model that purports to reenact and illustrate both the techniques and the results of the preceding chapters. In fact, this simple model can also be helpful in checking the accuracy of the preceding analysis. Moreover, the linear model is conducive to applications, that is, it can be estimated as more and more data are coming in and in the meantime it can be used for simulations, stochastic or otherwise.

The Fixed-Deposit-Rate Model

To develop a model that illustrates and reenacts the results of chapter 3, we must first specify the necessary structural or behavioral equations, namely, the demand for demand deposits, D^d, and the function for borrowed reserves, R_B.

The demand function is specified as

$$D^d = a_0 - a_1(i - \zeta) + a_2\beta, \qquad (7.1)$$

where a_0 is the "intercept" and β is the same shift parameter we examined in the preceding chapters. We note that the partial derivatives of 7.1 have the required signs: $\partial D^d/\partial(i - \zeta) = -a_1 < 0$ and $\partial D^d/\partial\beta = a_2 > 0$. For this model we fix the deposit rate by specifying that

$$\zeta = \bar{\zeta}. \qquad (7.2)$$

The borrowed-reserves function is given by 7.3:

$$R_B = b_0 + b_1 \cdot (i - \bar{d}) + b_2\theta, \qquad (7.3)$$

which also exhibits the desired characteristics; that is, from 7.3 we get the partial derivatives, $\partial R_B/\partial(i - \bar{d}) \equiv R_B' = b_1 > 0$ and $\partial R_B/\partial\theta = b_2 > 0$.

Next, we specify required reserves, R_R, by (7.4):

$$R_R = k \cdot D^d. \qquad (7.4)$$

Substituting 7.1 and 7.2 into 7.4, we have:

$$R_R = ka_0 - ka_1 i + k a_1 \bar{\zeta} + ka_2 \beta. \qquad (7.5)$$

The earning-assets, or bills, market will not be specified because we have chosen it as the omitted market. Therefore, we need to examine explicitly only the market for reserves. Since the excess demand for reserves (EDR) is specified as 7.6—that is,

$$EDR = R_R + R_E - R_B - \frac{R_*}{p}, \qquad (7.6)$$

we need to specify only excess reserves, R_E. As in the previous chapters, we assume that excess reserves are constant:

$$R_E = \bar{R}_E. \qquad (7.7)$$

Now setting $EDR = 0$ in 7.6 and substituting its components from 7.3, 7.5, and 7.7, we get the fundamental equation of our model:

$$EDR = ka_0 - ka_1 i + ka_1 \bar{\zeta} + ka_2 \beta + \bar{R}_E - b_0$$

$$- b_1 i + b_1 \bar{d} - b_2 \theta - \frac{R_*}{p} = 0. \qquad (7.8)$$

Collecting terms and solving for i, we have:

$$i_* = \frac{1}{ka_1 + b_1} \cdot \left\{ (ka_0 - b_0) + ka_1 \bar{\zeta} + ka_2 \beta - b_2 \theta \right.$$

$$\left. + \bar{R}_E + b_1 \bar{d} - \frac{R_*}{p} \right\}. \qquad (7.9)$$

Substituting 7.9 (and 7.2) into 7.1 we get D^*:

$$D^* \equiv D^d[i_*(\cdot) - \bar{\zeta}; \beta] \equiv a_0 - a_1(i_* - \bar{\zeta}) + a_2 \beta. \qquad (7.10)$$

From 7.9 we can derive immediately the effects of a change in a particular parameter on the interest rate:

$$\frac{\partial i_*}{\partial p} = \frac{\dfrac{R_*}{p^2}}{ka_1 + b_1} > 0 \qquad (7.10a)$$

$$\frac{\partial i_*}{\partial R_*} = -\frac{\frac{1}{p}}{ka_1 + b_1} < 0 \qquad (7.10b)$$

$$\frac{\partial i_*}{\partial \bar{d}} = \frac{b_1}{ka_1 + b_1} > 0 \qquad (7.10c)$$

$$\frac{\partial i_*}{\partial \bar{\zeta}} = \frac{ka_1}{ka_1 + b_1} > 0 \qquad (7.10d)$$

$$\frac{\partial i_*}{\partial \theta} = -\frac{b_2}{ka_1 + b_1} < 0 \qquad (7.10e)$$

$$\frac{\partial i_*}{\partial \bar{R}_E} = \frac{1}{ka_1 + b_1} > 0 \qquad (7.10f)$$

$$\frac{\partial i_*}{\partial \beta} = \frac{ka_2}{ka_1 + b_1} > 0 \qquad (7.10g)$$

$$\frac{\partial i_*}{\partial k} = \frac{D^*}{ka_1 + b_1} > 0 \qquad (7.10h)$$

where

$$B = ka_1 + b_1. \qquad (7.11)$$

The result in 7.10h is derived when we define the quantity of demand deposits, D^*, that is consistent with the equilibrium interest rate:

$$D^* = a_0 - a_1[i_*(\cdot) - \bar{\zeta}] + a_2 \beta,$$

or

$$D^* = a_0 - a_1 i_*(\cdot) + a_1 \bar{\zeta} + a_2 \beta, \qquad (7.12)$$

where $i_*(\cdot)$ is, of course, given by 7.9.

Now, appropriate differentiation of 7.12 and substitution of 7.10a through 7.10h gives the effects of policy and of shocks on the quantity of demand deposits:

$$\frac{\partial D^*}{\partial p} = - a_1 \frac{\partial i_*}{\partial p}$$

or, by 7.10a:

$$\frac{\partial D^*}{\partial p} = - \frac{a_1 \dfrac{R_*}{p^2}}{B} < 0. \qquad (7.13)$$

Similarly,

$$\frac{\partial D^*}{\partial R_*} = - a_1 \frac{\partial i_*}{\partial R_*} = \frac{a_1}{p \cdot B} > 0 \qquad (7.14)$$

$$\frac{\partial D^*}{\partial \bar{d}} = - a_1 \frac{\partial i_*}{\partial \bar{d}} = - \frac{a_1 b_1}{B} < 0 \qquad (7.15)$$

$$\frac{\partial D^*}{\partial \bar{\zeta}} = a_1 - a_1 \frac{\partial i_*}{\partial \bar{\zeta}} = \frac{a_1 b_1}{B} > 0 \qquad (7.16)$$

$$\frac{\partial D^*}{\partial \theta} = - a_1 \frac{\partial i_*}{\partial \theta} = \frac{a_1 b_1}{B} > 0 \qquad (7.17)$$

$$\frac{\partial D^*}{\partial \bar{R}_E} = - a_1 \frac{\partial i_*}{\bar{R}_E} = - \frac{a_1}{B} < 0 \qquad (7.18)$$

$$\frac{\partial D^*}{\partial \beta} = a_2 - a_1 \frac{\partial i_*}{\partial \beta} = \frac{a_2 b_1}{B} > 0 \qquad (7.19)$$

$$\frac{\partial D^*}{\partial k} = - a_1 \frac{\partial i_*}{\partial k} = - \frac{a_1 D^*}{B} < 0. \qquad (7.20)$$

Effects on Reserves Aggregates

Borrowed Reserves.   We define $R_{\hat{B}}^*$ as in 7.21:

$$R_{\hat{B}}^* = b_0 + b_1 [i_*(\cdot) - \bar{d}] + b_2 \theta$$
$$= b_0 + b_1 i_*(\cdot) - b_1 \bar{d} + b_2 \theta. \qquad (7.21)$$

This means that when we incorporate the solution for i—that is, 7.9 into 7.3—we can find the effects of shocks on borrowed reserves by simply differentiating 7.21:

$$\frac{\partial R_B^*}{\partial p} = b_1 \frac{\partial i_*}{\partial p} = \frac{b_1 \dfrac{R_*}{p^2}}{B} > 0 \tag{7.22}$$

$$\frac{\partial R_B^*}{\partial R_*} = b_1 \frac{\partial i_*}{\partial R_*} = -\frac{b_1}{p \cdot B} < 0 \tag{7.23}$$

$$\frac{\partial R_B^*}{\partial \bar{d}} = -b_1 + b_1 \frac{\partial i_*}{\partial \bar{d}} = -\frac{ka_1 b_1}{B} < 0 \tag{7.24}$$

$$\frac{\partial R_B^*}{\partial \bar{\zeta}} = b_1 \frac{\partial i_*}{\partial \bar{\zeta}} = \frac{ka_1 b_1}{B} > 0 \tag{7.25}$$

$$\frac{\partial R_B^*}{\partial \theta} = b_2 + b_1 \frac{\partial i_*}{\partial \theta} = \frac{ka_1 b_1 b_2}{B} > 0 \tag{7.26}$$

$$\frac{\partial R_B^*}{\partial \bar{R}_E} = b_1 \frac{\partial i_*}{\partial \bar{R}_E} = \frac{b_1}{B} > 0 \tag{7.27}$$

$$\frac{\partial R_B^*}{\partial \beta} = b_1 \frac{\partial i_*}{\partial \beta} = \frac{ka_2 b_1}{B} > 0 \tag{7.28}$$

$$\frac{\partial R_B^*}{\partial k} = b_1 \frac{\partial i_*}{\partial k} = \frac{b_1 D^*}{B} > 0. \tag{7.29}$$

Total Reserves. We use the following definition:

$$R_T^* = \frac{R_*}{p} + R_B^*(\cdot), \tag{7.30}$$

or

$$R_T^* = \frac{R_*}{p} + b_0 + b_1\, i_*(\cdot) - b_1\, \bar{d} + b_2\, \theta.$$ (7.31)

It is clear from 7.30 that with the exception of an exogenous change in R_* or in p, the effects of shocks on total reserves are precisely the same effects as those on borrowed reserves:

$$\frac{\partial R_T^*}{\partial \bar{d}} = \frac{\partial R_B^*}{\partial \bar{d}} = -\frac{ka_1 b_1}{B} < 0$$ (7.32)

$$\frac{\partial R_T^*}{\partial \bar{\zeta}} = \frac{\partial R_B^*}{\partial \bar{\zeta}} = \frac{ka_1 b_1}{B} > 0$$ (7.33)

$$\frac{\partial R_T^*}{\partial \theta} = \frac{\partial R_B^*}{\partial \theta} = \frac{ka_1 b_1 b_2}{B} > 0$$ (7.34)

$$\frac{\partial R_T^*}{\partial \bar{R}_E} = \frac{\partial R_B^*}{\partial \bar{R}_E} = \frac{b_1}{B} > 0$$ (7.35)

$$\frac{\partial R_T^*}{\partial \beta} = \frac{\partial R_B^*}{\partial \beta} = \frac{ka_2 b_1}{B} > 0$$ (7.36)

$$\frac{\partial R_T^*}{\partial k} = \frac{\partial R_B^*}{\partial k} = \frac{b_1 D^*}{B} > 0.$$ (7.37)

On the other hand, the effects of a change in R_* and in p are, respectively:

$$\frac{\partial R_T^*}{\partial R_*} = \frac{1}{p} + b_1 \frac{\partial i_*}{\partial R_*} = \frac{ka_1}{pB} > 0$$ (7.38)

and

$$\frac{\partial R_T^*}{\partial p} = -\frac{R_*}{p^2} + b_1 \frac{\partial i_*}{\partial p} = -\frac{ka_1 \dfrac{R_*}{p^2}}{B} < 0$$ (7.39)

The Market-Determined-Deposit-Rate Model

Clearance of the Deposit Market Alone

To specify the model with a flexible, market-determined deposit rate we need the supply of demand deposits, D^s:

$$D^s = c_0 + c_1 [(1 - k) i - \zeta] + c_2 \mu$$
$$= c_0 + (1 - k) c_1 \cdot i - c_1 \zeta + c_2 \mu. \qquad (7.40)$$

Clearance of the deposit market requires that

$$D^d = D^s. \qquad (7.41)$$

Substituting 7.1 and 7.40 into 7.41, solving for ζ, and denoting this solution by $\hat{\zeta}$, we get:

$$\hat{\zeta} \equiv \hat{\zeta}(i, \mu, \beta, k) \equiv \frac{1}{a_1 + c_1} \cdot \{(c_0 - a_0) + [a_1 + (1 - k)c_1]i$$
$$+ c_2\mu - a_2\beta\}. \qquad (7.42)$$

The effects of changes in the endogenous variable, i, and in the parameters, μ, β, and k, when the deposit market is required to clear, are given by the partial derivatives:

$$\frac{\partial \hat{\zeta}}{\partial i} = \frac{a_1 + (1 - k)c_1}{a_1 + c_1} > 0 \qquad (7.43)$$

$$\frac{\partial \hat{\zeta}}{\partial \mu} = \frac{c_2}{a_1 + c_1} > 0 \qquad (7.44)$$

$$\frac{\partial \hat{\zeta}}{\partial \beta} = -\frac{a_2}{a_1 + c_1} < 0 \qquad (7.45)$$

$$\frac{\partial \hat{\zeta}}{\partial k} = -\frac{c_2 \cdot i}{a_1 + c_1} < 0. \qquad (7.46)$$

We know that by 7.43

$$1 > \frac{\partial \hat{\zeta}}{\partial i} > 0. \qquad (7.47)$$

Substituting 7.42 into 7.40 and denoting the result by $\hat{D}$, we have:

$$\hat{D} \equiv \hat{D}(i; \mu, \beta, k) \equiv c_0 + (1 - k)c_1 i - c_1 \hat{\zeta}(i; \mu, \beta, k) + c_2 \mu,$$
$$(7.48)$$

which after tedious manipulations becomes:

$$\hat{D}(i; \mu, \beta, k) = \frac{1}{a_1 + c_1} \{(a_1 c_0 + c_1 a_0) + a_1 c_2 \mu + c_1 a_2 \beta - a_1 k c_1\}.$$
$$(7.49)$$

We shall leave it to the reader to show that formula 7.49 can be derived when we substitute 7.1 into 7.40 and that the result can be defined as $\hat{D}$.

Now, the effects of a change in i, μ, β, and k, taken one at a time, on the quantity of demand deposits when the deposit market alone is cleared are given by 7.50 through 7.53:

$$\frac{\partial \hat{D}}{\partial i} = -\frac{k a_1 c_1}{a_1 + c_1} < 0 \qquad (7.50)$$

$$\frac{\partial \hat{D}}{\partial \mu} = \frac{a_1 c_2}{a_1 + c_1} > 0 \qquad (7.51)$$

$$\frac{\partial \hat{D}}{\partial \beta} = \frac{c_1 a_2}{a_1 + c_1} > 0 \qquad (7.52)$$

$$\frac{\partial \hat{D}}{\partial k} = \frac{a_1 c_1 i}{a_1 + c_1} < 0. \qquad (7.53)$$

Clearance of All Financial-Asset Markets

The financial system is in equilibrium if EDD and EDR are simultaneously equal to zero. The equation, $EDD = 0$, is represented by its implications, 7.42 and 7.43 through 7.46, or by its implications, 7.49 and 7.50 through 7.53. Hence, we need to specify $EDR = 0$ and to use the characteristics 7.42 or 7.50, and so on. EDR was specified in 7.6 as:

$$EDR = R_R + R_E - R_B - \frac{R_*}{p}.$$

But now required reserves are given by

$$R_R = k \cdot \hat{D}(i; \mu, \beta, k). \qquad (7.54)$$

Continuing to assume that excess reserves are fixed at $\bar{R}_E$, we have the following for reserves and full-financial equilibrium:

$$EDR = k \cdot \hat{D}(i; \mu, \beta, k) + \bar{R}_E - R_B(\cdot) - \frac{R_*}{p} = 0,$$

or, by substitution of 7.49 and 7.2,

$$\frac{k}{a_1 + c_1} \cdot \{(a_1 c_0 + c_1 a_0) + a_1 c_2 \mu + c_1 a_2 \beta - a_1 k \, c_1 i\}$$

$$+ \bar{R}_E - b_0 - b_1 i + b_1 \bar{d} - b_2 \theta - \frac{R_*}{p} = 0. \qquad (7.55)$$

Solving 7.55 explicitly for i, we get:

$$i = \frac{1}{A} \cdot \left\{ [k(a_1 c_0 + c_1 a_0) - b_0(a_1 + c_1)] + [a_1 + c_1] \cdot \bar{R}_E \right.$$

$$+ b_1(a_1 + c_1) \cdot \bar{d} - b_2(a_1 + c_1) \cdot \theta + k a_1 c_2 \cdot \mu$$

$$\left. + k \, c_1 a_2 \cdot \beta - (a_1 + c_1) \cdot \frac{R_*}{p} \right\}, \qquad (7.56)$$

where

$$A \equiv a_1 b_1 + b_1 c_1 + a_1 k^2 \, c_1. \qquad (7.57)$$

Overall Effects on the (Bills) Interest Rate, i

The effects of monetary policy and of shocks on the interest rate when *all* asset markets are cleared are given by the respective partial derivatives of 7.56:

$$\frac{\partial i}{\partial p} = \frac{(a_1 + c_1)R_*}{Ap^2} > 0 \qquad (7.58)$$

$$\frac{\partial i}{\partial R_*} = -\frac{a_1 + c_1}{A \cdot p} < 0 \qquad (7.59)$$

$$\frac{\partial i}{\partial \bar{d}} = \frac{b_1(a_1 + c_1)}{A} > 0 \qquad (7.60)$$

$$\frac{\partial i}{\partial \theta} = -\frac{b_2(a_1 + c_1)}{A} < 0 \qquad (7.61)$$

$$\frac{\partial i}{\partial \bar{R}_E} = \frac{a_1 + c_1}{A} > 0 \qquad (7.62)$$

$$\frac{\partial i}{\partial \beta} = \frac{kc_1 a_2}{A} > 0 \qquad (7.63)$$

$$\frac{\partial i}{\partial \mu} = \frac{ka_1 c_2}{A} > 0 \qquad (7.64)$$

$$\frac{\partial i}{\partial k} = \frac{1}{A} \cdot [(a_1 c_0 + a_0 c_1) + a_1 c_2 \mu + c_1 a_2 \beta]$$

$$-\frac{2ka_1 c_1}{A} \cdot \left\{ (a_1 + c_1) b_1 \bar{d} - (a_1 + c_1) b_2 \theta \right.$$

$$+ k[(a_1 c_0 + a_0 c_1) + a_1 c_2 \mu + a_2 c_1 \beta] - (a_1 + c_1) b_0$$

$$\left. + (a_1 + c_1) \bar{R}_E - (a_1 + c_1) \cdot \frac{R_*}{p} \right\} \gtrless 0. \qquad (7.65)$$

Overall Effect on the Deposit Interest Rate, ζ

To find the effect of shocks on the deposit rate, ζ, when all asset markets are cleared, we must differentiate 7.42 and use 7.43 through 7.46 and 7.58 through 7.65. We shall denote this overall effect on ζ when parameter a_j is changed by $\Delta\zeta/\Delta a_j$.

$$\frac{\Delta\zeta}{\Delta p} = \frac{\partial \hat{\zeta}}{\partial i} \frac{\partial i}{\partial p} = \frac{R_*[a_1 + (1-k)c_1]}{Ap^2} > 0 \qquad (7.66)$$

$$\frac{\Delta\zeta}{\Delta R_*} = \frac{\partial\hat{\zeta}}{\partial i}\frac{\partial i}{\partial R_*} = -\frac{a_1 + (1-k)c_1}{Ap} < 0 \qquad (7.67)$$

$$\frac{\Delta\zeta}{\Delta\bar{d}} = \frac{\partial\hat{\zeta}}{\partial i}\frac{\partial i}{\partial\bar{d}} = \frac{b_1[a_1 + (1-k)c_1]}{A} > 0 \qquad (7.68)$$

$$\frac{\Delta\zeta}{\Delta\theta} = \frac{\partial\hat{\zeta}}{\partial i}\frac{\partial i}{\partial\theta} = -\frac{b_2[a_1 + (1-k)c_1]}{A} < 0 \qquad (7.69)$$

$$\frac{\Delta\zeta}{\Delta\bar{R}_E} = \frac{\partial\hat{\zeta}}{\partial i}\frac{\partial i}{\partial\bar{R}_E} = \frac{a_1 + (1-k)c_1}{A} > 0 \qquad (7.70)$$

$$\frac{\Delta\zeta}{\Delta\beta} = \frac{\partial\hat{\zeta}}{\partial\beta} + \frac{\partial\hat{\zeta}}{\partial i}\frac{\partial i}{\partial\beta} = -\frac{a_2}{A}\cdot\{k(k-1)c_1 + b_1\} \gtrless 0$$
$$\qquad (7.71)$$

$$\frac{\Delta\zeta}{\Delta\mu} = \frac{\partial\hat{\zeta}}{\partial\mu} + \frac{\partial\hat{\zeta}}{\partial i}\frac{\partial i}{\partial\mu} = \frac{c_2}{A}\cdot(b_1 + ka_1) > 0$$
$$\qquad (7.72)$$

$$\frac{\Delta\zeta}{\Delta k} = \frac{\partial\hat{\zeta}}{\partial k} + \frac{\partial\hat{\zeta}}{\partial i}\frac{\partial i}{\partial k},$$

or

$$\frac{\Delta\zeta}{\Delta k} \gtrless 0. \qquad (7.73)$$

We must now record the all-important condition for signing $\Delta\zeta/\Delta\beta$.

$$\frac{\Delta\zeta}{\Delta\beta} \lessgtr 0 \text{ when } \{k(k-1)c_1 + b_1\} \gtrless 0. \qquad (7.74)$$

Overall Effects on the Quantity of Demand Deposits

To find the effects on the quantity of demand deposits, we must differentiate 7.49 and substitute 7.50 through 7.53 and 7.58 through 7.65:

$$\frac{\Delta D}{\Delta p} = \frac{\partial \hat{D}}{\partial i}\frac{\partial i}{\partial p} = -\frac{ka_1c_1}{A}\cdot\frac{R_*}{p} < 0 \qquad (7.75)$$

$$\frac{\Delta D}{\Delta R_*} = \frac{ka_1c_1}{pA} > 0 \qquad (7.76)$$

$$\frac{\Delta D}{\Delta \bar{d}} = -\frac{ka_1b_1c_1}{A} < 0 \qquad (7.77)$$

$$\frac{\Delta D}{\Delta \theta} = \frac{ka_1b_2c_1}{A} > 0 \qquad (7.78)$$

$$\frac{\Delta D}{\Delta \bar{R}_E} = -\frac{ka_1c_1}{A} < 0 \qquad (7.79)$$

$$\frac{\Delta D}{\Delta \beta} = \frac{a_2b_1c_1}{A} > 0 \qquad (7.80)$$

$$\frac{\Delta D}{\Delta \mu} = \frac{a_1b_1c_2}{A} > 0 \qquad (7.81)$$

$$\frac{\Delta D}{\Delta k} \lesseqgtr 0. \qquad (7.82)$$

Effects on Reserves Aggregates

Borrowed Reserves. Substituting 7.56 into 7.3, we have the relevant borrowings function:

$$R_B = b_0 + b_1 i(\cdot) - b_1\bar{d} + b_2\theta, \qquad (7.83)$$

where $i(\cdot)$ is given by 7.56. Differentiating 7.83 and using 7.58 through 7.65, we get the usual effects of shocks, denoted by $\Delta R_B/\Delta a_j$:

$$\frac{\Delta R_B}{\Delta p} = b_1\frac{\partial i}{\partial p} = \frac{(a_1 + c_1)b_1R_*}{A\cdot p^2} > 0 \qquad (7.84)$$

$$\frac{\Delta R_B}{\Delta R_*} = b_1\frac{\partial i}{\partial R_*} = -\frac{(a_1 + c_1)b_1}{A\cdot p} < 0 \qquad (7.85)$$

$$\frac{\Delta R_B}{\Delta \bar{d}} = b_1 \left[\frac{\partial i}{\partial \bar{d}} - 1 \right] = -\frac{k^2 a_1 b_2 c_1}{A} < 0 \qquad (7.86)$$

$$\frac{\Delta R_B}{\Delta \theta} = b_2 + b_1 \frac{\partial i}{\partial \theta} = \frac{k^2 a_1 b_2 c_1}{A} > 0 \qquad (7.87)$$

$$\frac{\Delta R_B}{\Delta \bar{R}_E} = b_1 \frac{\partial i}{\partial \bar{R}_E} = \frac{b_1(a_1 + c_1)}{A} > 0 \qquad (7.88)$$

$$\frac{\Delta R_B}{\Delta \beta} = b_1 \frac{\partial i}{\partial \beta} = \frac{k a_2 b_1 c_1}{A} > 0 \qquad (7.89)$$

$$\frac{\Delta R_B}{\Delta \mu} = b_1 \frac{\partial i}{\partial \mu} = \frac{k a_1 b_1 c_2}{A} > 0 \qquad (7.90)$$

$$\frac{\Delta R_B}{\Delta k} = b_1 \frac{\partial i}{\partial k}$$

or,

$$\frac{\Delta R_B}{\Delta k} \gtrless 0. \qquad (7.91)$$

Total Reserves. Since total reserves, R_T, are defined as

$$R_T = R_B + \frac{R_*}{p}, \qquad (7.92)$$

the change in R_T is the same as the change in R_B for all shocks except p and R_*. Now, substituting 7.83 into 7.92, we get:

$$R_T = b_0 + b_1 i(\cdot) - b_1 \bar{d} + b_2 \theta + \frac{R_*}{p}. \qquad (7.93)$$

Differentiating with respect to p, we get:

$$\frac{\Delta R_T}{\Delta p} = b_1 \frac{\partial i}{\partial p} - \frac{R_*}{p^2} = -\frac{k^2 a_1 c_1 R_*}{A p^2} > 0. \qquad (7.94)$$

And differentiating with respect to R_*, we get:

$$\frac{\Delta R_T}{\Delta R_*} = b_1 \frac{\partial i}{\partial R_*} + \frac{1}{p} = \frac{k^2 a_1 c_1}{A \cdot p} > 0. \qquad (7.95)$$

The remaining effects are

$$\frac{\Delta R_T}{\Delta \bar{d}} = \frac{\Delta R_B}{\Delta \bar{d}} = -\frac{k^2 a_1 b_1 c_1}{A} < 0 \qquad (7.96)$$

$$\frac{\Delta R_T}{\Delta \theta} = \frac{\Delta R_B}{\Delta \theta} = \frac{k^2 a_1 b_2 c_1}{A} > 0 \qquad (7.97)$$

$$\frac{\Delta R_T}{\Delta \bar{R}_E} = \frac{\Delta R_B}{\Delta \bar{R}_E} = \frac{b_1 (a_1 + c_1)}{A} > 0 \qquad (7.98)$$

$$\frac{\Delta R_T}{\Delta \beta} = \frac{\Delta R_B}{\Delta \beta} = \frac{k a_2 b_1 c_1}{A} > 0 \qquad (7.99)$$

$$\frac{\Delta R_T}{\Delta \mu} = \frac{\Delta R_B}{\Delta \mu} = \frac{k a_1 b_1 c_2}{A} > 0 \qquad (7.100)$$

$$\frac{\Delta R_T}{\Delta k} = \frac{\Delta R_B}{\Delta k} \gtrless 0. \qquad (7.101)$$

Comparison of Interest-Rate Responses

We shall now compare the response of the (bills) interest rate to shocks when the deposit rate is fixed and when it is flexible (that is, when it is market determined). By 7.10a and 7.58, we get:

$$\frac{\partial i}{\partial p} - \frac{\partial i_*}{\partial p} = \frac{k a_1 R_*}{p^2 A B} \cdot \{(1 - k) c_1 + a_1\} > 0. \qquad (7.102)$$

That is,

$$\frac{\partial i}{\partial p} > \frac{\partial i_*}{\partial p} > 0. \qquad (7.103)$$

By 7.10b and 7.59, we get:

$$\frac{\partial i}{\partial R_*} - \frac{\partial i_*}{\partial R_*} = -\frac{ka_1}{pBA} \cdot \{(1 - k)c_1 + a_1\} < 0, \qquad (7.104)$$

or

$$\frac{\partial i}{\partial R_*} < \frac{\partial i_*}{\partial R_*} < 0. \qquad (7.105)$$

By 7.10c and 7.60, we get

$$\frac{\partial i}{\partial \bar{d}} - \frac{\partial i_*}{\partial d} = \frac{ka_1b_1}{A \cdot B} \cdot \{(1 - k)c_1 + a_1\} > 0, \qquad (7.106)$$

or

$$\frac{\partial i}{\partial \bar{d}} > \frac{\partial i_*}{\partial \bar{d}} > 0; \qquad (7.107)$$

and using 7.10e and 7.61, we get:

$$\frac{\partial i}{\partial \theta} - \frac{\partial i_*}{\partial \theta} = -\frac{ka_1b_2}{A \cdot B} \cdot \{(1 - k)c_1 + a_1\} < 0, \qquad (7.108)$$

or

$$\frac{\partial i}{\partial \theta} < \frac{\partial i_*}{\partial \theta} < 0. \qquad (7.109)$$

Using 7.10f and 7.62, we get

$$\frac{\partial i}{\partial \bar{R}_E} - \frac{\partial i_*}{\partial \bar{R}_E} = \frac{ka_1}{AB} \cdot \{(1 - k)c_1 + a_1\} > 0,$$

or

$$\frac{\partial i}{\partial \bar{R}_E} > \frac{\partial i_*}{\partial \bar{R}_E} = 0. \qquad (7.110)$$

Recalling that when the deposit rate is fixed and binding, a positive shift in the supply function has no effect on the interest rate—that is, $\partial i_*/\partial \mu = 0$—and by using 7.64, we get this result:

$$\frac{\partial i}{\partial \mu} > \frac{\partial i_*}{\partial \mu} = 0. \qquad (7.111)$$

Turning to demand-side shocks and using 7.10g and 7.63, we can derive the indeterminate result:

$$\frac{\partial i}{\partial \beta} - \frac{\partial i_*}{\partial \beta} = - \frac{ka_1 a_2}{A \cdot B} \cdot \{k(k-1)c_1 + b_1\} \gtreqless 0, \qquad (7.112)$$

and these results:

$$0 < \frac{\partial i}{\partial \beta} < \frac{\partial i_*}{\partial \beta} \text{ when } \{k(k-1)c_1 + b_1\} > 0 \qquad (7.113)$$

$$\frac{\partial i}{\partial \beta} > \frac{\partial i_*}{\partial \beta} > 0 \text{ when } \{k(k-1)c_1 + b_1\} < 0. \qquad (7.114)$$

Finally, we get indeterminate results when k changes. By 7.11h and 7.65, we get:

$$\frac{\partial i}{\partial k} - \frac{\partial i_*}{\partial k} \gtreqless 0. \qquad (7.115)$$

Comparison of Response in Monetary Aggregates

Of course, the only monetary aggregate in our system is demand deposits. Beginning with the effects of an exogenous change in the price level, we subtract 7.75 from 7.13 and find that

$$\frac{\partial D^*}{\partial p} - \frac{\Delta D}{\Delta p} = - \frac{a_1 b_1}{A \cdot B} \cdot \frac{R_*}{p^2} \; [(1-k)c_1 + a_1] < 0 \qquad (7.116)$$

and that

$$\frac{\partial D^*}{\partial p} < \frac{\Delta D}{\Delta p} < 0. \tag{7.117}$$

To compare the effects of a change in the nominal reserve base, R_*, we use 7.76 and 7.14 and get:

$$\frac{\partial D^*}{\partial R_*} - \frac{\Delta D}{\Delta R_*} = \frac{a_1 b_1}{pAB} \cdot [(1 - k)c_1 + a_1] > 0, \tag{7.118}$$

and

$$\frac{\partial D^*}{\partial R_*} > \frac{\Delta D}{\Delta R_*} > 0. \tag{7.119}$$

Continuing with the remaining shocks, we record the following:

$$\frac{\partial D^*}{\partial \bar{d}} - \frac{\Delta D}{\Delta \bar{d}} = -\frac{a_1 b_1^2}{A \cdot B} \cdot [(1 - k)c_1 + a_1] < 0; \tag{7.120}$$

and

$$\frac{\partial D^*}{\partial \bar{d}} < \frac{\Delta D}{\Delta \bar{d}} < 0 \tag{7.121}$$

$$\frac{\partial D^*}{\partial \theta} - \frac{\Delta D}{\Delta \theta} = \frac{a_1 b_1 b_2}{A \cdot B} [(1 - k)c_1 + a_1] > 0; \tag{7.122}$$

and finally

$$\frac{\partial D^*}{\partial \theta} > \frac{\Delta D}{\Delta \theta} > 0, \tag{7.123}$$

$$\frac{\partial D^*}{\partial \bar{R}_E} - \frac{\Delta D}{\Delta \bar{R}_E} = -\frac{a_1 b_1}{AB} \cdot [(1 - k)c_1 + a_1] < 0. \tag{7.124}$$

and

$$\frac{\partial D^*}{\partial \bar{R}_E} < \frac{\Delta D}{\Delta \bar{R}_E} < 0. \tag{7.125}$$

Now, recalling that under a fixed, binding deposit rate we have $\partial D^*/\partial\mu = 0$, and using 7.81, we get

$$\frac{\Delta D}{\Delta\mu} = \frac{a_1 b_1 c_2}{A} > \frac{\partial D^*}{\partial\mu} = 0. \qquad (7.126)$$

We now turn to the two shocks that give interdeterminate results without additional conditions. First, comparing the effects of a positive shift in demand for demand deposits, we get

$$\frac{\partial D^*}{\partial\beta} - \frac{\Delta D}{\Delta\beta} = \frac{a_1 a_2 b_1}{A \cdot B} \cdot [k(k-1)c_1 + b_1] \gtrless 0, \qquad (7.127)$$

from which we see that

$$\frac{\partial D^*}{\partial\beta} > \frac{\Delta D}{\Delta\beta} > 0 \text{ when } [k(k-1)c_1 + b_1] > 0, \qquad (7.128)$$

and that

$$\frac{\Delta D}{\Delta\beta} > \frac{\partial D^*}{\partial\beta} > 0 \text{ when } [k(k-1)c_1 + b_1] < 0. \qquad (7.129)$$

Finally, we have:

$$\frac{\partial D^*}{\partial k} - \frac{\Delta D}{\Delta k} \gtrless 0. \qquad (7.130)$$

Comparison of Responses in Reserves Aggregates

Borrowed Reserves

We shall begin by comparing the effects on borrowed reserves. Using 7.22 and 7.84, we find that

$$\frac{\Delta R_B}{\Delta p} - \frac{\partial R_B^*}{\partial p} = \frac{k a_1 b_1 R_*}{p^2 \cdot A B} \cdot \{(1-k)c_1 + a_1\} > 0 \qquad (7.131)$$

and, hence, that

$$\frac{\Delta R_B}{\Delta p} > \frac{\partial R_B^*}{\partial p} > 0. \qquad (7.132)$$

Comparing the corresponding effects of a change in R_*, we get

$$\frac{\Delta R_B}{\Delta R_*} - \frac{\partial R_B^*}{\partial R_*} = -\frac{ka_1b_1}{p \cdot A \cdot B} \cdot \{(1-k)c_1 + a_1\} < 0, \qquad (7.133)$$

and

$$\frac{\Delta R_B}{\Delta R_*} < \frac{\partial R_B^*}{\partial R_*} < 0. \qquad (7.134)$$

In contrast, we see that the results change direction when shocks originating in the function of borrowed reserves are examined. In particular, when the discount rate—$\bar{d}$—is changed, we get

$$\frac{\Delta R_B}{\Delta \bar{d}} - \frac{\partial R_B^*}{\partial \bar{d}} = \frac{ka_1b_1^2}{A \cdot B}\{(1-k)c_1 + a_1\} > 0, \qquad (7.135)$$

or

$$\frac{\partial R_B^*}{\partial \bar{d}} < \frac{\Delta R_B}{\Delta \bar{d}} < 0. \qquad (7.136)$$

When the administration of the discount window is loosened, we have

$$\frac{\Delta R_B}{\Delta \theta} - \frac{\partial R_B^*}{\partial \theta} = -\frac{ka_1b_1b_2}{A \cdot B} \cdot \{(1-k)c_1 + a_1\} < 0 \qquad (7.137)$$

and, hence,

$$\frac{\partial R_B^*}{\partial \theta} > \frac{\Delta R_B}{\Delta \theta} > 0. \qquad (7.138)$$

On the other hand, the effects of an exogenous change in excess reserves give us this result:

$$\frac{\Delta R_B}{\Delta \bar{R}_E} - \frac{\partial R_{\tilde{B}}^*}{\partial \bar{R}_E} = \frac{k a_1 b_1}{A \cdot B} \cdot \{(1 - k)c_1 + a_1\} > 0 \qquad (7.139)$$

and

$$\frac{\Delta R_B}{\Delta \bar{R}_E} > \frac{\partial R_{\tilde{B}}^*}{\partial \bar{R}_E} > 0. \qquad (7.140)$$

Now comparing the effects of a shift in the supply function for demand deposits, we get

$$\frac{\Delta R_B}{\Delta \mu} = \frac{k a_1 b_1 c_2}{A} > \frac{\partial R_{\tilde{B}}^*}{\partial \mu} = 0. \qquad (7.141)$$

Turning now to the crucial shift in the demand function, we get

$$\frac{\Delta R_B}{\Delta \beta} - \frac{\partial R_{\tilde{B}}^*}{\partial \beta} = - \frac{k a_1 a_2 b_1}{A \cdot B} \cdot \{k(k-1)c_1 + b_1\} \gtrless 0, \quad (7.142)$$

from which we derive the special cases:

$$\frac{\Delta R_B}{\Delta \beta} > \frac{\partial R_{\tilde{B}}^*}{\partial \beta} > 0 \text{ when } \{k(k-1)c_1 + b_1\} < 0 \qquad (7.143)$$

and

$$\frac{\partial R_{\tilde{B}}^*}{\partial \beta} > \frac{\Delta R_B}{\Delta \beta} > 0 \text{ when } \{k(k-1)c_1 + b_1\} > 0. \qquad (7.144)$$

Finally, we can compare the effects of a change in the reserve requirement, k:

$$\frac{\Delta R_B}{\Delta k} - \frac{\partial R_{\tilde{B}}^*}{\partial k} \gtrless 0. \qquad (7.145)$$

Total Reserves. We expect to find that the relative magnitudes of the effects on total reserves are identical to the effects on borrowed reserves—even for shocks in the price level, p, and in the nominal reserve base, R_*. Comparing 7.94 and 7.39, we get:

$$\frac{\Delta R_T}{\Delta p} - \frac{\partial R_T^*}{\partial p} = \frac{ka_1b_1R_*}{p^2 \cdot A \cdot B} \cdot \{(1-k)c_1 + a_1\} > 0 \qquad (7.146)$$

and, hence,

$$\frac{\partial R_T^*}{\partial p} < \frac{\Delta R_T}{\Delta p} < 0. \qquad (7.147)$$

We note that the right-hand side of 7.146 is the same as the right-hand side of 7.131.

Similarly, using 7.96 and 7.38, we get

$$\frac{\Delta R_T}{\Delta R_*} - \frac{\partial R_T^*}{\partial R_*} = -\frac{ka_1b_1}{pAB} \cdot \{(1-k)c_1 + a_1\} < 0 \qquad (7.148)$$

and, hence,

$$\frac{\partial R_T^*}{\partial R_*} > \frac{\Delta R_T}{\Delta R_*} > 0. \qquad (7.149)$$

Again, we note that the right hand side of 7.148 and 7.133 coincide.

For completeness we record the remaining comparisons:

$$\frac{\Delta R_T}{\Delta \bar{d}} - \frac{\partial R_T^*}{\partial \bar{d}} = \frac{\Delta R_B}{\Delta \bar{d}} - \frac{\partial R_B^*}{\partial \bar{d}} = \frac{ka_1b_1^2}{A \cdot B}\{(1-k)c_1 + a_1\} > 0 \qquad (7.150)$$

$$\frac{\Delta R_T}{\Delta \theta} - \frac{\partial R_T^*}{\partial \theta} = \frac{\Delta R_B}{\Delta \theta} - \frac{\partial R_B^*}{\partial \theta} = -\frac{ka_1b_1b_2}{A \cdot B}\{(1-k)c_1 + a_1\} < 0 \qquad (7.151)$$

$$\frac{\Delta R_T}{\Delta \bar{R}_E} - \frac{\partial R_T^*}{\partial \bar{R}_E} = \frac{\Delta R_B}{\Delta \bar{R}_E} - \frac{\partial R_B^*}{\partial \bar{R}_E} = \frac{ka_1b_1}{A \cdot B}\{(1-k)c_1 + a_1\} > 0 \qquad (7.152)$$

$$\frac{\Delta R_T}{\Delta \mu} = \frac{\Delta R_B}{\Delta \mu} > \frac{\partial R_T^*}{\partial \mu} = \frac{\partial R_B^*}{\partial \mu} \equiv 0 \qquad (7.153)$$

$$\frac{\Delta R_T}{\Delta \beta} - \frac{\partial R_T^*}{\partial \beta} = \frac{\Delta R_B}{\Delta \beta} - \frac{\partial R_B^*}{\partial \beta} = -\frac{ka_1a_2b_1}{A \cdot B} \cdot \{k(k-1)c_1 + b_1\} \gtrless 0. \qquad (7.154)$$

And finally,

$$\frac{\Delta R_T}{\Delta k} - \frac{\partial R_T^*}{\partial k} = \frac{\Delta R_B}{\Delta k} - \frac{\partial R_B^*}{\partial k} \gtreqless 0. \qquad (7.155)$$

**Part III
The Financial and the
Real Sectors Combined**

8

Fixed Deposit Rates and the Real Sector: Price Level, Actual and Expected Inflation, and Interest Rates

Until now we have examined the financial sector in isolation. Beginning with this chapter, we shall extend the model to include the real sector also.[1] In this chapter the real sector is added to the financial system characterized by a fixed deposit rate; in other words, the analysis of chapter 3 is extended to include the real sector. In chapter 9 we shall attach the same real sector to the financial sector that permits a market-determined deposit rate and in chapter 10 we shall compare the implications of the two regimes.

The completion of the model is undertaken in the next section. The real sector consists of a price-adjustment mechanism based on the goods and services market and on a simple expectations-adjustment mechanism, that is, an adaptive expectations mechanism. In this book we are interested in designing a full employment, neoclassical model that emphasizes inflation and the neutrality of inflation with respect to the real rate of interest (that is, the Fisher hypothesis).[2] For this reason, that is, to derive such properties, we shall assume that investment and savings depend only on the real interest rate on bills, which is defined as the nominal interest rate (on bills) minus the expected rate of inflation. In particular, we shall deliberately avoid assuming that investment and saving (and, hence, consumption) depend on the real reserve base, or, more generally, on the real reserve base plus the real quantity of earning assets (bills). Shocks originating in the real sector can be considered by strategically incorporating a shift parameter in the investment function—to represent, for example, animal spirits.

In this chapter, as well as in the rest of this book, we shall examine two variants of the model. The first concentrates on the *level* of the nominal reserve base, that is, on the case where its rate of growth is fixed at zero, which permits determination of the price level and the expected rate of inflation. Such a model is useful in examining once-and-for-all shocks in the nominal reserve base or in any other parameter. In the second variant of the model, we shall assume a nonzero rate of growth in the nominal monetary base, which permits a nonzero expected and actual rate of inflation. This model is also useful for examining comparative dynamics, that is, the effects of continuous changes in the nominal reserve base and, in particular, effects of a change in the rate of growth, not simply in the level of the nominal reserve base.

In the third section, we shall explain the method of solution of the entire model, a method that permits us to use the results derived when we examined

169

the corresponding financial sector in isolation, that is, the results of chapter 3. The method permits equilibrium and disequilibrium analysis, but it assumes that the financial markets clear considerably faster than the goods market. Of course, for equilibrium analysis and for the comparative statics of the remaining chapters, the assumption of different speeds of response is immaterial.

In the next section, Comparative Statics, we shall derive the full variants of the model and show that they are identical. Moreover, we shall prove that the entire model can be stable if a Cagan-type stability condition is satisfied. This Cagan stability condition imposes, as usual, an upper bound on the speed of revision in expectations (of inflation).

In the next section, Comparative Statics, we shall derive the full equilibrium, comparative statics effects of one-shot shocks on the price level, on expected inflation, and on the interest rate. These shocks can be one-shot changes in a monetary instrument or one-shot stochastic shocks originating in the financial or in the real sector. The derived results are standard. We show, for example, that a one-shot increase in the nominal reserve base causes an equiproportionate increase in the price level, but no change in expectations. The ultimate effect on the interest rate is zero. This means that the initial decrease in the interest rate is eventually matched by the increase in the interest rate caused by the consequent increase in the price level.

Finally, in the section, Comparative Dynamics, we shall examine the effects of a change in the *rate of growth* of the nominal reserve base on expected and on actual inflation, on the real reserve base, and on the nominal and real interest rate. We shall derive an important result, namely that an increase in the rate of growth of the nominal reserve base will affect a real variable; in particular, it will diminish the real reserve base. In other words, money cannot be superneutral.

The Models

First we shall extend the financial model under a fixed deposit rate—that is, the model in chapter 3—to include the real sector. To the equations of financial equilibrium,

$$EDB = 0 \qquad\qquad (8.1)$$

$$EDR = 0 \qquad\qquad (8.2)$$

$$D = D^d(\,\cdot\,) \qquad\qquad (8.3)$$

we append the equations corresponding to real-sector equilibrium—namely, the equations depicting that the goods market is cleared (excess demand for goods and services is zero),

$$EDG = 0, \tag{8.4}$$

and that actual inflation $\dot{p}/p$, is equal to expected inflation, π:

$$\frac{\dot{p}}{p} = \pi. \tag{8.5}$$

As in chapter 3, we can reduce the entire financial system of 8.1 through 8.3 to one equation. First, we specify EDR:

$$EDR = R_R + R_E - R_B - R. \tag{8.6}$$

But since in this case demand deposits are demand determined, the quantity of required reserves, R_R, is

$$R_R = k \cdot D^d(i - \bar{\zeta}; \beta). \tag{8.7}$$

Excess reserves, R_E, are assumed fixed at $\bar{R}_E$:

$$R_E = \bar{R}_E \tag{8.9}$$

Borrowed reserves, R_B, are specified as earlier:

$$R_B = R_B(i - \bar{d}; \theta). \tag{8.9}$$

And the real reserve base, R, is found by deflating the nominal reserve base, R_*:

$$R = \frac{R_*}{p}. \tag{8.10}$$

Substituting 8.7 through 8.10 into 8.6, we get:

$$EDR = k \cdot D^d(i - \bar{\zeta}; \beta) + \bar{R}_E - R_B(i - \bar{d}; \theta) - \frac{R_*}{p}. \tag{8.11}$$

We now have only two equations—8.1 and 8.11—but according to Walras'

Law we need to examine explicitly only one. Thus we choose to examine the market for reserves. Hence the equilibrium of the entire financial system is found by setting $EDR = 0$ in 8.11:

$$EDR = k \cdot D^d(i - \bar{\zeta}; \beta) + R_E - R_B(i - \bar{d}; \theta) - \frac{R_*}{p} = 0. \quad (8.12)$$

If we are interested only in continuous equilibrium of the financial system, we may simply attach 8.12 to the real sector. But if we want to examine disequilibrium as well—that is, if we want to specify how the financial-market equilibrium is brought about—we must use the following differential equation:

$$\frac{di}{dt} = \delta \cdot EDR, \ \delta > 0 \quad (8.13)$$

Equation 8.13 states that the interest rate rises (falls) if and only if there is excess demand for (excess supply of) reserves. In other words, 8.13 is an idealization of the law of supply and demand.

As we briefly stated in chapter 3, continuous financial-sector equilibrium is a special case of 8.13—that is, when $\delta \to \infty$, since

$$\lim_{\delta \to \infty} \frac{di}{dt} \cdot \frac{1}{\delta} = EDR \to 0. \quad (8.14)$$

In summary, we see that the dynamics of the entire financial system is captured by the differential equation in 8.13 (and that its equilibrium is stated by 8.12) However, to this specification we must add the real sector.

The Real Sector—Expectations

We now turn to the examination of the real sector, for which we need to specify the investment, I, and savings, S, functions because in a closed economy without a government sector excess demand for goods and services, EDG, is the difference between the two:

$$EDG = I(\cdot) - S(\cdot). \quad (8.15)$$

Following standard procedures, we assume that real investment depends negatively on the real rate of interest, $i - \pi$, whereas real savings depends positively on the same rate, that is

$$I = I(i - \pi), I' < 0 \tag{8.16'}$$

$$S = S(i - \pi), S' > 0, \tag{8.17}$$

where I' and S' are the partial derivatives of I and S, with respect to the real rate of interest. In 8.16, keeping the same notation, we shall insert a shift parameters, α, into the investment function since we shall later examine the consequences of such a shock.

$$I = I(i - \pi; \alpha), I' < 0, \frac{\partial I}{\partial \alpha} > 0. \tag{8.16}$$

The dynamics of price inflation—that is, how equality 8.4 is brought about—will also be specified in the orthodox manner, as in 8.18:

$$\frac{\dot{p}}{p} = \varepsilon \cdot EDG + \pi. \tag{8.18}$$

In words, we see that actual inflation has an expected component, π, and an unexpected component, $\varepsilon \cdot EDG$; the latter is positive when there is excess demand, $EDG > 0$; negative when there is excess supply, $EDG < 0$; and zero when the market for goods and services is cleared. In the final case, of course, actual inflation, $\dot{p}/p$, is equal to expected inflation, π, that is,

$$\frac{\dot{p}}{p} = \pi, \tag{8.19}$$

which is a condition for equilibrium for both the goods market and the expectations-adjustment mechanism.

We shall adopt Cagan's (1956) adaptive scheme as our expectations adjustment mechanism. Hence,

$$\dot{\pi} = \gamma \left(\frac{\dot{p}}{p} - \pi \right), \gamma > 0 \tag{8.20}$$

where γ, the "Cagan coefficient," is the speed of adjustment of expectations. When this speed is infinite (that is, when $\gamma \to \infty$) expected inflation is always equal to actual inflation and 8.19 always prevails. When γ is not infinite, condition 8.19 prevails only at equilibrium. Substituting 8.18 into 8.20, we get:

$$\dot{\pi} = \gamma\varepsilon \cdot EDG, \tag{8.21}$$

which states that expected inflation rises or falls if and only if there is excess demand for or excess supply of goods and services.

Equations 8.18 and 8.21 together describe the real sector of our stylized economy; upon substitution of 8.15, 8.16, and 8.17, equations 8.18 and 8.21 become 8.22 and 8.23:

$$\frac{\dot{p}}{p} = \varepsilon[I(i - \pi; \alpha) - S(i - \pi)] + \pi \tag{8.22}$$

$$\dot{\pi} = \gamma\varepsilon[I(i - \pi; \alpha) - S(i - \pi)]. \tag{8.23}$$

To these two equations we must attach the equation specifying the dynamics of the interest rate. This equation is, of course, 8.13. Substituting 8.11 into 8.13, we get:

$$\frac{di}{dt} = \delta\left\{ kD^d(i - \bar{\zeta}; \beta) + \bar{R}_E - R_B(i - \bar{d}; \theta) - \frac{R_*}{p} \right\}. \tag{8.24}$$

Attaching this equation to 8.22 through 8.23, we get a dynamic system of three differential equations, di/dt, $\dot{p}$, and $\dot{\pi}$, in three unknowns, (i, p, π).

Alternatively, we can specify a system of three differential equations, di/dt, $\dot{R}$, and $\dot{\pi}$, in the unknowns (i, R, π). The latter is more relevant if we choose to focus on the dynamics of inflation rather than of the price level. To derive the alternative system we substitute R, the real reserve base for R_*/p and get 8.25:

$$\frac{di}{dt} = \delta\{kD^d(i - \bar{\zeta}; \beta) + \bar{R}_E - R_B(i - \bar{d}; \theta) - R\}. \tag{8.25}$$

We then time differentiate 8.10 to get:

$$\frac{\dot{R}}{R} = \frac{\dot{R}_*}{R_*} - \frac{\dot{p}}{p}.$$

Substituting 8.22, we get:

$$\frac{\dot{R}}{R} = \frac{\dot{R}_*}{R_*} - \varepsilon[I(i - \pi; \alpha) - S(i - \pi)] - \pi. \tag{8.26}$$

Equations 8.25, 8.26, and 8.23 comprise a system of three differential equations, di/dt, $\dot{R}$, and $\dot{\pi}$, in the triplet (i, R, π). It is clear that this model includes the model consisting of 8.24, 8.22, and 8.23, as a special case. We see that when $\dot{R}_*/R_* = 0$—that is, when the nominal reserve base is kept fixed—the two models coincide. Their difference is only cosmetic because there is a one-to-one relation between $R \equiv R_*/p$ and p. But R rises if and only if p falls, and similarly, R, falls if and only if p rises.

Rearranging equations 8.22 and 8.26 and renumbering all the equations that are involved, we have the two alternative dynamic systems. System 8.27 through 8.29, below, emphasizes the dynamics of the price level and the effects of changing the nominal quantity of nonborrowed reserves, R_*.

$$\left\{ \quad \frac{di}{dt} = \delta\left\{ kD^d(i - \bar{\zeta}; \beta) + \bar{R}_E - R_B(i - \bar{d}; \theta) - \frac{R_*}{p} \right\} \right. \qquad (8.27)$$

$$\dot{p} = \varepsilon p[I(i - \pi; \alpha) - S(i - \pi)] + p\pi \qquad (8.28)$$

$$\dot{\pi} = \gamma\varepsilon[I(i - \pi; \alpha) - S(i - \pi)]. \qquad (8.29)$$

On the other hand, system 8.30 through 8.32 emphasizes the dynamics of inflation and the role of the rate of reserve expansion, $\dot{R}_*/R_*$.

$$\left\{ \quad \frac{di}{dt} = \delta\{kD^d(i - \bar{\zeta}; \beta) + \bar{R}_E - R_B(i - \bar{d}; \theta) - R\} \right. \qquad (8.30)$$

$$\dot{R} = R \cdot \left\{ \frac{\dot{R}_*}{R_*} - \varepsilon[I(i - \pi; \alpha) - S(i - \pi)] - \pi \right\} \qquad (8.31)$$

$$\dot{\pi} = \gamma\varepsilon[I(i - \pi; \alpha) - S(i - \pi)]. \qquad (8.32)$$

The Method of Solution[3]

We can examine these models as they stand—that is, we can examine simultaneously, and in one step, all three differential equations for each model. However, we shall follow a two-step procedure, beginning with an examination of the financial sector, as represented by 8.27 (or by 8.30). For the issues examined here, this procedure involves no essential loss of information and it greatly simplifies the analysis. More important, this approach allows us to incorporate the results of our earlier analysis.

Our approach employs the realistic assumption that the financial markets clear faster than the goods and services market, or, that the speed of adjustment, δ, is greater than the speed of adjustment, ε. Moreover, the financial markets adjust faster than the expectations of inflation—that is, δ is also greater than γ. We can go to the limit and assume that δ is infinite—that is, we can assume that the financial markets clear simultaneously. Note that

$$\lim_{\delta \to \infty} \frac{di}{dt} \cdot \frac{1}{\delta} \to 0,$$

which implies that EDR also tends to zero. That is, using 8.27, we get

$$kD^d(i - \bar{\zeta}; \beta) + \bar{R}_E - R_B(i - \bar{d}; \theta) - \frac{R_*}{p} = 0. \qquad (8.33)$$

Equation 8.33 is an equation in two endogenous variables, i and p, and in the parameters, R_*, $\bar{\zeta}$, $\bar{d}$, θ, β, $\bar{R}_E$, and k. We can solve this equation explicitly for i in terms of the endogenous variable, p, and the exogenous variables. We can write this solution as:

$$i = i_*(p; R_*, \bar{\zeta}, \bar{d}, \theta, \beta, \bar{R}_E, k). \qquad (8.34)$$

In chapter 3 we found the partial derivatives of 8.34, which are reproduced as 8.35 through 8.42 below:

$$\frac{\partial i_*}{\partial p} = -\frac{R_*}{p^2} \cdot C^{-1} > 0 \qquad (8.35)$$

$$\frac{\partial i_*}{\partial R_*} = \frac{1}{p} \cdot C^{-1} < 0 \qquad (8.36)$$

$$\frac{\partial i_*}{\partial \bar{\zeta}} = k \frac{\partial D^d}{\partial z_h} \cdot C^{-1} > 0 \qquad (8.37)$$

$$\frac{\partial i_*}{\partial \bar{d}} = -R'_B \cdot C^{-1} > 0 \qquad (8.38)$$

$$\frac{\partial i_*}{\partial \theta} = \frac{\partial R_B}{\partial \theta} \cdot C^{-1} < 0 \qquad (8.39)$$

$$\frac{\partial i_*}{\partial \beta} = -k \frac{\partial D^d}{\partial \beta} \cdot C^{-1} > 0 \qquad (8.40)$$

$$\frac{\partial i_*}{\partial \bar{R}_E} = - C^{-1} > 0, \tag{8.41}$$

$$\frac{\partial i_*}{\partial k} = - D^d(\cdot) \cdot C^{-1} > 0 \tag{8.42}$$

where

$$C = k \frac{\partial D^d}{\partial z_h} - R'_B < 0 \tag{8.43}$$

and C^{-1} is the inverse of C.

When we use the alternative model, equations 8.30 through 8.32, we must set $\delta \to \infty$ in 8.30. Differentiating the resulting $EDR = 0$ equation, we get the same results as just given, with modifications for 8.35 and 8.36. In place of 8.35 and 8.36 we have a single equation,

$$\frac{\partial i_*}{\partial R} = C^{-1} < 0. \tag{8.44}$$

An increase in the *real* reserve base, R, causes excess supply of real reserves which lowers the interest rate. But an increase in the real reserve base can result either from an increase in the nominal reserve base, R_*, while the price level is constant, or from a fall in the price level, p, while the nominal reserve base, R_*, is fixed. This, of course, is consistent with 8.35 and 8.36. But we can derive this from 8.44:

$$\frac{\partial i_*}{\partial R_*} = \frac{\partial i_*}{\partial R} \frac{\partial R}{\partial R_*} = \frac{1}{p} C^{-1}$$

$$\frac{\partial i_*}{\partial p} = \frac{\partial i_*}{\partial R} \frac{\partial R}{\partial p} = - \frac{R_*}{p^2} C^{-1}.$$

The Solution of 8.30 when $\delta \to \infty$ can be written as:

$$i = i_*(R; R_*, \bar{\zeta}, \bar{d}, k, \beta, \bar{R}_E), \tag{8.45}$$

with partials 8.44 and 8.36 through 8.42.

Stability

Substituting 8.34 (and its characteristics embodied in 8.35 through 8.42) into 8.28 and 8.29, we can reduce the three-differential-equation system—8.27 through 8.29—to a two-differential-equation system—8.46 through 8.47—in $\dot{p}$ and $\dot{\pi}$ alone:

$$\dot{p} = \varepsilon p\{I[i_*(p; R_*, \bar{\zeta}, \bar{d}, \theta, k, \beta, \bar{R}_E) - \pi; \alpha]$$

$$- S[i_*(p; R_*, \bar{\zeta}, \bar{d}, \theta, k, \beta, \bar{R}_E) - \pi]\} + p\pi \qquad (8.46)$$

$$\dot{\pi} = \gamma\varepsilon\{I[i_*(p; R_*, \bar{\zeta}, \bar{d}, \theta, k, \beta, \bar{R}_E) - \pi; \alpha]$$

$$- S[i_*(p; R_*, \bar{\zeta}, \bar{d}, \theta, k, \beta, \bar{R}_E) - \pi\}. \qquad (8.47)$$

Similarly, by substituting 8.45 into 8.31 through 8.32, we have the corresponding two-differential-equation system—8.48 through 8.49—in the variables $\dot{R}$ and $\dot{\pi}$:

$$\dot{R} = R\left\{\frac{\dot{R}_*}{R_*} - \varepsilon\{I[i_*(R; R_*, \bar{\zeta}, \bar{d}, \theta, k, \beta, \bar{R}_E) - \pi; \alpha]\right.$$

$$\left. - S[i_*(R; R_*, \bar{\zeta}, \bar{d}, \theta, k, \beta, \bar{R}_E) - \pi]\} - \pi\right\} \qquad (8.48)$$

$$\dot{\pi} = \gamma\varepsilon\{I[i_*(R; R_*, \bar{\zeta}, \bar{d}, \theta, k, \beta, \bar{R}_E) - \pi; \alpha]$$

$$- S[i_*(R; R_*, \bar{\zeta}, \bar{d}, \theta, k, \beta, \bar{R}_E) - \pi]\}. \qquad (8.49)$$

The equilibrium of system 8.46 through 8.47 is found by setting $\dot{p} = \dot{\pi} = 0$. By 8.47 (and by the original equation on which 8.47 relies—that is, 8.20), the requirement $\dot{\pi} = 0$ implies that

$$\frac{\dot{p}}{p} = \pi. \qquad (8.50)$$

The same requirement, $\dot{\pi} = 0$, implies:

$$I - S = 0. \qquad (8.51)$$

Because the requirement $\dot{p} = 0$ is satisfied if and only if

$$\varepsilon(I - S) + \pi = 0,$$

it follows that $\pi = 0$ and, hence, that

$$\frac{\dot{p}}{p} = \pi = 0. \tag{8.52}$$

That is, at equilibrium the actual rate of inflation is not only equal to the expected rate, but it is zero. We must note that system 8.46 through 8.47 assumes a fixed level of nonborrowed reserves, which means that it assumes a zero rate of growth in the amount of nominal nonborrowed reserves. We can therefore extend 8.52 to become 8.53:

$$\frac{\dot{p}}{p} = \pi = \frac{\dot{R}_*}{R_*} = 0. \tag{8.53}$$

For situations when the steady-state (equilibrium) rate of inflation is different from zero, we must use a model with a nonzero rate of growth in the nominal reserve base. Model 8.48 through 8.49 was designed to analyze these situations. Setting $\dot{\pi} = 0$ in 8.49, we again get 8.50 and 8.51—that is,

$$\frac{\dot{p}}{p} = \pi$$

$$I - S = 0.$$

But setting $\dot{R} = 0$ in 8.48 and using 8.50 and 8.51, we also get:

$$\pi = \frac{\dot{R}_*}{R_*}. \tag{8.54}$$

And it follows, then, that at the steady state we have:

$$\frac{\dot{p}}{p} = \pi = \frac{\dot{R}_*}{R_*}. \tag{8.55}$$

In words, equation 8.55 states that the actual rate of inflation is equal to and caused by the rate of growth in the nominal reserve base and that eventually this growth and inflation rates come to be expected.

We shall now examine local dynamic stability, beginning with model 8.46 through 8.47. Taking the Taylor linear expansion at the equilibrium point, $\dot{p} = \dot{\pi} = 0$, we can set up the matrix of the dynamic system, which is matrix F, as follows:

$$F = \begin{bmatrix} \varepsilon p(I' - S') \dfrac{\partial i_*}{\partial p} & p[1 - \varepsilon(I' - S')] \\[2em] \gamma\varepsilon(I' - S') \dfrac{\partial i_*}{\partial p} & -\gamma\varepsilon(I' - S') \end{bmatrix} \qquad (8.56)$$

This system is locally stable if and only if the trace of F is negative and its determinant positive. We see from 8.57,

$$\det F = -\gamma\varepsilon(I' - S') \, p \, \frac{\partial i_*}{\partial p} > 0 \qquad (8.57)$$

that the determinant is indeed positive. Therefore, the system is stable if and only if the trace is negative. The trace is:

$$\operatorname{tr} F = \varepsilon(I' - S') \left[p \frac{\partial i_*}{\partial p} - \gamma \right]. \qquad (8.58)$$

Since $(I' - S')$ is negative, it follows that $\operatorname{tr} F$ is negative and the system is stable if an only if

$$p \frac{\partial i_*}{\partial p} - \gamma > 0, \qquad (8.59)$$

or, if and only if

$$\gamma < p \frac{\partial i_*}{\partial p}. \qquad (8.60)$$

This is a variant of Cagan's stability condition: The speed of adjustment in expectations must be smaller than some positive number.[4]

When condition 8.60 is satisfied, the phase graph of the dynamic system is similar to that in figure 8–1.

We now turn to system 8.48 through 8.49. Taking the Taylor linear expansion around the equilibrium position, $R = \pi = 0$, we get the matrix of the dynamic system—that is, matrix H.

$$H = \begin{bmatrix} -\varepsilon(I' - S')R \dfrac{\partial i_*}{\partial R} & R \cdot [\varepsilon(I' - S') - 1] \\[2em] \gamma\varepsilon(I' - S') \dfrac{\partial i_*}{\partial R} & -\gamma\varepsilon(I' - S') \end{bmatrix} \qquad (8.61)$$

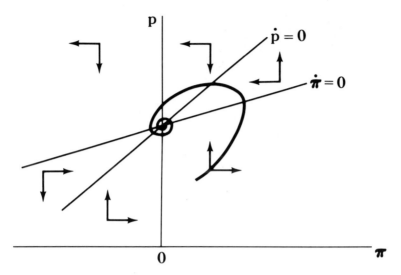

Figure 8–1. Fixed-Deposit Rate Regime: Price Level—Expected Inflation Dynamics

First we find the determinant of H. In 8.62 we see that it is positive.

$$\det H = \gamma\varepsilon(I' - S') R \frac{\partial i_*}{\partial R} > 0. \tag{8.62}$$

Next we examine the trace.

$$\operatorname{tr} H = -\varepsilon(I' - S') R \frac{\partial i_*}{\partial R} - \gamma\varepsilon(I' - S').$$

Collecting terms, we get:

$$\operatorname{tr} H = -\gamma\varepsilon(I' - S')\left(\frac{R \dfrac{\partial i_*}{\partial R}}{\gamma} + 1\right). \tag{8.63}$$

Because $-\gamma\varepsilon(I' - S') > 0$, $\operatorname{tr} H$ is negative if and only if

$$\frac{R \dfrac{\partial i_*}{\partial R}}{\gamma} + 1 < 0$$

—that is, if and only if

$$\gamma < -R \frac{\partial i_*}{\partial R}.$$
(8.64)

This is the *necessary and sufficient* condition for stability of system 8.48 through 8.49. Comparing 8.64 to 8.60, we see that this Cagan condition is similar to the Cagan condition for stability of system 8.46 through 8.47. In fact, by 8.44 and 8.37 we see that they are *identical*. By 8.44 we get:

$$-R \frac{\partial i_*}{\partial R} = -R \cdot C^{-1}.$$

But by 8.37 we get:

$$p \frac{\partial i_*}{\partial p} = - \frac{pR_*}{p^2} \cdot C^{-1} = - \frac{R_*}{p} \cdot C^{-1} = -R \cdot C^{-1}.$$

Therefore, conditions 8.60 and 8.64 coincide. When this stability condition is satisfied, the phase graph of the dynamic system[5] 8.48 through 8.49 is given by figure 8–2.

Comparative Statics: The Effect of One-Shot Shocks on the Price Level and the Interest Rate

We shall now examine the effects of several parameters—considered one at a time—on the equilibrium price level, interest, inflation, and on real non-borrowed reserves. We shall start with the equilibrium position of system 8.46 through 8.47—that is, by setting $p = 0$ and $\pi = 0$, and by deriving respectively, equations 8.65 through 8.66.

$$\varepsilon\{I[i_*(p; R_*, \bar{\zeta}, \bar{d}, \theta, k, \beta, \bar{R}_E) - \pi; \alpha]$$

$$- S[i_*(p; R_*, \bar{\zeta}, \bar{d}, \theta, k, \beta, \bar{R}_E) - \pi]\} + \pi = 0$$
(8.65)

$$I[i_*(p; R_*, \bar{\zeta}, \bar{d}, \theta, k, \beta, \bar{R}_E) - \pi; \alpha]$$

$$- S[i_*(p; R_*, \bar{\zeta}, \bar{d}, \theta, k, \beta, \bar{R}_E) - \pi] = 0.$$
(8.66)

Differentiating these two equations totally, permitting changes in the monetary parameters—R_*, $\bar{\zeta}$, $\bar{d}$, θ, k, β, and $\bar{R}_E$—and in the real sector parameter—α—we can derive the equations of change. These equations of

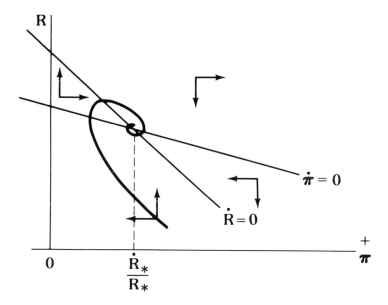

Figure 8–2. Fixed-Deposit-Rate Regime: Real Reserve Base—Expected Inflation Dynamics

change for monetary shocks can be given compactly if we define the monetary parameters as $a_j, j = 1, \ldots, 7$, where $a_1 = R_*$; $a_2 = \bar{d}$; $a_3 = \theta$; $a_4 = \bar{R}_E$; $a_5 = \beta$; $a_6 = \zeta$; and $a_7 = k$. Thus the effects of a change in these parameters, one at a time, on the price level, p, and on expected inflation, π, are given compactly by the following matrix system:

$$\tilde{F} \cdot \begin{bmatrix} dp \\ \\ d\pi \end{bmatrix} = - \begin{bmatrix} \varepsilon(I' - S')\dfrac{\partial i_*}{\partial a_j}\, da_j \\ \\ (I' - S')\dfrac{\partial i_*}{\partial a_j}\, da_j \end{bmatrix} \qquad (8.67)$$

$$j = 1, 2, \ldots, 7.$$

The equations of change for a real-sector shock are given by 8.68:

$$\tilde{F} \cdot \begin{bmatrix} dp \\ \\ d\pi \end{bmatrix} = - \begin{bmatrix} \varepsilon I_\alpha\, d\alpha \\ \\ I_\alpha\, d\alpha \end{bmatrix} \qquad (8.68)$$

In both expressions, 8.67 and 8.68, $\tilde{F}$ is given by 8.69:

$$\tilde{F} = \begin{bmatrix} \varepsilon(I' - S')\dfrac{\partial i_*}{\partial p} & 1 - \varepsilon(I' - S') \\[2mm] (I' - S')\dfrac{\partial i_*}{\partial p} & -(I' - S') \end{bmatrix} \qquad (8.69)$$

Comparing 8.69 with 8.56, and using 8.57, we see that

$$\det \tilde{F} = \frac{\det F}{\gamma \varepsilon p} = -(I' - S')\frac{\partial i_*}{\partial p} > 0. \qquad (8.70)$$

Solving 8.67 for dp/da_j, we get:

$$\frac{dp}{da_j} = -\frac{\dfrac{\partial i_*}{\partial a_j}}{\dfrac{\partial i_*}{\partial p}} \qquad j = 1,2,\ldots,7. \qquad (8.71)$$

In applying formula 8.71, we first examine the effects of a one-shot increase in the nominal reserve base, R_*.

$$\frac{dp}{dR_*} = -\frac{\dfrac{\partial i_*}{\partial R_*}}{\dfrac{\partial i_*}{\partial p}} > 0. \qquad (8.72)$$

An increase in the nominal reserve base increases the price level, as expected. But we can be more specific. Substituting 8.35 and 8.36 into 8.72, we derive:

$$\frac{dp}{dR_*} = \frac{p}{R_*} \qquad (8.73')$$

and, rearranging, we get:

$$\frac{dp}{p} = \frac{dR_*}{R_*}. \qquad (8.73)$$

As expected, the percentage increase in the price level is equal to the percentage increase in the nominal reserve base—a quantity theory result.

The effect of an increase in the discount rate, $\bar{d}$, on the price level is:

$$\frac{dp}{d\bar{\zeta}} = -\frac{\dfrac{\partial i_*}{\partial \bar{\zeta}}}{\dfrac{\partial i_*}{\partial p}}.$$

Substituting 8.35 and 8.37, we get:

$$\frac{dp}{d\bar{\zeta}} = \frac{k\dfrac{\partial D^d}{\partial z_h}\cdot p^2}{R_*} = \frac{p\dfrac{\partial D^d}{\partial z_h}}{R} < 0. \qquad (8.74)$$

We see that an increase in the deposit interest rate is clearly contractionary. Of course, this is the expected result because we saw in 8.37 that the increase in $\bar{\zeta}$ raises the (bills) interest rate, which in turn causes excess supply of goods and services. The effect of a change in the discount rate is given by:

$$\frac{dp}{d\bar{d}} = -\frac{pR'_B}{R}; \qquad (8.75')$$

Rearranging, we get:

$$\frac{dp}{p} = -\frac{R'_B \cdot d\bar{d}}{R} < 0. \qquad (8.75)$$

That is, the percentage decrease in the price level is equal to the percentage decrease in reserves caused by the reduction in borrowed reserves. The increase in the discount rate is, as expected, contractionary. On the other hand, easing in the administration of the discount window is, as expected, expansionary:

$$\frac{dp}{d\theta} = \frac{p\dfrac{\partial R_B}{\partial \theta}}{R} > 0. \qquad (8.76)$$

Continuing, an increase in the reserve-requirement ratio is contractionary as we can see from 8.77:

$$\frac{dp}{dk} = -\frac{p^2 D^d}{R_*} < 0 \qquad (8.77)$$

An increase in the demand function for demand deposits is contractionary and, hence, lowers the price level:

$$\frac{dp}{d\beta} = -\frac{kp^2 \frac{\partial D^d}{\partial \beta}}{R_*} < 0. \tag{8.78}$$

Finally, an exogenous increase in the demand for excess reserves is also contractionary:

$$\frac{dp}{d\bar{R}_E} = -\frac{p^2}{R_*}. \tag{8.79}$$

We now turn to the examination of the effects, if any, of the same parameters on the expected rate of inflation. Solving 8.67 for $d\pi/da_j$, we get:

$$\frac{d\pi}{da_j} = -\frac{\varepsilon}{\det \widetilde{F}} \begin{vmatrix} (I'-S')\frac{\partial i_*}{\partial p} & (I'-S')\frac{\partial i_*}{\partial a_j} \\ (I'-S')\frac{\partial i_*}{\partial p} & (I'-S')\frac{\partial i_*}{\partial a_j} \end{vmatrix}$$

$$j = 1,2,\ldots,7.$$

We see that the two rows of the determinant are the same. Therefore, we have proved that

$$\frac{d\pi}{da_j} = 0 \qquad j = 1,2,\ldots,7. \tag{8.80}$$

That is, a one-shot change in any one of the monetary parameters will leave the expected rate of inflation unaffected at zero. This is a good test for the accuracy of our analysis. We know that, at equilibrium, model 8.46 through 8.47 must satisfy the condition that $\pi = 0$ and that this is borne out by our comparative-statics analysis.

The effects of shocks originating in the real sector can be found by solving 8.68 for $dp/d\alpha$ and $d\pi/d\alpha$.

$$\frac{dp}{d\alpha} = \frac{I_\alpha}{\det \widetilde{F}} > 0. \tag{8.81}$$

$$\frac{d\pi}{d\alpha} = 0. \tag{8.82}$$

As expected, a positive shift in the investment function is expansionary, whereas the same shift leaves expected inflation unaffected—namely, at zero.

Effects on the Interest Rate

To find the overall effects of the shift parameters we must use equation 8.34, reproduced here as 8.83:

$$i = i_*(p; a_1, a_2, \ldots, a_7). \tag{8.83}$$

The effects of the seven monetary shocks, taken one at a time, are found by total differentiation of 8.83:

$$\frac{di}{da_j} = \frac{\partial i_*}{\partial a_j} + \frac{\partial i_*}{\partial p}\frac{dp}{da_j} \quad j = 1,2,\ldots,7. \tag{8.84}$$

Equation 8.84 means that there are two effects of a monetary shock on the interest rate. The first—$\partial i_*/\partial a_j$—is the immediate, direct effect. The second—$(\partial i_*/\partial p)(dp/\partial a_j)$—is indirect, working through a change in the price level. For example, an increase in the nominal reserve base first lowers the interest rate, $\partial i_*/\partial R_* < 0$. But this is expansionary, raising the price level, $dp/dR_* > 0$, which, in turn, raises the interest rate, $(\partial i_*/\partial p)(dp/dR_*) > 0$. The key question, here, is whether the indirect effect (which is of opposite sign) negates exactly the direct effect. If it does, money (that is, the nominal reserve base) is neutral.

Substituting 8.71 into 8.84, we get:

$$\frac{di}{da_j} = \frac{\partial i_*}{\partial a_j} - \frac{\partial i_*}{\partial p} \cdot \frac{\dfrac{\partial i_*}{\partial a_j}}{\dfrac{\partial i_*}{\partial p}} = \frac{\partial i_*}{\partial a_j} - \frac{\partial i_*}{\partial a_j},$$

or,

$$\frac{di}{da_j} = 0 \quad j = 1,2,\ldots,7. \tag{8.85}$$

We have just proved that the ultimate effects of all seven monetary shocks are zero. In this sense, money is neutral.

On the other hand, the effect of a real-sector shock is not neutral. A positive shift in the investment function will have a lasting positive effect on the interest rate:

$$\frac{di}{d\alpha} = \frac{\partial i*}{\partial p}\frac{dp}{d\alpha} > 0. \tag{8.86}$$

It is worth noting that both the nominal rate of interest, i, and the real rate of interest, r, increase since expected inflation remains the same—namely, at zero.

Comparative Dynamics: Effects of a Change in the Rate of Growth of the Nominal Reserve Base

We shall now examine the comparative statics of model $(\dot{R}\partial\,\dot{\pi})$—that is, of model 8.48 through 8.49. However, we shall concentrate on the effects of a change in the rate of growth of the nominal reserve base, $\dot{R}*/R*$, which we shall define as v:

$$v \equiv \frac{\dot{R}*}{R*}. \tag{8.87}$$

The effects of one-shot changes in the parameters—$R*$, $\bar{\zeta}$, $\bar{d}$, θ, k, β, and $\bar{R}_E$—are the same as in the previous section. First, the effect on π is zero. To find the effect on R we differentiate the definition, $R \equiv R*/p$, which establishes the relation between p and R:

$$dR = \frac{dR*}{p} - R\cdot\frac{dp}{p}. \tag{8.88}$$

With $R*$ given (that is, $dR* = 0$), there is a negative relation between R and p. Hence, for a change in parameters—$\bar{\zeta}$, $\bar{d}$, θ, k, β, and $\bar{R}_E$—the effects on R are opposite in sign to those derived for p. For a change in the parameter $R*$, the effect on R is zero because $dR/R = dR*/R* - dp/p$ and $dR*/R* = dp/p$. One can establish these one-shot effects formally by using the equations of change that we shall derive for this model. We shall, however, spare the reader all of these details.

Now, setting $\dot{R}$ and $\dot{\pi}$ equal to zero in equations 8.48 through 8.49, we have the equilibrium conditions, 8.89 through 8.90. (We suppress most parameters because we shall not use them.)

$$v - \varepsilon\{I[i_*(R; R_*, \ldots) - \pi; \alpha]$$

$$- S[i_*(R; R_*, \ldots) - \pi]\} - \pi = 0 \tag{8.89}$$

$$I[i_*(R; R_*, \ldots) - \pi]; \alpha]$$

$$- S[i_*(R; R_*, \ldots) - \pi] = 0. \tag{8.90}$$

Differentiating 8.89 through 8.90 with respect to v, we have the equations of change in matrix form:

$$\tilde{H} \cdot \begin{bmatrix} dR \\ d\pi \end{bmatrix} = \begin{bmatrix} dv \\ 0 \end{bmatrix} \tag{8.91}$$

where

$$\tilde{H} = \begin{bmatrix} -\varepsilon(I' - S')\dfrac{\partial i_*}{\partial R} & \varepsilon(I' - S') - 1 \\ (I' - S')\dfrac{\partial i_*}{\partial R} & -(I' - S') \end{bmatrix} \tag{8.92}$$

Comparing 8.92 to 8.61 and using 8.62, we see that

$$\det \tilde{H} = \frac{\det H}{\gamma \varepsilon R} = (I' - S')\frac{\partial i_*}{\partial R}. \tag{8.93}$$

We expect that the solution fo 8.91 for $d\pi/dv$ should be equal to one because we already know that at any equilibrium $\pi = v$ must hold and, therefore, that $d\pi = dv$. Indeed, solving 8.91, we derive the following result:

$$\frac{d\pi}{dv} = \frac{d(\dot{p}/p)}{dv} = 1. \tag{8.94}$$

Now, solving for dR/dv, we get:

$$\frac{dR}{dv} = \frac{1}{\dfrac{\partial i_*}{\partial R}} < 0. \tag{8.95}$$

This is an important result.[6] It establishes the nonneutrality of money in the sense that an increase in the rate of growth of the nominal reserve base affects a real variable—namely, it reduces the real reserve base. This result is important because the model, by construction, must yield neutrality of money with regard to employment and output (since the system is a full-employment model) and with regard to the *real* interest rate, $r \equiv i - \pi$. The reason for the real-interest-rate neutrality property lies in the specification of both the investment and savings functions. Since $I = I(r)$ and $S = S(r)$, r is the solution of the equilibrium condition $I(r) - S(r) = 0$ and, by construction, no other variable can influence it. Had we used a more exotic investment and/or savings function,[7] we could have derived nonneutrality of v on r.

To formally derive the result $dr/dv = 0$ and, hence, to check for the accuracy of our results, we differentiate 8.45 with respect to v:

$$i = i_*(R; R_*, \ldots, \bar{R}_E). \qquad (8.45)$$

We get:

$$\frac{di}{dv} = \frac{\partial i_*}{\partial R} \frac{dR}{dv}$$

and, upon substitution of 8.95, we derive:

$$\frac{di}{dv} = \frac{\dfrac{\partial i_*}{\partial R}}{\dfrac{\partial i_*}{\partial R}} = 1. \qquad (8.96)$$

Thus we see that the nominal interest rate changes by the same percentage as v does. Because expected inflation, π, changes by the same percentage—that is, since $d\pi = dv$—we have proved that the real rate remains unchanged.

Notes

1. Several contributions integrating the real and the financial sectors are W.C. Brainard and J. Tobin (1968); J. Tobin (1969); M.G. Hadjimichalakis (1975a, 1975b); D. Backus, W. Brainard, G. Smith, and J. Tobin (1980); F. Modigliani and L. Papademos (1980); and J. Tobin (1981).

2. Our integration of the financial and real sectors is in the neoclassical tradition. See J. Tobin (1981).

3. This method, introduced by M.G. Hadjimichalakis (1975a) in a five-asset Tobin-Brainard model, was dubbed "nested dynamics" by J. Tobin in a conversation with the author.

4. The positive number, $p(\partial i_*/\partial p)$, is related to an elasticity. Defining η as the percentage increase in the nominal interest rate, i, due to a percentage rise in the price level—that is,

$$\eta = \frac{\partial i_*}{\partial p} \cdot \frac{p}{i},$$

we see that

$$p\frac{\partial i_*}{\partial p} = i \cdot \eta.$$

For the original Cagan stability condition see P. Cagan (1956). Also see M. Sidrauski (1967) and M.G. Hadjimichalakis (1971b).

5. Figures 8–1 and 8–2 are identical to those in M.G. Hadjimichalakis (1971b). It may be of interest to note that the 1971 model had no loans (credit) market and its "money market" consisted of money from the "helicopter"—that is, the model also lacked fractional reserve banking and a Central Bank. The model in this chapter has a loans market, fractional reserve banking, and a Central Bank; it nevertheless can be reduced to a model indistinguishable from that simple 1971 model.

6. This result differs from the standard result in the literature. For example, in a Wicksell-type model when real balances are not an argument in the investment or savings function, money is superneutral. The key difference is the presence of a Central Bank.

7. See M.G. Hadjimichalakis (1981e).

Market-Determined Deposit Rates and the Real Sector

In this chapter we shall add the same real sector as in chapter 8 to the financial sector that relies on a market-determined deposit rate in addition to a market-determined (bills) interest rate. In other words, we shall extend the model and the analysis of chapters 4 and 5 to incorporate feedback from and to the real sector.

In the second section of this chapter we shall undertake a detailed derivation of the two basic models: One concentrates on levels of monetary instruments and, hence, on the price level and zero-equilibrium inflation—actual and expected; the other concentrates on a continuous change in the nominal reserve base that permits examination of nonzero, equilibrium, expected, and actual inflation.

In the next section, we shall examine the consistency of the two models by establishing their stability properties. As in the previous chapter, we shall establish that the models are stable provided some Cagan-type restriction is imposed on the speed of revision of expectations. Then we shall further examine the consistency of the models by deriving the comparative statics effects on the price level of one-shot shocks. We again show the expected result that an increase in the level of the nominal reserve base causes an equiproportionate increase in the price level and has no lasting effect on expected inflation. Similarly, any one-shot monetary shock—such as a change in the discount rate, a change in the administration of the discount window, or a change in the demand for excess reserves—changes the price level by a percentage equal to the consequent percentage change in nominal reserves. Finally, we shall show that a positive shift in the *supply* of demand deposits—for example, because of cost-reducing financial innovations—is contractionary because it reduces the equilibrium price level. This confirms a partial result noted in chapter 5. Of course, a positive shift in the *demand* for demand deposits is also contractionary, as expected.

In the section titled The Price Level and Interest Rates—still using the model that assumes zero growth in the nominal reserve base and, hence, zero-equilibrium inflation—we shall examine the effects of one-shot shocks on the interest rates. As expected, we shall find that no one-shot monetary shock has any lasting effect on the bills rate; only a shock emanating from the real sector can affect this rate. But this is not true for the second interest rate that we must also examine in this chapter, namely the deposit rate. In particular, we shall find that one-shot shocks in the demand for or in the supply of demand deposits will have a lasting effect on the deposit rate; that changes in the reserve requirement ratio may have a lasting effect on the deposit rate; and that one-shot changes in the remaining parameters will have no ultimate effect on the deposit rate.

In the final section, Inflation and Interest Rates, we shall examine the consequences of a change in the rate of growth of the nominal reserve base. Of course, we shall use the second variant of our model. We shall find that an increase in the rate of growth of the nominal reserve base by a given percentage will increase the expected and actual rate of inflation by the same percentage. Because of the way we construct the real sector, however, the change in the rate of growth of the nominal reserve base will have no effect on the real bills rate; that is, it will increase the nominal bills rate by the same percentage.

However, we shall show that there are two nonneutralities. First, we find that an increase in the rate of growth of the nominal reserve base will erode the real reserve base. Second, we find that the same increase in the rate of growth of the nominal reserve base increases the nominal deposit rate by a greater percentage, thereby increasing the real deposit rate. In this sense, money—or more precisely, reserves—cannot be superneutral.

Development of the Models

To build our model we need to add the real-sector equations to those that represent the financial system. Of course, equilibrium in the financial sector requires that the markets for these three assets be cleared—that is, that the excess demand for each of these assets be zero:

$$EDB = 0 \qquad \text{Bills market}$$

$$EDR = 0 \qquad \text{Reserves market}$$

$$EDD = 0 \qquad \text{Demand-deposits market}$$

But the financial sector is constrained by Walras' Law (for stocks):

$$EDB + EDR + EDD = 0. \tag{9.1}$$

This equality holds whether the assets markets are cleared or not. Since we can, therefore, eliminate any one of the three assets markets, we shall choose to eliminate the market for earning assets, or bills. Then we shall examine only EDR and EDD.

Equilibrium in the "real" or current-account, or flow, sector requires that the single market for goods and services be cleared—that is,

$$EDG = 0,$$

and that expectations of inflation be fulfilled, or,

$$\frac{\dot{p}}{p} = \pi,$$

where $\dot{p}/p$ is the actual and π the expected rate of inflation. Thus the equilibrium position of the system is described by the following equations:

$$EDD = 0 \tag{9.2}$$

$$EDR = 0 \tag{9.3}$$

$$EDG = 0 \tag{9.4}$$

$$\frac{\dot{p}}{p} = \pi. \tag{9.5}$$

In order to examine later the consistency and stability of this equilibrium specification, we must also spell out the dynamic adjustments by which this equilibrium is achieved. For the three markets, we rely on the law of supply and demand. The deposit rate rises, with a speed of adjustment equal to λ, if and only if there is excess supply of deposits; similarly, the bills or earning-assets rate rises, with a speed of adjustment equal to δ, if and only if there is excess demand for reserves—that is, excess supply of bills; and, of course, the price level—that is, the price of goods and services—rises above expected inflation with a speed of adjustment equal to ε, if and only if there is excess demand for goods and services. Finally, we introduce the expectations-adjustment mechanism. We simply rely on an adaptive scheme (although other mechanisms can also be considered) with a speed of adjustment, or a Cagan coefficient equal to γ. All of these adjustment mechanisms are summarized as follows:

$$\dot{\zeta} = -\lambda EDD, \ \lambda > 0 \tag{9.2'}$$

$$\frac{di}{dt} = \delta EDR, \ \delta > 0 \tag{9.3'}$$

$$\frac{\dot{p}}{p} = \varepsilon EDG + \pi, \ \varepsilon > 0 \qquad (9.4')$$

$$\dot{\pi} = \gamma \left(\frac{\dot{p}}{p} - \pi \right), \ \gamma > 0. \qquad (9.5')$$

Now we can make the realistic assumption that financial markets clear faster than goods markets. But we go to the limit by assuming that the financial markets clear instantaneously, that is, that λ and δ (and, in the background, the bills-market speed) are infinite. This implies that the demand deposits, the reserves, and the bills markets are always cleared whether or not the goods market is cleared and whether or not expectations are fulfilled. Thus the system is represented by:

$$EDD = 0 \qquad (9.6)$$

$$EDR = 0 \qquad (9.7)$$

$$\frac{\dot{p}}{p} = \varepsilon EDG + \pi \qquad (9.8)$$

$$\dot{\pi} = \gamma \left[\frac{\dot{p}}{p} - \pi \right]. \qquad (9.9)$$

Our system is one of four equations in four unknowns—ζ, i, p, and π. Our strategy in solving and describing the system is first to solve equations 9.6 and 9.7 for the two interest rates, ζ and i, as functions of the remaining endogenous variables, p and π, and of the exogenous variables (that is, policy and shock parameters), that will later be introduced fully.[1] Then we substitute these solutions in the final two equations and thereby reduce the entire system to two differential equations—$\dot{p}$ and $\dot{\pi}$—in two unknowns—p and π.

A variant of the model considers the system as one of four equations in four unknowns (ζ, i, R, and π); as earlier, R denotes the real reserve base, $R \equiv R_*/p$. This specification is needed in order to examine equilibrium nonzero inflation rates. In this case, we solve the system first for ζ and i as functions of the remaining endogenous variables, R and π, and of the exogenous variables. Substituting back into the remaining equations (including, $\dot{R}/R = \dot{R}_*/R_* - \dot{p}/p$), we reduce the entire system to the two differential equations—$\dot{R}$ and $\dot{\pi}$—in the two unknowns—R and π.

In chapters 4 and 5, we solved equations 9.6 and 9.7 for ζ and i as functions of p and of the remaining variables. Therefore, we shall merely record them here, and we shall also modify the solutions i and ζ to be functions of the real reserve base. The solution of 9.6 and 9.7 for i is:

$$i = i(p; R_*, \bar{d}, \theta, \bar{R}_E, \beta, \mu, k), \tag{9.10}$$

with partials given by expressions 9.11 through 9.18 as follows. It is important to note that i does not depend on the expected rate of inflation (that is, $\partial i / \partial \pi \equiv 0$ in 9.10).

$$\frac{\partial i}{\partial p} = \frac{\dfrac{R_*}{p^2}\left(\dfrac{\partial D^d}{\partial z_h} - \dfrac{\partial D^s}{\partial z_f}\right)}{Q} > 0 \tag{9.11}$$

$$\frac{\partial i}{\partial R_*} = -\frac{\dfrac{1}{p}\left(\dfrac{\partial D^d}{\partial z_h} - \dfrac{\partial D^s}{\partial z_f}\right)}{Q} < 0 \tag{9.12}$$

$$\frac{\partial i}{\partial \bar{d}} = \frac{R'_B\left(\dfrac{\partial D^d}{\partial z_h} - \dfrac{\partial D^s}{\partial z_f}\right)}{Q} > 0 \tag{9.13}$$

$$\frac{\partial i}{\partial \theta} = -\frac{\dfrac{\partial R_B}{\partial \theta}\left(\dfrac{\partial D^d}{\partial z_h} - \dfrac{\partial D^s}{\partial z_f}\right)}{Q} < 0 \tag{9.14}$$

$$\frac{\partial i}{\partial \bar{R}_E} = \frac{\left(\dfrac{\partial D^d}{\partial z_h} - \dfrac{\partial D^s}{\partial z_f}\right)}{Q} > 0 \tag{9.15}$$

$$\frac{\partial i}{\partial \beta} = -\frac{k\,\dfrac{\partial D^d}{\partial \beta} \cdot \dfrac{\partial D^s}{\partial z_f}}{Q} > 0 \tag{9.16}$$

$$\frac{\partial i}{\partial \mu} = \frac{k\,\dfrac{\partial D^d}{\partial z_h} \cdot \dfrac{\partial D^s}{\partial \mu}}{Q} > 0 \tag{9.17}$$

$$\frac{\partial i}{\partial k} = \frac{\hat{D} \cdot \left(\frac{\partial D^d}{\partial z_h} - \frac{\partial D^s}{\partial z_f} \right) - ik \frac{\partial D^s}{\partial z_f} \cdot \frac{\partial D^d}{\partial z_h}}{Q} \gtrless 0, \quad (9.18)$$

where

$$Q = k^2 \frac{\partial D^s}{\partial z_f} \frac{\partial D^d}{\partial z_h} + R'_B \left(\frac{\partial D^d}{\partial z_h} - \frac{\partial D^s}{\partial z_f} \right). \quad (9.19)$$

Since we have not included the deposit rate, ζ, as an argument in either the investment or in the savings function, we do not need to record here the solution $\zeta(p; \dots)$ and its partials. These will be recorded in a later section, where they are needed for a different purpose. We need, however, to extend the solution for i so that it can be considered as a function of the real reserve base, $R_*/p \equiv R$, rather than as a function of p:

$$i = i(R; R_*, \bar{d}, \theta, \bar{R}_E, \beta, \mu, k), \quad (9.20)$$

with

$$\frac{\partial i}{\partial R} = - \frac{\frac{\partial D^d}{\partial z_h} - \frac{\partial D^s}{\partial z_f}}{Q} < 0 \quad (9.21)$$

and

$$\frac{\partial i}{\partial R_*} = \frac{\partial i}{\partial R} \frac{\partial R}{\partial R_*} = - \frac{\frac{1}{p}\left(\frac{\partial D^d}{\partial z_h} - \frac{\partial D^s}{\partial z_f} \right)}{Q} < 0. \quad (9.22)$$

Furthermore, we note here that 9.22 coincides with 9.12.

To connect the financial sector with the real sector, we again need to specify EDG, the excess demand for goods and services. As earlier, we see that it is equal to investment, I, minus savings, S, and that those behavioral structural relations have already been specified as:

$$I = I(i - \pi; \alpha), I' \equiv \frac{\partial I}{\partial(i - \pi)} < 0, \frac{\partial I}{\partial \alpha} \equiv I_\alpha > 0 \quad (9.23)$$

$$S = S(i - \pi), S' \equiv \frac{\partial S}{\partial(i - \pi)} > 0. \quad (9.24)$$

That is, investment is related negatively and savings positively to the real interest rate, $r \equiv i - \pi$. The partial $\partial I/\partial \alpha$ represents a positive shift in investment demand. Therefore, EDG is specified by:

$$EDG = I(i - \pi; \alpha) - S(i - \pi). \qquad (9.25)$$

Equation 9.8 is now specified as:

$$\frac{\dot{p}}{p} = \varepsilon[I(i - \pi; \alpha) - S(i - \pi)] + \pi, \qquad (9.26)$$

which incorporates the stipulation that actual inflation, $\dot{p}/p$, has an expected component, π, and an unexpected component, $\varepsilon[I - S]$, which is based on excess demand or excess supply of goods and services.

Now, substituting 9.26 into 9.9, we get:

$$\dot{\pi} = \gamma\varepsilon\{I(i - \pi; \alpha) - S(i - \pi)\}. \qquad (9.27)$$

The final step involves substituting 9.10 into both 9.26 and 9.27 in order to display the ultimate dynamic system, as seen in 9.28 and 9.29, a system of two differential equations, $\dot{p}$ and $\dot{\pi}$, in two unknowns, p and π, with all the policy and other shock parameters.

$$\dot{p} = \varepsilon p \cdot \{I[i(p; R_*, \bar{d}, \theta, \bar{R}_E, \mu,\beta,k) - \pi; \alpha]$$
$$- S[i(p; R_*, \bar{d}, \theta, \bar{R}_E, \mu, \beta, k) - \pi]\} + p\pi \qquad (9.28)$$

$$\dot{\pi} = \gamma\varepsilon \cdot \{I[i(p; R_*, \bar{d}, \theta, \bar{R}_E, \mu, \beta, k) - \pi; \alpha]$$
$$- S[i(p; R_*, \bar{d}, \theta, \bar{R}_E, \mu, \beta, k]\}. \qquad (9.29)$$

Alternatively, we can use the definition in 9.30,

$$R \equiv \frac{R_*}{p}, \qquad (9.30)$$

to get

$$\frac{\dot{R}}{R} = \frac{\dot{R}_*}{R_*} - \frac{\dot{p}}{p}. \qquad (9.31)$$

Now, using 9.20 in 9.26 and 9.27 and substituting into 9.31, we can reduce our system to two equations—$\dot{R}$ and $\dot{\pi}$—in two unknowns—R and π:

$$\dot{R} \equiv R \cdot \left[\frac{\dot{R}_*}{R_*} - \varepsilon \cdot \{I[i(R; \ldots) - \pi; \alpha] - S[i(R; \ldots) - \pi]\} - \pi \right]$$

$$(9.32)$$

$$\dot{\pi} = \gamma\varepsilon\{I[i(R; \ldots) - \pi; \alpha] - S[i(R; \ldots) - \pi]\}. \quad (9.33)$$

Stability of the System

A full equilibrium—that is, equilibrium in the goods market and the fulfill-
ment of expectations as well are equilibrium in the three assets markets—
occurs when all motion stops. This happens when we set $p = \pi = 0$ in 9.28
and 9.29, or when we use the second model, setting $\dot{R} = \dot{\pi} = 0$ in 9.32 and
9.33.

First we shall examine the stability of the system 9.28 through 9.29.
Setting $p = \pi = 0$ in 9.28 through 9.29, we can describe the properties of this
equilibrium. By 9.28, $p = 0$ if and only if

$$\varepsilon(I - S) + \pi = 0.$$

But by 9.29,

$$(I - S) = 0. \quad (9.34)$$

Therefore, at equilibrium,

$$\frac{\dot{p}}{p} = \pi = 0. \quad (9.35)$$

Now taking the Taylor linear expansion of 9.28 through 9.29 in the
neighborhood of this equilibrium, we can form the matrix of the dynamic
system

$$A = \begin{bmatrix} \varepsilon p(I' - S')\dfrac{\partial i}{\partial p} & p\{l - \varepsilon(I' - S')\} \\[2em] \gamma\varepsilon(I' - S')\dfrac{\partial i}{\partial p} & -\gamma\varepsilon(I' - S') \end{bmatrix} \quad (9.36)$$

The system is stable—that is, the system converges to its equilibrium if and only if the trace of matrix A is negative and its determinant is positive:

$$\det A = -\gamma \varepsilon p(I' - S') \frac{\partial i}{\partial p} > 0. \tag{9.37}$$

The determinant is, indeed, positive, since $(I' - S') < 0$ and $\partial i / \partial p > 0$, the latter by 9.11. We see that the trace is

$$\operatorname{tr} A = \varepsilon(I' - S') \cdot \left\{ p \frac{\partial i}{\partial p} - \gamma \right\}. \tag{9.38}$$

Since $(I' - S') < 0$, it follows that tr A is negative if and only if the expression in braces is positive—that is, if and only if

$$p \frac{\partial i}{\partial p} - \gamma > 0. \tag{9.39}$$

This condition is satisfied if and only if[2]

$$\gamma < p \frac{\partial i}{\partial p}. \tag{9.40}$$

This is a variant of the Cagan stability condition. We have shown, therefore, that the system is stable if and only if a Cagan stability condition is satisfied. The phase plane of the dynamic system is presented in figure 9–1.

Now we turn to system 9.32 through 9.33. At full equilibrium,

$$\frac{\dot{p}}{p} = \pi \text{ by 9.5' and 9.33 when } \dot{\pi} = 0,$$

$$\pi = \frac{\dot{R}_*}{R_*} \text{ by 9.32 and 9.33,}$$

and

$$I(\cdot) - S(\cdot) = 0, \tag{9.41}$$

by 9.33. That is, at equilibrium all markets are cleared and expected inflation

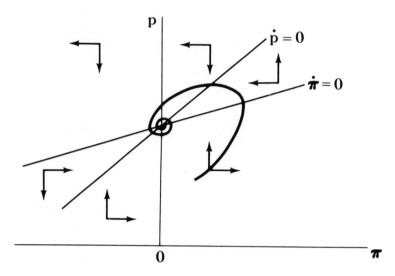

Figure 9–1. Flexible-Deposit-Rate Regime: Price Level—Expected Inflation Dynamics

is equal to the actual rate of inflation, which, in turn, is equal to the rate of growth in the nominal reserve base:

$$\frac{\dot{p}}{p} = \pi = \frac{\dot{R}_*}{R_*} . \tag{9.42}$$

Now, taking the Taylor linear expansion of 9.32 through 9.33 around the equilibrium point, $\dot{R} = \pi = 0$, we form the matrix of the dynamic system. We denote this matrix with B:

$$B = \begin{bmatrix} -\varepsilon R(I' - S')\dfrac{\partial i}{\partial R} & R[\varepsilon(I' - S') - 1] \\[2em] \gamma\varepsilon(I' - S')\dfrac{\partial i}{\partial R} & -\gamma\varepsilon(I' - S') \end{bmatrix} \tag{9.43}$$

We can prove that the determinant of B is positive and, in particular, that

$$\det B = \gamma\varepsilon R(I' - S')\frac{\partial i}{\partial R} > 0. \tag{9.44}$$

Next we examine the trace of B:

$$\text{tr } B = -\varepsilon R(I' - S')\frac{\partial i}{\partial R} - \gamma\varepsilon(I' - S'),$$
$$(9.45)$$

or

$$\text{tr } B = -\gamma\varepsilon(I' - S')\left[1 + \frac{R\dfrac{\partial i}{\partial R}}{\gamma}\right].$$
$$(9.46)$$

It is clear that tr B is negative if and only if

$$1 + \frac{R\dfrac{\partial i}{\partial R}}{\gamma} < 0,$$
$$(9.47)$$

that is, if and only if

$$\gamma < -R\frac{\partial i}{\partial R}.$$
$$(9.48)$$

Of course, 9.48 is, again, a variant of the Cagan stability condition. We see that when this condition is satisified, the phase diagram[3] of system 9.32 through 9.33 is the one shown in figure 9–2.

Comparative Statics:
Ultimate Effects on the Price Level

Starting from a position of full equilibrium, described by setting $p = 0$ and $\pi = 0$ in 9.28 and 9.29—that is, described by equations 9.49 and 9.50,

$$\varepsilon\{I[i(p; R_*, \bar{d}, \theta, \mu, \beta, \bar{R}_E, k) - \pi; \alpha]$$
$$- S[i(p; R_*, \bar{d}, \theta, \mu, \beta, \bar{R}_E, k) - \pi]\} + \pi = 0 \quad (9.49)$$

$$I[i(p; R_*, \bar{d}, \theta, \mu, \beta, \bar{R}_E, k) - \pi; \alpha]$$
$$- S[i(p; R_*, \bar{d}, \theta, \mu, \beta, \bar{R}_E, k) - \pi] = 0, \quad (9.50)$$

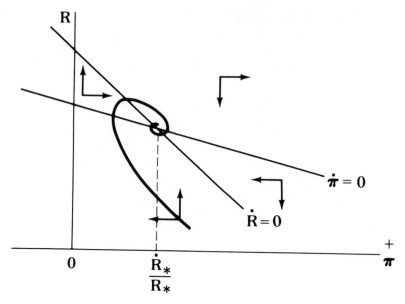

Figure 9–2. Flexible-Deposit-Rate Regime: Real Reserve Base—Expected
Inflation Dynamics

we shall examine the effects of a change in any one of several policy and
shock parameters on endogenous variables. In particular, we shall permit
changes, one at a time, in all of the following: in the reserve base, R^*; the
nominal discount rate, $\bar{d}$; the reserve requirement ratio, k; outside shocks in
the demand for demand deposits, β; the supply of demand deposits, μ; and in
investment, α(say, when the "animal spirits" of entrepreneurs rise).

In matrix form the equations of change for monetary shocks, deliberate or
inadvertent, are given by 9.51:

$$\tilde{A} \cdot \begin{bmatrix} \dfrac{dp}{da_j} \\[2ex] \dfrac{d\pi}{da_j} \end{bmatrix} = - \begin{bmatrix} \varepsilon(I' - S')\dfrac{\partial i}{\partial a_j} \\[2ex] (I' - S')\dfrac{\partial i}{\partial a_j} \end{bmatrix} \tag{9.51}$$

$$j = 1, 2, \ldots, 7,$$

where $a_1 = R_*$; $a_2 = \bar{d}$; $a_3 = \theta$; $a_4 = \bar{R}_E$; $a_5 = \beta$; $a_6 = \mu$; and $a_7 = k$. The
equations of change for the real-sector shock—namely, an increase in the
investment function—are given by 9.52:

$$
\tilde{A} \cdot \begin{bmatrix} \dfrac{dp}{d\alpha} \\[2ex] \dfrac{d\pi}{d\alpha} \end{bmatrix} = - \begin{bmatrix} \varepsilon I_\alpha \\[2ex] I_\alpha \end{bmatrix}
\tag{9.52}
$$

In both expressions $\tilde{A}$ is given by 9.53:

$$
\tilde{A} = \begin{bmatrix} \varepsilon(I' - S')\dfrac{\partial i}{\partial p} & 1 - \varepsilon(I' - S') \\[3ex] (I' - S')\dfrac{\partial i}{\partial p} & -(I' - S') \end{bmatrix}
\tag{9.53}
$$

Comparing 9.53 with 9.36, we see that

$$
\det \tilde{A} = \frac{\det A}{\gamma \varepsilon p} = -(I' - S')\frac{\partial i}{\partial p} > 0.
\tag{9.54}
$$

We can now solve dp/da_j, $d\pi/da_j$ and $dp/d\alpha$, $d\pi/d\alpha$. It is clear, however, that if our model is consistent and our analysis is correct, we must always find that $d\pi/da_j$ and $d\pi/d\alpha$ are zero. We already know that at any full equilibrium, π is zero. Therefore, the new equilibrium must also have this property. In the following discussion, we shall derive $d\pi/da_j$ only the first time, with the understanding that for the remainder of comparative-statics excercises $d\pi/da_j$ and $d\pi/d\alpha$ are indeed zero.

Change in Reserves Base, R_*

The effect of an increase in R_* on the price level is given by:

$$
\frac{dp}{dR_*} = \frac{(I' - S')}{\det \tilde{A}} \cdot \frac{\partial i}{\partial R_*}
$$

Substituting 9.54, we have:

$$
\frac{dp}{dR_*} = - \frac{\dfrac{\partial i}{\partial R_*}}{\dfrac{\partial i}{\partial p}} \cdot
\tag{9.55}
$$

As expected, $d\pi/dR_* = 0$, as can be seen by the following:

$$\frac{d\pi}{dR_*} = -\frac{1}{\det \tilde{A}} \cdot \begin{vmatrix} \varepsilon(I' - S')\dfrac{\partial i}{\partial p} & \varepsilon(I' - S')\dfrac{\partial i}{\partial R_*} \\ (I' - S')\dfrac{\partial i}{\partial p} & (I' - S')\dfrac{\partial i}{\partial R_*} \end{vmatrix}$$

$$= 0. \tag{9.56}$$

Let us now concentrate on 9.55, an expression that denotes the effect of a one-shot increase in the amount of nominal reserves on the price level. This is the ultimate effect—that is, the effect after all interrelationships have worked themselves out. But the ultimate effect on the price level depends on the impact and on the intermediate effects on interest rates. In fact, according to 9.55, the ultimate effect on the price level is the negative of the ratio of the immediate effect of the increase in reserves on the nominal interest rate on earning assets, or bills, and the intermediate effect of the consequent increase in the price level on the same interest rate. Since this pattern emerges with all other monetary shocks, we can substitute the specific parameter for the word *reserves* in the statement already given and get all other results. Mathematically, we have:

$$\frac{dp}{da_j} = -\frac{\dfrac{\partial i}{\partial a_j}}{\dfrac{\partial i}{\partial p}} \qquad j = 1, \ldots, 7. \tag{9.57}$$

Change in Other Parameters

Substituting for $j = 2, \ldots, 7$, we get:

$$\frac{dp}{d\bar{d}} = -\frac{\dfrac{\partial i}{\partial \bar{d}}}{\dfrac{\partial i}{\partial p}} \tag{9.58}$$

$$\frac{dp}{d\theta} = -\frac{\dfrac{\partial i}{\partial \theta}}{\dfrac{\partial i}{\partial p}} \qquad (9.59)$$

$$\frac{dp}{d\bar{R}_E} = -\frac{\dfrac{\partial i}{\partial \bar{R}_E}}{\dfrac{\partial i}{\partial p}} \qquad (9.60)$$

$$\frac{dp}{d\mu} = -\frac{\dfrac{\partial i}{\partial \mu}}{\dfrac{\partial i}{\partial p}} \qquad (9.61)$$

$$\frac{dp}{\partial \beta} = -\frac{\dfrac{\partial i}{\partial \beta}}{\dfrac{\partial i}{\partial p}} \qquad (9.62)$$

$$\frac{dp}{dk} = -\frac{\dfrac{\partial i}{\partial k}}{\dfrac{\partial i}{\partial p}} \qquad (9.63)$$

Turning to the effect of an increase in investment demand on the price level, we can solve 9.52 for $dp/d\alpha$ and get:

$$\frac{dp}{d\alpha} = \frac{I_\alpha}{\det \tilde{A}} > 0. \qquad (9.64)$$

The ultimate effect of the increase in investment on the price level is positive, as one would expect. But to find the ultimate effects of monetary shocks and policies, we need to use the impact, or immediate, effect of these shocks, or policy changes, on the interest rate; that is, we need to substitute expressions

9.11 through 9.18 into 9.55 and 9.58 through 9.63. Substituting 9.11 and 9.12 into 9.55, we get:

$$\frac{dp}{dR_*} = \frac{p}{R_*} > 0. \qquad (9.65)$$

As expected, an increase in the amount of nonborrowed reserves increases the price level. In fact, the percentage increase in the price level is equal to the percentage increase in the nominal reserve base, as rearrangement of expression 9.65 reveals:

$$\frac{dp}{p} = \frac{dR_*}{R_*}. \qquad (9.65')$$

We should note that the result itself is not as important as the fact that our model has produced this result, which is expected of any consistent model.

Now, substituting 9.13 into 9.58, we get this result:

$$\frac{dp}{d\bar{d}} = -\frac{P^2 R_B'}{R_*}; \qquad (9.66)$$

that is, we see that an increase in the discount rate is, indeed, deflationary. More significantly, we can rearrange and get the following expression:

$$\frac{dp}{p} = -\frac{p R_B'}{R_*} d\bar{d} < 0, \qquad (9.66')$$

which simply means that the percentage decrease in the price level (caused by a rise in the discount rate) is equal to the decrease in borrowed reserves expressed as a percentage of the reserve base.

The effect of a positive shock in the borrowings function, that is, the effect of a loosening in the administration of the discount window, is

$$\frac{dp}{d\theta} = \frac{P^2 \frac{\partial R_B}{\partial \theta}}{R_*}, \qquad (9.67)$$

which is positive, and, as expected, opposite in sign to 9.66; it can be rearranged as

$$\frac{dp}{p} = \frac{p \dfrac{\partial R_B}{\partial \theta}}{R_*} \, d\theta > 0. \qquad (9.67')$$

The explanation of 9.67' is similar to that of 9.66' but in the opposite direction.

Continuing, we see that an exogenous increase in the demand for excess reserves is deflationary:

$$\frac{dp}{d\bar{R}_E} = -\frac{p^2}{R_*}. \qquad (9.68)$$

Rearranging, we get:

$$\frac{dp}{p} = -\frac{p d\bar{R}_E}{R_*}. \qquad (9.68')$$

This expression means that an increase in the demand for excess reserves causes a percentage fall in the price level equal to the fall in excess reserves, $-p d\bar{R}_E$, expressed as a percentage of the nominal reserve base.

The effect of a positive shock in the supply function for demand deposits is:

$$\frac{dp}{d\mu} = -\frac{k \, p^2 \, \dfrac{\partial D^s}{\partial \mu} \cdot \dfrac{\partial D^d}{\partial z_h}}{R_* \left(\dfrac{\partial D^d}{\partial z_h} - \dfrac{\partial D^s}{\partial z_f} \right)} < 0, \qquad (9.69)$$

which is negative. At first this result may seem surprising, but closer inspection reveals that it is not. This is one case when an increase in the money supply (that is, supply of demand deposits) may, in fact, be contractionary. The reasoning is simple: An increase in the supply function of demand deposits—say, because of cost-reducing innovations in the banking industry—necessitates a rise in the deposit rate paid by banks. This rise pulls the earning assets rate, i, upward, which creates an excess supply of goods and services.

Turning to demand-side shocks—that is, to a positive shift in the demand function for demand deposits—we see that it is, once again, deflationary; the

amount of demand deposits, and, hence, of money in our system, is
increased, but economic activity falls, causing a fall in the price level:

$$\frac{dp}{d\beta} = \frac{k\,p^2\,\dfrac{\partial D^d}{\partial \beta} \cdot \dfrac{\partial D^s}{\partial z_f}}{R_*\left(\dfrac{\partial D^d}{\partial z_h} - \dfrac{\partial D^s}{\partial z_f}\right)} < 0. \qquad (9.70)$$

This time the fall in the price level results from an increase in the amount of
demand deposits which creates an excess demand for reserves and raises the
earning-assets interest rate. This increase, in turn, stifles economic activity.[4]

Finally, we find that without additional assumptions the effect of
an increase in the reserve-requipment ratio is indeterminate; it may be
either deflationary, as expected, or inflationary. But it is deflationary if
$D + k\partial\hat{D}/\partial k > 0$, as the following expression reveals:[5]

$$\frac{dp}{dk} = -\frac{p^2\left[D + k\dfrac{\partial\hat{D}}{\partial k}\right]}{R_*}. \qquad (9.71)$$

The Price Level and Interest Rates

In this section we shall examine the effects of the price level on the two
interest rates—the bills rate, i, and the deposit rate, ζ. Of course, one-shot
increases (decreases) in the price level result from one-shot increases
(decreases) in the nominal reserve base, R_*, or from a one-shot change (in
the appropriate direction) of another parameter, $a_j, j = 2, \ldots, 7$. Therefore,
we shall examine the overall, or ultimate, effects of deliberate or inadvertent
shocks on the interest rates when all markets—that is, when both the
financial sector and the real sector—are equilibrated. We shall begin with the
effect on the bills interest rate, i.

Ultimate Effect on the Bills Interest Rate, i

To find the overall, or ultimate, effect on i, we need only to differentiate
totally, with respect to the relevant parameter, a_j, expression 9.10. Since $d\pi/da_j = 0$ and $j = 1, \ldots, 7$, we have:

$$\frac{di}{da_j} = \frac{\partial i}{\partial p}\frac{dp}{da_j} + \frac{\partial i}{\partial a_j} \qquad j = 1, \ldots, 7. \qquad (9.72)$$

Substituting 9.57, we derive:

$$\frac{di}{da_j} = -\frac{\partial i}{\partial p} \cdot \frac{\dfrac{\partial i}{\partial a_j}}{\dfrac{\partial i}{\partial p}} + \frac{\partial i}{\partial a_j} = -\frac{\partial i}{\partial a_j} + \frac{\partial i}{\partial a_j},$$

or

$$\frac{di}{da_j} = 0 \qquad j = 1, \ldots, 7. \qquad (9.73)$$

We have derived the result that a once-and-for-all change in a monetary parameter changes the interest rate in the beginning, but as time passes the price level changes, moving the interest rate in the opposite direction, until the initial interest rate is reestablished. For example, an increase in the level of the nominal reserve base first lowers i, by 9.12. This later causes excess demand for goods and services and raises the price level, which, in turn, shrinks the supply of *real* reserves and raises the interest rate by 9.11. This rise in i continues until the price level increases by the same percentage as the amount of the reserve base (by 9.65′), at which point the original level of i is reestablished. This example is illustrated in figure 9–3.

On the other hand, a contractionary policy, such as an increase in the discount rate, is illustrated in figure 9–4.

Ultimate Effect on the Deposit Rate

To find the ultimate effects on the deposit rate, ζ, we need to use the solution of $EDD = 0$ and $EDR = 0$. In the section on Development of the Models we avoided recording that solution because it was not needed until now. This solution is:

$$\zeta = \zeta(p; R_*, \bar{d}, \ldots) \equiv \hat{\zeta}[i(p; R_*, \bar{d}, \theta, \bar{R}_E, \mu, \beta, k); \mu, \beta, k]. \qquad (9.74)$$

We shall distinguish between two kinds of shocks. First, for the three parameters, μ, β, and k, we have separately and in that order:

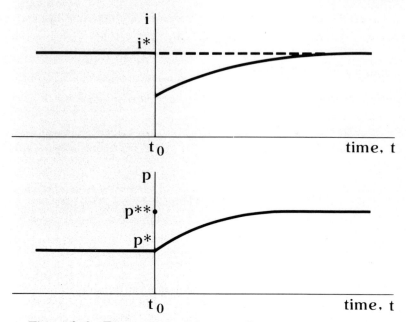

Figure 9–3. Expansionary Monetary Policy and the Bills Rate

$$\frac{d\zeta}{d\mu} = \frac{\partial \zeta}{\partial p}\frac{dp}{d\mu} + \frac{\partial \zeta}{\partial \mu} = \frac{\partial \hat{\zeta}}{\partial i}\frac{\partial i}{\partial p}\frac{dp}{d\mu} + \frac{\partial \hat{\zeta}}{\partial i}\frac{\partial i}{\partial \mu} + \frac{\partial \hat{\zeta}}{\partial \mu}$$

$$= \frac{\partial \hat{\zeta}}{\partial i}\left[\frac{\partial i}{\partial p}\frac{dp}{d\mu} + \frac{\partial i}{\partial \mu}\right] + \frac{\partial \hat{\zeta}}{\partial \mu} . \qquad (9.75)$$

By 9.72 and 9.73, we have:

$$\frac{d\zeta}{d\mu} = \frac{\partial \hat{\zeta}}{\partial i}\frac{di}{d\mu} + \frac{\partial \hat{\zeta}}{\partial \mu} = \frac{\partial \hat{\zeta}}{\partial \mu} > 0. \qquad (9.76)$$

That is, the overall, ultimate effect of an increase in the supply function for demand deposits is equal to the first effect. We note that by 9.75 there are three effects: First, $\partial \hat{\zeta}/\partial \mu$, the deposit rate rises to clear the deposit market alone; second, as shown by $\partial \hat{\zeta}/\partial i \cdot \partial i/\partial \mu$, the deposit rate rises further since the bills rate must also rise if all asset markets are to clear; and third, as shown by $\partial \hat{\zeta}/\partial i \cdot \partial i/\partial p \cdot dp/d\mu$, the rise in the bills rate, which causes excess supply of goods and services, reduces the price level, which in turn lowers both rates and, in particular, the deposit rate. By 9.73, the second effect is exactly negated by the third and, hence, only the first effect remains.

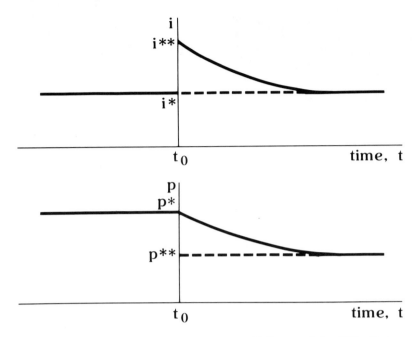

Figure 9–4. Contractionary Monetary Policy and the Bills Rate

The effects of a change in β and a change in k are derived in a similar fashion and are recorded as 9.77 and 9.78:

$$\frac{d\zeta}{d\beta} = \frac{\partial\hat{\zeta}}{\partial\beta} < 0 \qquad (9.77)$$

$$\frac{d\zeta}{dk} = \frac{\partial\hat{\zeta}}{\partial k} < 0. \qquad (9.78)$$

Now we turn to the effects of the remaining shocks—that is, of a change in any one of the four parameters, R_*, $\bar{d}$, θ, and $\bar{R}_E$. We shall illustrate the difference in results by examining a change in the nominal reserve base, R_*. Differentiating 9.74 totally, we get:

$$\frac{d\zeta}{dR_*} = \frac{\partial\zeta}{\partial p}\frac{dp}{dR_*} + \frac{\partial\zeta}{\partial R_*} = \frac{\partial\hat{\zeta}}{\partial i}\frac{\partial i}{\partial p}\frac{dp}{dR_*} + \frac{\partial\hat{\zeta}}{\partial i}\frac{\partial i}{\partial R_*}. \qquad (9.79)$$

We see that the increase in the nominal reserve base has only two effects on the deposit rate and that these effects correspond to the second and third effects in 9.75.

Now, collecting terms in 9.79 and relying on 9.72 and 9.73, we get:

$$\frac{d\zeta}{dR_*} = \frac{\partial \hat{\zeta}}{\partial i} \left[\frac{\partial i}{\partial p} \frac{dp}{dR_*} + \frac{\partial i}{\partial R_*} \right],$$

or,

$$\frac{d\zeta}{dR_*} = 0. \qquad (9.80)$$

Similarly, we have:

$$\frac{d\zeta}{d\bar{d}} = \frac{d\zeta}{d\theta} = \frac{d\zeta}{d\bar{R}_E} = \frac{d\zeta}{dR_*} = 0. \qquad (9.81)$$

In other words, the ultimate effect of any of these shocks on the deposit rate, ζ, is zero.

Inflation and Interest Rates

Now we shall examine the comparative statics of model 9.32 through 9.33. Since this model exhibits nonzero-equilibrium actual and expected inflation, engineered by a nonzero rate of growth in the nominal reserve base, we shall be referring to these exercises as comparative *dynamics*. These exercises will concentrate on the effects of a change in the rate of growth of the nominal reserve base.

First, we shall denote the rate of growth of the nominal reserve base by v—that is,

$$v = \frac{\dot{R}_*}{R_*}. \qquad (9.82)$$

Recalling the equilibrium property (9.42), we get 9.83:

$$v = \pi = \frac{\dot{p}}{p}. \qquad (9.83)$$

Then we can substitute 9.82 into 9.32 and set $\dot{R}$ and $\dot{\pi}$ equal to zero in 9.32 and 9.33 to derive the equilibrium conditions 9.84 through 9.85 as follows:

$$v - \varepsilon\{I[i(R;\dots) - \pi] - S[i(R;\dots) - \pi]\} - \pi = 0 \qquad (9.84)$$

$$I[i(R; \ldots) - \pi] - S[i(R; \ldots) - \pi] = 0. \qquad (9.85)$$

To find the equations of change we differentiate 9.84 to 9.85 totally, with respect to v and set up the resulting system in matrix form as follows:

$$\tilde{B} \cdot \begin{bmatrix} \dfrac{dR}{dv} \\[2mm] \dfrac{d\pi}{dv} \end{bmatrix} = - \begin{bmatrix} 1 \\[2mm] 0 \end{bmatrix} \qquad (9.86)$$

where

$$\tilde{B} = \begin{bmatrix} -\varepsilon(I' - S')\dfrac{\partial i}{\partial R} & \varepsilon(I' - S') - 1 \\[4mm] (I' - S')\dfrac{\partial i}{\partial R} & -(I' - S') \end{bmatrix} \qquad (9.87)$$

The determinant of $\tilde{B}$, which is positive, is related to the determinant of B by 9.44:

$$\det \tilde{B} = \frac{\det B}{\gamma \varepsilon R} = (I' - S')\frac{\partial i}{\partial R} > 0. \qquad (9.88)$$

Now, solving 9.86 for dR/dv and $d\pi/dv$, we find:

$$\frac{dR}{dv} = \frac{\dfrac{1}{\dfrac{\partial i}{\partial R}}}{} < 0 \qquad (9.89)$$

and

$$\frac{d\pi}{dv} = 1. \qquad (9.90)$$

The result in 9.90 is expected because direct differentiation of 9.83 gives the same result, that a given percentage increase in the rate of growth of the nominal base increases expected and actual inflation by the same percentage.

The result in 9.89, similar to the result of the same exercise under a fixed deposit rate, is important; it says that an increase in the rate of growth of the nominal reserve base will reduce the *level* of the *real* reserve base. That is, it says that *money is not superneutral*: A change in v changes real magnitudes.

Inflation and the Real (Bills) Rate of Interest

But what about the other real variable—the real rate of interest, r? Can it be influenced by a change in v? To see that the answer is no, we recall that the real rate of interest is defined as

$$r = i - \pi. \tag{9.91}$$

Differentiating r with respect to v and using 9.90. we get:

$$\frac{dr}{dv} = \frac{di}{dv} - 1. \tag{9.92}$$

Therefore, we see that monetary policy, reflected as a change in the rate of growth of the nominal reserve base, v, can have an influence on the real interest rate, r, only if di/dv is different from one—that is only if a given percentage increase in the rate of growth of the nominal reserve base, dv, increases the nominal interest rate, di, by a different percentage (that is, $di \neq dv$). But we have designed our model from the beginning to exclude such an eventuality. This property, called the Fisher hypothesis, is embedded in the following assumptions: first, that we are examining a fully employed economy; and second, that both investment, I, and savings, S, depend only on the real interest rate, r. It follows, then, that r is the solution of the single equation $I(r) - S(r) = 0$ and that no monetary instrument can influence its level.[6]

We can confirm the just-mentioned property of the model and also test the accuracy of our exercises by deriving di/dv. Using 9.20, we find:

$$\frac{di}{dv} = \frac{\partial i}{\partial R}\frac{dR}{dv}.$$

Substituting 9.89, we get

$$\frac{di}{dv} = \frac{\frac{\partial i}{\partial R}}{\frac{\partial i}{\partial R}} = 1. \tag{9.93}$$

Hence, by 9.92, we get the Fisher property:

$$\frac{dr}{dv} = 0. \tag{9.94}$$

Inflation, the Nominal Deposit Rate,
and the Real Deposit Rate

The real deposit rate, ρ, is defined as:

$$\rho = \zeta - \pi. \tag{9.95}$$

Hence, the effect of a change in the rate of growth of the nominal reserve base is:

$$\frac{d\rho}{dv} = \frac{d\zeta}{dv} - 1. \tag{9.96}$$

We see from 9.96 that whether or not there is an effect on the real variable, ρ, depends on whether $d\zeta/dv$ is equal to one or not. To find $d\zeta/dv$ we differentiate the analogue of 9.74—that is, 9.97:

$$\zeta = \zeta(R; \ldots) = \hat{\zeta}[i(R; \ldots); \mu, \beta, k]. \tag{9.97}$$

Now, differentiating the left-hand side of 9.97, we get:

$$\frac{d\zeta}{dv} = \frac{\partial \zeta}{\partial R} \frac{dR}{dv} \tag{9.98}$$

or, by 9.89

$$\frac{d\zeta}{dv} = \frac{\dfrac{\partial \zeta}{\partial R}}{\dfrac{\partial i}{\partial R}}. \tag{9.99}$$

But by the right-hand side of 9.97, we see that

$$\frac{\partial \zeta}{\partial R} = \frac{\partial \hat{\zeta}}{\partial i} \frac{\partial i}{\partial R}. \tag{9.100}$$

And substituting 9.100 into 9.99, we get:

$$\frac{d\zeta}{dv} = \frac{\dfrac{\partial \hat{\zeta}}{\partial i}\,\dfrac{\partial i}{\partial R}}{\dfrac{\partial i}{\partial R}}$$

or

$$\frac{d\zeta}{dv} = \frac{\partial \hat{\zeta}}{\partial i}. \tag{9.101}$$

But we know from chapter 4 (expression 4.49), that

$$\frac{\partial \hat{\zeta}}{\partial i} = \frac{\dfrac{\partial D^d}{\partial z_h} - (1 - k)\,\dfrac{\partial D^s}{\partial z_f}}{\dfrac{\partial D^d}{\partial z_h} - \dfrac{\partial D^s}{\partial z_f}} = 1 + k\,\frac{\partial D^s}{\partial z_f}. \tag{9.102}$$

It follows, therefore, that

$$\frac{d\zeta}{dv} = 1 + k\,\frac{\partial D^s}{\partial z_f} \tag{9.103}$$

and that

$$\frac{d\rho}{dv} = k\,\frac{\partial D^s}{\partial z_f}. \tag{9.104}$$

Expression 9.104 says that as long as the reserve-requirement ratio, k, is positive, an increase in the rate of growth of the nominal reserve base will increase the nominal deposit rate by more, thereby increasing the real deposit rate. We must note that it is because of the positive reserve requirement that the deposit rate must rise by more than the increase in the bills rate (that is, $\partial \hat{\zeta}/\partial i > 1$).

Notes

1. Alternatively and equivalently we can solve only the first equation for ζ and substitute the solution into the remaining equations in order to reduce

the system to three equations, di/dt, $\dot{p}$, and $\dot{\pi}$, as functions of the triplet, (i, p, π).

2. As in note 4 of chapter 8, we can express this condition in terms of an elasticity.

3. We note that figures 9–1 and 9–2 are identical to figures 8–1 and 8–2, respectively, and also identical to those in M.G. Hadjimichalakis (1971b). Hence the message in note 5 of chapter 8 is strengthened: Even if the model is extended to encompass fractional reserve banking and a Central Bank, a market for loans, and a market for deposits, it nevertheless can be reduced to a model indistinguishable from the simple 1971 model.

4. For some policy implications of supply-side shocks and of demand-side shocks, see Concluding Comments in chapter 5.

5. We know from chapter 5 that if the absolute value of the interest elasticity of the demand for demand deposits is less than or equal to one, the inequality $D + k(\partial \hat{D}/\partial k) > 0$, is satisfied.

6. But as mentioned in chapter 8, and in the accompanying note 7, a more complicated savings and/or investment function will negate this result.

10

Comparison of Entire Regimes: Monetary Policy, Real-Sector Shocks, Inflation, and Real Variables

In the preceding chapters we examined the effects of one-shot shocks originating in both the financial sector and in the real sector; and we examined the effects of a continuous shock originating in the financial sector—namely, the effects of a change in the rate of growth of the nominal reserve base.

We have shown that the effects of one-shot financial shocks on the price level, on expected inflation, and on the (bills) interest rate are identical whether the deposit rate is fixed or market determined. Therefore, in this chapter we shall compare the consequences of only one of the two kinds of one-shot shocks, namely, the ones originating in the real sector. In the second section we shall show that the price level is less sensitive to (and, therefore, more immune from) shocks originating in the real sector when the deposit rate is market determined than when it is fixed. Next, we shall compare the consequences of the aforementioned continuous monetary shock. And we shall show that an increase in the rate of growth of the nominal reserve base (and, hence, an increase in the equilibrium rate of inflation) reduces the real reserve base by less under a flexible deposit rate than under a fixed deposit rate. In other words, we shall show that inflation erodes the real reserve base by less when the deposit rate is market determined than when it is fixed by the Central Bank.

However, the most important difference lies in the dynamic structure of the models. In chapters 8 and 9 we have seen that the two models are stable under some reasonable Cagan-type stability conditions. In the final section of this chapter, we shall prove that the entire model is more stable under a market-determined deposit rate than under a fixed deposit rate. In particular, we shall prove that the economy moves faster from one equilibrium to another when the deposit rate is flexible than when it is fixed. This stability property has profound policy implications: With a flexible deposit rate, monetary policy is more effective, in the sense that it achieves results faster. And, of course, the effects of inadvertent shocks also disappear faster.

**One-Shot Shocks in the Real Sector: Comparison of
Effects on Price Levels and Interest Rates**

We shall first examine the consequences of a one-shot shock originating in
the real sector. In particular, we shall consider a positive shock in investment
demand—say, an increase in the "animal spirits" of the entrepreneurs, which
is denoted by $\partial I/\partial \alpha = I_\alpha > 0$. Since we already know that this shock will
have no effect on equilibrium expected inflation whether the deposit rate is
fixed or market determined, we shall restrict our comparison to the effects on
the price level and on the interest rate.

We have seen in chapter 8 that under a fixed-deposit-rate regime the
increase in the price level is

$$\frac{dp}{d\alpha}\Big|_{\bar\zeta} = \frac{I_\alpha}{\det \tilde F} > 0. \tag{10.1}$$

With a flexible deposit rate the effect on the price level is also positive and
given by 10.2:

$$\frac{dp}{d\alpha} = \frac{I_\alpha}{\det \tilde A} > 0. \tag{10.2}$$

Substracting 10.1 from 10.2, we get:

$$\frac{dp}{d\alpha} - \frac{dp}{d\alpha}\Big|_{\bar\zeta} = I_\alpha \cdot \left\{ \frac{1}{\det \tilde A} - \frac{1}{\det \tilde F} \right\} \tag{10.3}$$

Now, $\det \tilde A$ and $\det \tilde F$ are given by 10.4 and 10.5:

$$\det \tilde A = -(I' - S')\frac{\partial i}{\partial p} \tag{10.4}$$

$$\det \tilde F = -(I' - S')\frac{\partial i_*}{\partial p}. \tag{10.5}$$

Therefore, it follows that

$$\frac{dp}{d\alpha} - \frac{dp}{d\alpha}\Big|_{\bar\zeta} = \frac{I_\alpha}{(I' - S')}\left\{ \frac{1}{\frac{\partial i_*}{\partial p}} - \frac{1}{\frac{\partial i}{\partial p}} \right\}. \tag{10.6}$$

Since $I_\alpha/(I' - S')$ is negative, the entire right-hand side of 10.6 is
negative if and only if the expression in braces is positive—that is,

$$\frac{dp}{d\alpha} - \frac{dp}{d\alpha}\Big|_{\zeta} < 0 \qquad (10.7)$$

if and only if

$$\frac{1}{\dfrac{\partial i_*}{\partial p}} - \frac{1}{\dfrac{\partial i}{\partial p}} > 0. \qquad (19.8)$$

But in chapter 6 we proved that

$$\frac{\partial i}{\partial p} > \frac{\partial i_*}{\partial p} > 0, \qquad (10.9)$$

which, indeed, establishes 10.8 and, hence, 10.7.

We can prove this result directly by substituting the expressions for $\partial i_*/\partial p$ and $\partial i/\partial p$ into 10.6. As we have seen in chapter 3 and 5, these expressions are

$$\frac{\partial i_*}{\partial p} = -\frac{\dfrac{R_*}{p^2}}{C} > 0, \qquad (10.10)$$

where

$$C = k\frac{\partial D^d}{\partial z_h} - R'_B < 0, \qquad (10.11)$$

and

$$\frac{\partial i}{\partial p} = \frac{\dfrac{R_*}{p^2} \cdot \left(\dfrac{\partial D^d}{\partial z_h} - \dfrac{\partial D^s}{\partial z_f}\right)}{Q} > 0, \qquad (10.12)$$

where

$$Q = k^2\frac{\partial D^s}{\partial z_f}\frac{\partial D^d}{\partial z_h} + R'_B\left(\frac{\partial D^d}{\partial z_h} - \frac{\partial D^s}{\partial z_f}\right) < 0. \qquad (10.13)$$

Substituting 10.10 through 10.13 into 10.6 and rearranging, we get:

$$\frac{dp}{d\alpha} - \frac{dp}{d\alpha}\Big|_{\zeta} = -\frac{kI_{\alpha}\dfrac{\partial D^d}{\partial z_h}}{(I' - S')\dfrac{R_*}{p^2}\left(\dfrac{\partial D^d}{\partial z_h} - \dfrac{\partial D^s}{\partial z_f}\right)}$$

$$\cdot \left\{ \frac{\partial D^d}{\partial z_h} - (1-k)\frac{\partial D^s}{\partial z_f} \right\} < 0. \qquad (10.14)$$

Expression 10.14 establishes 10.7. That is, we have proved that a positive shift in investment demand increases the price level by less when the deposit rate is flexible than when it is fixed. In other words, the price level is more immune to real-sector shocks when the deposit rate is market determined than when it is fixed.

But what about the effects on the interest rate? We note that any change in the nominal interest rate is also a change in the real interest rate because this particular shock leaves expected inflation unchanged. Second, the real sector is assumed the same whether the deposit rate is fixed or flexible. Moreover, this identical real sector assumes that investment and savings depend only on the interest rate. Hence the real interest rate must be the same under either regime. This means that our analysis, if it is correct, must show that the positive shift in investment demand causes the same increase in the interest rate under either regime.

The proof is simple: Differentiating 10.15—that is,

$$i = i_*(p; \ldots), \qquad (10.15)$$

we get:

$$\frac{di}{d\alpha}\Big|_{\zeta} = \frac{\partial i_*}{\partial p} \cdot \frac{dp}{d\alpha}\Big|_{\zeta}. \qquad (10.16)$$

Substituting 10.1 into 10.16, we get:

$$\frac{di}{d\alpha}\Big|_{\zeta} = -\frac{I_{\alpha}\dfrac{\partial i_*}{\partial p}}{(I' - S')\dfrac{\partial i_*}{\partial p}},$$

or,

$$\frac{di}{d\alpha}\bigg|_{\zeta} = -\frac{I_\alpha}{(I' - S')} > 0. \qquad (10.17)$$

Similarly, differentiating (10.18)

$$i = i(p; \dots), \qquad (10.18)$$

and substituting 10.2, we get:

$$\frac{di}{d\alpha} = \frac{\partial i}{\partial p} \frac{dp}{d\alpha} = -\frac{I_\alpha \dfrac{\partial i}{\partial p}}{(I' - S')\dfrac{\partial i}{\partial p}},$$

or,

$$\frac{di}{d\alpha} = -\frac{I_\alpha}{(I' - S')} > 0. \qquad (10.19)$$

By 10.17 and 10.19, we see that the positive effects on the interest rate coincide.

Continuous Shocks and Inflation: Comparison of Effects on Real Reserve Base

Now we turn to the consequences of a change—say, of an increase in the rate of growth of the nominal reserve base, $\dot{R}_*/R_*$—which we have denoted by v. First, we have shown that whether the deposit rate is fixed or flexible, in equilibrium the expected rate of inflation and the actual rate of inflation coincide with the rate of growth in the nominal reserve base:

$$\frac{\dot{p}}{p} = \pi = v. \qquad (10.20)$$

Therefore, it follows that there cannot be any difference in the effects of a change in v on the expected and actual rates of inflation between the two monetary regimes: Whether the deposit rate is fixed or flexible, a given increase in the rate of growth of the nominal reserve base will cause an equal increase in inflation.

Second, because of the way the model is constructed, the Fisher hypothesis holds under both a fixed and a flexible deposit rate. That is, an increase in expected inflation increases the nominal (bills) interest rate by the same percentage, leaving the real (bills) rate unchanged. Since equilibrium inflation is changed by the same percentage that the rate of growth in the nominal reserve base is changed, it follows that the impact of such a change on the real rate of interest is the same under both monetary regimes.

Finally, we examine the effects on the only other common real variable—namely, the real reserve base, $R \equiv R_*/p$. In chapter 8 we found that when the deposit rate is fixed, the effect of a change in v on R is given by

$$\frac{dR}{dv}\Big|_{\zeta} = \frac{1}{\frac{\partial i_*}{\partial R}} < 0 \tag{10.21}$$

—that is, we found that an increase in the rate of growth of the nominal reserve base, by increasing the rate of inflation, erodes the quantity of the real reserve base. In chapter 9 we derived the same qualitative result when the deposit rate is market determined:

$$\frac{dR}{dv} = \frac{1}{\frac{\partial i}{\partial R}} < 0. \tag{10.22}$$

Now we shall undertake a quantitative comparson; we shall inquire whether the erosion in R, caused by an increase in v, differs between the two monetary regimes. To begin, we see that by 10.21 and 10.22 we get:

$$\frac{dR}{dv}\Big|_{\zeta} - \frac{dR}{dv} = \frac{1}{\frac{\partial i_*}{\partial R}} - \frac{1}{\frac{\partial i}{\partial R}}. \tag{10.23}$$

We can determine the sign of expression 10.23 and, hence, we can find which effect predominates if we can find the sign of $(\partial i_*/\partial R - \partial i/\partial R)$; that is, the relative effect of a change in the rate of growth of the nominal reserve base on the level of the real reserve base depends on the relative effect of a change in the real reserve base on the nominal bills interest rate. Here, we shall examine 10.23 directly and derive the sign of $[(\partial i_*/\partial R) - (\partial i/\partial R)]$ as a corollary.

In chapter 3 we derived $\partial i_*/\partial R$ as

$$\frac{\partial i_*}{\partial R} = \frac{1}{k \frac{\partial D^d}{\partial z_h} - R'_B} < 0. \tag{10.24}$$

Hence its inverse is·

$$\frac{1}{\frac{\partial i_*}{\partial R}} = k \frac{\partial D^d}{\partial z_h} - R'_B. \tag{10.25}$$

In chapter 5 we found $\partial i / \partial R$ as

$$\frac{\partial i}{\partial R} = -\frac{\frac{\partial D^d}{\partial z_h} - \frac{\partial D^s}{\partial z_f}}{Q} < 0. \tag{10.26}$$

Therefore, the inverse of $\partial i / \partial R$ is:

$$\frac{1}{\frac{\partial i}{\partial R}} = -\frac{1}{\frac{\partial D^d}{\partial z_h} - \frac{\partial D^s}{\partial z_f}}. \tag{10.27}$$

Now, substituting 10.25 and 10.27 into 10.23 and collecting terms, we get:

$$\frac{dR}{dv}\bigg|_{\zeta} - \frac{dR}{dv} = \frac{k \frac{\partial D^d}{\partial z_h}}{\frac{\partial D^d}{\partial z_h} - \frac{\partial D^s}{\partial z_f}} \cdot \left\{ \frac{\partial D^d}{\partial z_h} - (1-k)\frac{\partial D^s}{\partial z_f} \right\} < 0.$$

We have therefore proved that

$$\frac{dR}{dv}\bigg|_{\zeta} < \frac{dR}{dv} < 0. \tag{10.29}$$

That is, we have proved that an increase in the rate of growth of the nominal reserve base erodes the real reserve base by more when the deposit rate is fixed than when it is flexible. Because an increase in the inflation rate is equal to the increase in the rate of growth of the nominal reserve base under both regimes, we have proved that an increase in the inflation rate erodes the real reserve base by more when the deposit rate is fixed than when it is flexible. Finally, we derive, as a corollary to our basic theorem, the following result:

$$\frac{\partial i}{\partial R} < \frac{\partial i_*}{\partial R} < 0; \qquad (10.30)$$

that is, we have shown that an increase in the real reserve base lowers the interest rate by more when the deposit rate is market determined than when it is fixed. Of course, this result is in line with a basic theme in chapter 6.

Comparisons of Speeds of Convergence to Equilibrium

At this point we should take stock of some of our results. We have shown that, as long as the nominal reserve base is the same, the equilibrium of each model is characterized by the same price level and by the same expected inflation and, as a corollary, that an increase in the nominal reserve base causes an equiproportionate increase in the price level with no lasting change in the interest rate.

These results are interesting in themselves and warrant notice because they confirm that our specification of the two models is consistent. However, we can say more about the two models—in particular, something that is of interest to the policymaker. In chapter 6 we saw that the interest rate responds more to a change in the nominal reserve base or in the discount rate when the deposit rate is market determined than when it is fixed by the Central Bank. But because we have stipulated that excess demand for goods and services depends only on the interest rate, this result means that the real sector and, hence, the price level, is more responsive to monetary policy and shocks when the deposit rate is market determined. But there is more. We have also shown that the interest rate is more responsive to a change in the price level when the deposit rate is market determined than when it is fixed. These results, along with the result that the equilibrium is the same under both regimes, point to the conjecture that the same equilibrium position can be reached *faster* when the deposit rate is market determined.

Zero Growth Rate in the Nominal Reserve Base

In the discussion that follows we shall investigate the conjecture that the transmission mechanism from the monetary sector to the real sector is faster when the deposit rate is market determined than when it is fixed. To this end, we shall compare the stability properties of these two systems in their entirety. First, we shall examine the special case where the rate of growth in the nominal reserve base, v, is fixed at zero and, hence, examine stability in the (p, π) plane. After detailed examination of this case, we must only briefly examine the general case. Under the assumption that the rate of growth of the nominal reserve base is zero, the fixed-deposit-rate regime is described by system 10.31 to 10.32:

$$\dot{p} = \varepsilon p \{ I[i_*(p; \ldots) - \pi; \alpha] - S[i_*(p; \ldots) - \pi] \} + p\pi \quad (10.31)$$

$$\dot{\pi} = \gamma\varepsilon \{ I[i_*(p; \ldots) - \pi; \alpha] - S[i_*(p; \ldots) - \pi] \}. \quad (10.32)$$

As we know, the stability properties of system 10.31 to 10.32 are embodied in the matrix of this system that is derived by taking the Taylor linear expansion at the equilibrium point, $p = \pi = 0$. We have denoted this matrix by F in 10.33:

$$F = \begin{bmatrix} \varepsilon p(I' - S') \dfrac{\partial i_*}{\partial p} & p[1 - \varepsilon(I' - S')] \\[2ex] \gamma\varepsilon(I' - S') \dfrac{\partial i_*}{\partial p} & -\gamma\varepsilon(I' - S') \end{bmatrix} \quad (10.33)$$

The corresponding flexible-deposit-rate regime is described by system 10.34 to 10.35:

$$\dot{p} = \varepsilon p \cdot \{ I[i(p; \ldots) - \pi; \alpha] - S[i(p; \ldots) - \pi] \} + p\pi \quad (10.34)$$

$$\dot{\pi} = \gamma\varepsilon \cdot \{ I[i(p; \ldots) - \pi; \alpha] - S[i(p; \ldots) - \pi] \}. \quad (10.35)$$

The matrix of this dynamic system is A in 10.36:

$$A = \begin{bmatrix} \varepsilon p(I' - S') \dfrac{\partial i}{\partial p} & p\{1 - \varepsilon(I' - S')\} \\[2ex] \gamma\varepsilon(I' - S') \dfrac{\partial i}{\partial p} & -\gamma\varepsilon(I' - S') \end{bmatrix} \quad (10.36)$$

Any two-differential equation system is stable if and only if the determinant is positive and its trace is negative. But we have already derived the determinant of F, which is positive:

$$\det F = -\gamma\varepsilon(I' - S')p\,\frac{\partial i_*}{\partial p} > 0. \qquad (10.37)$$

Furthermore, we have shown that the determinant of A is also positive:

$$\det A = -\gamma\varepsilon(I' - S')p\,\frac{\partial i}{\partial p} > 0. \qquad (10.38)$$

Hence the stability of each system depends entirely on the trace of its relevant matrix. In the case of a fixed deposit rate, tr F in 10.39,

$$\operatorname{tr} F = \varepsilon(I' - S')\left[p\,\frac{\partial i_*}{\partial p} - \gamma\right] \qquad (10.39)$$

is negative and, hence, system 10.31 to 10.32 is stable if and only if condition 10.40 is satisfied:

$$\gamma < p\,\frac{\partial i_*}{\partial p}. \qquad (10.40)$$

On the other hand, tr A is given in 10.41:

$$\operatorname{tr} A = \varepsilon(I' - S')\cdot\left\{p\,\frac{\partial i}{\partial p} - \gamma\right\}. \qquad (10.41)$$

By 10.41, tr A is negative and the flexible-deposit-rate regime is stable if and only if condition 10.42 is satisfied:

$$\gamma < p\,\frac{\partial i}{\partial p}. \qquad (10.42)$$

If these two conditions—10.40 and 10.42—are satisfied, the phase plane of each model is similar to that depicted in figure 10–1.

We can also depict separately the paths that the price level and expected inflation follow as time passes. Figure 10–2 illustrates the behavior of the price level, and figure 10–3 illustrates the behavior of expected inflation. In these graphs, t_0 is the time of origin; p_0 and π_0 the price level and expected inflation at this point in time; and $\bar{p}$ the equilibrium price level. Each path in figures 10–2 and 10–3 illustrates the dynamic behavior of the price level and of expected inflation under both regimes. But we shall prove in the following discussion that the equilibrium point—$p = \bar{p}$ and $\pi = 0$—can be reached

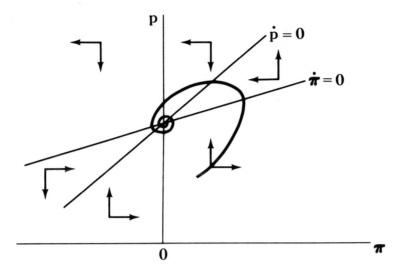

Figure 10–1. Price Level—Expected Inflation Dynamics

faster and with smaller oscillations under a flexible deposit rate than under a fixed deposit rate. In other words, we shall prove that the solid-line paths are for the fixed-deposit-rate model whereas the dotted-line paths represent the price level and expected inflation behavior in the flexible-deposit-rate model.

To prove this proposition we must compare the trace of A with the trace of F and the determinant of A with the determinant of F. By 10.41 and 10.39, we get:

$$\operatorname{tr} A - \operatorname{tr} F = \varepsilon (I' - S') p \left(\frac{\partial i}{\partial p} - \frac{\partial i_*}{\partial p} \right). \tag{10.43}$$

Since we have proved in chapter 6 that

$$\frac{\partial i}{\partial p} - \frac{\partial i_*}{\partial p} > 0, \tag{10.44}$$

it follows that

$$\operatorname{tr} A < \operatorname{tr} F. \tag{10.45}$$

Of course, when conditions 10.42 and 10.40 are satisfied we have:

$$\operatorname{tr} A < \operatorname{tr} F < 0. \tag{10.46}$$

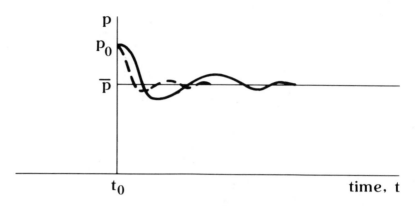

Figure 10–2. Price Level over Time

Now comparing the respective determinants, we have, by 10.38 and 10.37:

$$\det A - \det F = -\gamma \varepsilon p (I' - S') \left(\frac{\partial i}{\partial p} - \frac{\partial i_*}{\partial p} \right),$$

and by 10.44 we have the result:

$$\det A > \det F > 0. \tag{10.47}$$

The proof in 10.46—that the absolute value of the trace of A is greater than the absolute value of the trace of F—and the proof in 10.47—that the positive determinant of A is greater than the determinant of F—establish that equilibrium is reached faster with a flexible deposit rate than with a fixed deposit rate. We shall illustrate this proof for the case depicted in figures 10–1, 10–2, and 10–3—that is, when the approach to equilibrium is oscillatory.

We can approximate the fixed-deposit-rate model[1] by the following, second-order differential equation in p:

$$\ddot{p} - \operatorname{tr} F \dot{p} + \det F \, p = 0. \tag{10.48}$$

Similarly, we can approximate the flexible-deposit-rate model by:

$$\ddot{p} - \operatorname{tr} A \dot{p} + \det A \, p = 0. \tag{10.49}$$

The stability of each model and the speed at which the economy converges to equilibrium depend on the sign and on the magnitude of roots of the

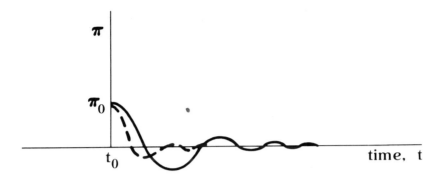

Figure 10–3. Expected Inflation over Time with Zero Equilibrium Rate

respective characteristic equation—that is, of equation 10.50 for the first
model and of 10.51 for the second model:

$$\lambda_*^2 - \text{tr } F \, \lambda_* + \det F = 0 \tag{10.50}$$

$$\lambda^2 - tr A \, \lambda + \det A = 0. \tag{10.51}$$

The roots of 10.50, denoted by λ_1^* and λ_2^*, are found by the formula,

$$\lambda_1^*, \lambda_2^* = \frac{\text{tr } F \pm \sqrt{\text{tr } F^2 - 4 \det F}}{2} \tag{10.52}$$

and the roots of 10.51—λ_1, λ_2—are found by:

$$\lambda_1, \lambda_2 = \frac{\text{tr } A \pm \sqrt{\text{tr } A^2 - 4 \det A}}{2} \tag{10.53}$$

Now, oscillations occur if and only if the roots are complex, which, in
turn, occurs when the discriminant (of each system) is negative. For the first
model this occurs when

$$\text{tr } F^2 - 4 \det F < 0 \tag{10.54}$$

and for the second model when

$$\text{tr } A^2 - 4 \det A < 0. \tag{10.55}$$

When 10.54 holds, the two roots of 10.50 are of the form,

$$\lambda_1^* = a_* + ib_* \tag{10.56}$$

$$\lambda_2^* = a_* - ib_*, \tag{10.57}$$

where $i = \sqrt{-1}$ and where the real part, a_*, is the same—namely,

$$a_* = \frac{\text{tr } F}{2}. \tag{10.58}$$

For the second model, when 10.55 holds, the roots of 10.51—λ_1, λ_2—are of the form,

$$\lambda_1 = a + ib \tag{10.59}$$

$$\lambda_2 = a - ib, \tag{10.60}$$

and the real part, a, is

$$a = \frac{\text{tr } A}{2}. \tag{10.61}$$

The solution of the second-order differential equation 10.48 can be written as:

$$p_*(t) = e^{\text{tr } F/2} \cdot \left\{ F_1 \cos b_* t + F_2 \sin b_* t \right\} \tag{10.62}$$

and the solution of 10.49 can be written as:

$$p(t) = e^{\text{tr } A/2} \cdot \left\{ A_1 \cos bt + A_2 \sin bt \right\} \tag{10.63}$$

(where F_1, F_2, A_1, and A_2 are constants).

Because tr F and tr A are negative, it is clear that the real part of each characteristic root is negative and that both $p_*(t)$ and $p(t)$ converge to equilibrium. However, because tr $A/2 <$ tr $F/2 < 0$, $p(t)$ converges to equilibrium faster than $p_*(t)$ does. This completes the proof for the case of oscillations.

*The General Case: Positive Rate of Growth
in the Nominal Reserve Base*

We shall now examine briefly the general case when the rate of growth in the
nominal reserve base, v, is different from zero. We shall conduct our analysis
in the (R, π) plane and prove the proposition that equilibrium is reached
faster and with narrower oscillations when the deposit rate is market
determined than when it is fixed. The fixed-deposit-rate dynamic model is
now represented by 10.64 to 10.65:

$$\dot{R} = R\{v - \varepsilon\{I[i_*(R; \dots) - \pi; \alpha] - S[i_*(R; \dots) - \pi[\} - \pi\} \tag{10.64}$$

$$\dot{\pi} = \gamma\varepsilon\{I[i_*(R; \dots) - \pi; \alpha] - S[i_*(R; \dots) - \pi]\}. \tag{10.65}$$

The matrix of this dynamic system is H:

$$H = \begin{bmatrix} -\varepsilon(I' - S')R\dfrac{\partial i_*}{\partial R} & R \cdot [\varepsilon(I' - S') - 1] \\ \gamma\varepsilon(I' - S')\dfrac{\partial i_*}{\partial R} & -\gamma\varepsilon(I' - S') \end{bmatrix} \tag{10.66}$$

The determinant and the trace of H are given by 10.67 and 10.68,
respectively:

$$\det H = \gamma\varepsilon(I' - S')R\frac{\partial i_*}{\partial R} > 0 \tag{10.67}$$

$$\operatorname{tr} H = -\varepsilon(I' - S')R\frac{\partial i_*}{\partial R} - \gamma\varepsilon(I' - S'). \tag{10.68}$$

The alternative model, when the deposit rate is market determined, is
given by 10.69 to 10.70:

$$\dot{R} = R \cdot \{v - \varepsilon\{I[i(R; \dots) - \pi; \alpha] - S[i(R; \dots) - \pi]\} - \pi\} \tag{10.69}$$

$$\dot{\pi} = \gamma\varepsilon \cdot \{I[i(R; \dots) - \pi; \alpha] - S[i(R; \dots) - \pi]\}. \tag{10.70}$$

The matrix of the dynamic system 10.69 to 10.70 is denoted by B and given in 10.71; its positive determinant is given by 10.72 and its trace is given by 10.73.

$$B = \begin{bmatrix} -\varepsilon R(I' - S')\dfrac{\partial i}{\partial R} & R[\varepsilon(I' - S') - 1] \\[2em] \gamma\varepsilon(I' - S')\dfrac{\partial i}{\partial R} & -\gamma\varepsilon(I' - S') \end{bmatrix} \qquad (10.71)$$

$$\det B = \gamma\varepsilon R(I' - S')\frac{\partial i}{\partial R} > 0 \qquad (10.72)$$

$$\operatorname{tr} B = -\varepsilon R(I' - S')\frac{\partial i}{\partial R} - \gamma\varepsilon(I' - S'). \qquad (10.73)$$

As earlier, we shall compare the determinants and the traces and find that

$$\det B - \det H = \gamma\varepsilon R(I' - S')\left[\frac{\partial i}{\partial R} - \frac{\partial i_*}{\partial R}\right] \qquad (10.74)$$

$$\operatorname{tr} B - \operatorname{tr} H = -\varepsilon R(I' - S')\left[\frac{\partial i}{\partial R} - \frac{\partial i_*}{\partial R}\right]. \qquad (10.75)$$

But, by 10.30 we see that

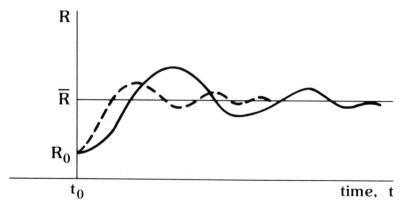

Figure 10–4. Real Reserve Base over Time

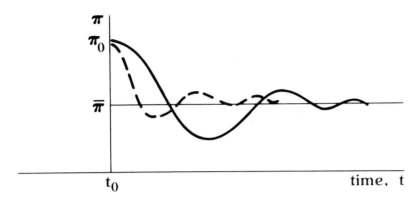

Figure 10–5. Expected Inflation over Time with a Positive Equilibrium Rate

$$\frac{\partial i}{\partial R} - \frac{\partial i_*}{\partial R} < 0.$$

Hence,

$$\det B > \det H > 0. \tag{10.76}$$

Provided these stability conditions hold,

$$\gamma < - R \frac{\partial i_*}{\partial R}$$

$$\gamma < - R \frac{\partial i}{\partial R}$$

we also have

$$\operatorname{tr} B < \operatorname{tr} H < 0. \tag{10.77}$$

Now we can proceed, as earlier, and use 10.77 to prove that equilibrium is reached faster under a flexible deposit rate than under a fixed deposit rate. In figures 10–4 and 10–5 the dotted line represents the paths of the real reserve base and of expected inflation under a flexible-deposit-rate regime, whereas the solid lines represent the paths under a fixed-deposit-rate regime.

Note

1. See G. Gandolfo (1971).

Bibliography

Arak, M. "Innovations in the Financial Markets." *Quarterly Review*, Federal Reserve Bank of New York 6, no. 4, Winter 1981–1982, pp. 1–3.

Backus, D., Brainard, W., Smith, G., and Tobin, J. "A Model of U.S. Financial and Nonfinancial Economic Behavior." *Journal of Money, Credit, and Banking*, Special Issue, 12, no. 2, May 1980, pp. 259–293.

Barro, R.J. and Santomero, A.M. "Household Money Holdings and the Demand Deposit Rate." *Journal of Money, Credit, and Banking* 4, no. 2, May 1972, pp. 397–413.

Brainard, W.C. "Financial Intermediaries and a Theory of Monetary Control." *Yale Economic Essays* 4, no. 1, Fall 1964, pp. 431–482.

———. "Uncertainty and the Effectiveness of Policy." *American Economic Review* 57, *Papers and Proceedings*, May 1967, pp. 411–425.

Brainard, W.C. and Tobin, J., "Pitfalls in Financial Model-Building." *American Economic Review* 58, *Papers and Proceedings*, May 1968, pp. 99–122.

Brunner, K., and Meltzer, A. H. "Money, Debt, and Economic Activity." *Journal of Political Economy* 80, September/October 1972, pp. 951–977.

———. "Some Further Investigations of Demand and Supply Functions for Money." *Journal of Finance*, May 1964, pp. 240–283.

———. "A Credit Market Theory of the Money Supply and an Explanation of Two Puzzles in U.S. Monetary Policy," in T. Baggiotti (ed.), *Essays in Honor of Marco Fanno* (Padova Cedam, 1966), pp. 151–176.

———. "The Meaning of Monetary Indicators," in G. Horwich (ed.), *Monetary Process and Policy: A Symposium*. Homewood, Ill.: R. D. Irwin, 1967, pp. 187–217.

———. "Liquidity Traps for Money, Bank Credit, and Interest Rates." *Journal of Political Economy* 76, January/February 1968, pp. 1–37.

Cagan, P. "The Monetary Dynamics of Hyperinflation," in Milton Friedman (ed.), *Studies in the Quantity Theory of Money*. Chicago: University of Chicago Press, 1956, pp. 25–117.

———. "Financial Innovations and the Erosion of Monetary Control," in William Fellner, Project Director, *Contemporary Economic Problems* (Washington, D.C.: American Enterprise Institute, 1979), pp. 117–151.

Dotsey, M., Englander, S., and Partlan, J.C. "Money Market Mutal Funds and Monetary Control." *Quarterly Review*, Federal Reserve Bank of New York. 6, no. 4. Winter 1981–1982, pp. 9–17.

Enzler, J., Johnson, L. and Paulus, J. "Some Problems of Money Demand." *Brookings Papers on Economic Activity* 1, 1976, pp. 261–280.

239

Farr, H.T. "The Monthly Money Market Model." Federal Reserve Board Working Paper, July 1981.

Federal Reserve System, Board of Governors. "The Impact of the Payment of Interest on Demand Deposits," A Staff Study Prepared by Stephen H. Axilrod with Collaboration of John D. Paulus and others, January 1977.

———. *The New Monetary Control Procedures*, Vols. I and II, Federal Reserve Staff Study, Washington, D.C., February 1981.

———. "The Depository Institutions Deregulation and Monetary Control Act of 1980," staff study by Charles R. McNeill and Denise M. Rechter, *Federal Reserve Bulletin*, June 1980, pp. 444–453.

Federal Reserve System, Federal Reserve Bank of Chicago. "The Depository Institutions Deregulation and Monetary Control Act of 1980." *Economic Perspectives* 4, no. 5, September/October, 1980.

Friedman, M. *A Program for Monetary Stability*. New York: Fordham University Press, 1960.

Gandolfo, G. *Mathematical Methods and Models in Economic Dynamics*. Amsterdam: North-Holland Publishing Company, 1971.

Goldfeld, S.M. *Commercial Bank Behavior and Economic Activity*. Amsterdam: North-Holland Publishing Company, 1966.

———. "The Case of Missing Money." *Brookings Papers on Economic Activity*, 3, 1976, pp. 683–730.

Goldfeld, S.M. and Kane, E.J. "The Determinants of Member-Bank Borrowing: An Econometric Study." *The Journal of Finance*, September 1966, pp. 499–514.

Goodfriend, M., Parthemos, J., and Summers, B. "Recent Financial Innovations: Causes, Consequences for the Payments System, and Implications for Monetary Control." *Economic Review*, Federal Reserve Bank of Richmond, March/April 1980, pp. 14–27.

Gramley, L.E. Statement by Lyle E. Gramley, Member Board of Governors of the Federal Reserve System, before the Subcommittee on Domestic Monetary Policy of the Committee on Banking, Finance, and Urban Affairs, U.S. House of Representatives, March 3, 1982, *Federal Reserve Bulletin*, March 1982, pp. 174–178.

Gurley, J.G. and Shaw, E.S. *Money in a Theory of Finance*. Washington, D.C.: Brookings Institution, 1960.

Hadjimichalakis, K.G. and Hadjimichalakis, M.G. "Bank Credit and Managed Liabilities: A General Equilibrium Analysis," Federal Reserve Board, Washington, D.C., Processed, April 1982.

Hadjimichalakis, M.G. (1971a) "Equilibrium and Disequilibrium Growth with Money: the Tobin Models." *Review of Economic Studies* 38, no. 4, October 1971, pp. 457–479.

———. (1971b). "Money, Expectations, and Dynamics: An Alternative View." *International Economic Review* 12, no. 3, October 1971, pp. 381–402.

_____. (1975a). "A Contribution to the 'Yale Model' of Monetary Theory and Policy: The Integration with the Current Account." Institute for Economic Research Discussion Paper No. 75-2, University of Washington, January 1975. (Also presented at the San Francisco Meeting of the *Econometric Society*, December 1974).

_____. (1975b). "Price Flexibility and Alternative Tools of Monetary Policy: Their Effects on the Rates of Return on Assets." Institute for Economic Research Discussion Paper No. 75-3, University of Washington, March 1975.

_____. (1980a). "The Effects of 'NOW' Accounts on Monetary Aggregates, Interest Rates, and the Economy: Some Theoretical and Early Empirical Results." *Economics Letters* 6, 1980, pp. 349–356.

_____. (1980b). "Precision of Monetary Control and Volatility of Rates: A Comparative Analysis of the Reserves and the Federal Funds Operating Targets." *Special Studies Paper No. 150.* Washington, D.C.: Federal Reserve Board, December 1980.

_____. (1981a). " 'NOW' Accounts and Monetary Control: Reserves *vs.* Federal Funds Operating Procedures." Washington, D.C.: Federal Reserve Board, 1981. Processed.

_____. (1981b). "Reserves *vs.* Federal Funds Operating Monetary Procedures: A General Equilibrium Analysis." *Economics Letters* 7, 1981, pp. 167–175.

_____. (1981c). "Monetary Control: The Role of the Discount Rate and Other Supplemental Monetary Instruments." *Economics Letters* 7, 1981, pp. 159–165.

_____. (1981d). "The Regulation Q Phaseout: The Effects on Monetary Aggregates, on Interest Rates, and on the Economy." *Special Studies Paper No. 148.* Washington, D.C.: Federal Reserve Board, January 1981.

_____. (1981e). "Expectations of the 'Myopic Perfect Foresight' Variety in Monetary Dynamics: Stability and Nonneutrality of Money." *Journal of Economic Dynamics and Control* 3, 1981, pp. 157–176.

_____. (1981f). "The Rose-Wicksell Model: Inside Money, Stability, and Stabilization Policies," *Journal of Macroeconomics* 3, no. 3, pp. 369–390.

_____. *Modern Macroeconomics: An Intermediate Text.* Englewood Cliffs, N.J.: Prentice-Hall, 1982.

Hester, D.D. "Innovations and Monetary Control." *Brookings Papers on Economic Activity* 1, 1981, pp. 141–199.

Judd, J.P. and Scadding, J.L. "Liability Management, Bank Loans and Deposit 'Market' Disequilibrium." *Economic Review*, Federal Reserve Bank of San Francisco, Summer 1981.

Klein, B. "The Competitive Supply of Money." *Journal of Money, Credit and Banking* 6, no. 4, November 1974, pp. 423–453.

Klein, M.A. "A Theory of the Banking Firm," *Journal of Money, Credit and Banking* 3, no. 2, Part 1, May 1971, pp. 205–218.

Lindsey, D.E. "The Implications of Removing the Demand Deposit Rate Prohibition for Monetary Control and the Conduct of Monetary Policy." *Special Studies Paper No. 104*, Washington, D.C.: Federal Reserve Board, September 1977.

Meigs, A.J. *Free Reserves and the Money Supply.* Chicago: University of Chicago Press, 1962.

Modigliani, F. and Papademos, L., "The Structure of Financial Markets and the Monetary Mechanism," in *Controlling Monetary Aggregates III.* Boston: Federal Reserve Bank of Boston, 1980, pp. 111–155.

Opper, B.N. "Major Deposit Developments: 1966–80," Appendix A in "Strategies for Deregulating Deposit Rate Ceilings." Washington, D.C.: Staff Paper Prepared for the Depository Institutions Deregulation Committee, March 18, 1981.

Poole, W. "Optimal Choice of Monetary Policy Instruments in a Simple Stochastic Model." *Quarterly Journal of Economics* 84, 1970, pp. 197–216.

Porter, R.C. "A Model of Bank Portfolio Selection." *Yale Economic Essays* 1, no. 2, Fall 1961, pp. 323–359.

Porter, R.D., Simpson, T.D., and Mauskopf, E. "Financial Innovation and the Monetary Aggregates." *Brookings Papers on Economic Activity* 1, 1979, pp. 213–229.

Rose, H. "Effective Demand in the Long Run," in J.A. Mirrlees and N.H. Stern, (eds.) *Models of Economic Growth.* New York: Wiley, 1973, pp. 25–47.

Santomero, A.M. and Siegel, J.J. "Bank Regulation and Macro-Economic Stability." *American Economic Review* 71, no. 1, March 1981, pp. 39–53.

Sidrauski, M. "Inflation and Economic Growth." *Journal of Political Economy* 75, December 1967, pp. 796–810.

Silber, W.L., ed. *Financial Innovation.* Lexington, Mass.: Lexington Books, D.C. Heath and Company, 1975.

———. "Commercial Bank Liability Management," A Study Prepared for the Trustees of the Banking Research Fund Association of Reserve City Bankers, 1978.

Simpson, T.D. and Porter, R.D. "Some Issues Involving the Definition and Interpretation of the Monetary Aggregates," in *Controlling Monetary Aggregates III.* Boston: Federal Reserve Bank of Boston, 1980, pp. 161–234.

Solomon, A.M. "Financial Innovation and Monetary Policy." *67th Annual Report*, Federal Reserve Bank of New York, January 1982, pp. 3–17.

Startz, R. "Implicit Interest on Demand Deposits." *Journal of Monetary Economics* 5, no. 4, October 1979, pp. 515–534.

Tobin, J. "Money and Finance in the Macro-economic Process." *Journal of Money, Credit and Banking* 14, May 1982, pp. 171–204.

_____. (1963*a*). "Commercial Banks as Creators of Money," in Deane Carson (ed.) *Banking and Monetary Studies.* Homewood, Ill.: Richard D. Irwin, 1963, pp. 241–247.

_____. (1963*b*). "An Essay on Principles of Debt Management," in *Fiscal and Debt Management Policies*, Commission on Money and Credit. Englewood Cliffs, N.J.: Prentice-Hall, 1963, pp. 143–218.

_____. "A General Equilibrium Approach to Monetary Theory." *Journal of Money, Credit and Banking* 1, February 1969, pp. 15–29.

_____. *Asset Accumulation and Economic Activity: Reflections on Contemporary Macroeconomic Theory.* Chicago: University of Chicago Press, 1980.

Tobin, J. and Brainard, W.C. "Financial Intermediaries and the Effectiveness of Monetary Controls." *American Economic Review*, (*Papers and Proceedings*) 53, no. 2, May 1963, pp. 383–400.

White, B.B. "Monetary Policy Without Regulation Q." *Quarterly Review*, Federal Reserve Bank of New York. 6, no. 4. Winter 1981–1982, pp. 4–8.

Index of Names

Index of Subjects

Adjustable-rate mortgages, 27
Assets, 17, 27–28; diversification, 33
Automatic transfer services (ATSs), 18, 20

Banking, old view of, 106–108
Banking Act of 1933, 19
Banking Act of 1935, 19
Banking firm, theory of, 66–73
Base money, 45, 46, 73–74
Bills rate, 8; demand for demand deposits and, 87; shocks and, 14
Borrowed reserves. *See* Reserves
Brainard, W.C., 3, 7, 28, 45
Brunner, K., 3, 7, 45

"Cagan coefficient," 173
Certificates of deposit (CDs), negotiable, 19, 24
Checking accounts, interest on, 32. *See also* Demand deposits
Consumer Checking Account Equity Act of 1980 (Title III, DIDMCA), 30, 32
Credit (loans), other checkable deposits and, 21
Credit-union-share drafts, 18–19, 20

Data processing, service innovations and, 28
Demand deposits, 45, 46; circumventing prohibition of interest on, 19–26; comparison of effects of monetary policy and shocks on, 128–136; cost of servicing, 67–68; demand for, bills rate and, 87; effects of monetary policy on, 102–108; effects of shocks on, 9, 10–11, 55–58; and interest rate 47; market-determined interest on, 65–86; market-determined-deposit-rate model and, 155–156; and other checkable deposits, 20–21; supply of, 3–4, 8; variability, comparison of, 10

Depository Institutions Deregulation Act of 1980 (Title II, DIDMCA), 29–30, 31–32
Depository Institutions Deregulation and Monetary Control Act, 1980 (DIDMCA), 6, 17, 20, 29–33; Title I, 29, 30–31; Title II, 29–30, 31–32; Title III, 30, 32; title IV, 30, 33; Title V, 30, 33
Depository Institutions Deregulation Committee (DIDC), 32
Deposit rate, 7, 8–9; fixed, 7, 45–64, 119–120, 129–130, 145–150, 169–191; market-clearing determination of, 79–85; market-determined, model, 155–156; market-determined, and real sector, 193–219; monetary policy and shocks, effects of on, 14, 96–102
Discount Corporation of New York, 24
Discount rate, demand for earning assets and, 63
Discount-rate policy, Federal Reserve, 37–38
"Discount window," 50, 68

Earning assets, discount rate and, 63
Electronic funds transfer system (EFTS), 28
Equilibrium, comparison of speeds of convergenct to, 228–237
Excess demand for reserves (EDR), 88–89

Federal funds (FFs), 23
Federal Home Loan Bank Board, 27
Federal Reserve: discount-rate policy, 37–38; NOW accounts, 38–39; open-market operations, 36–37; operating procedures, change in, 6, 18, 34–39
Federal Reserve Act of 1913, 29
Fed watchers, 9

About the Author

Michael G. Hadjimichalakis received the undergraduate degree in economics from the Athens School of Economics and Business Science, Athens, in 1964, and the Ph.D. in economics from the University of Rochester in 1970. Since 1969 he has been on the faculty of the University of Washington in Seattle. From September 1980 until September 1982 he was a visiting scholar at the Board of Governors of the Federal Reserve System in Washington. Professor Hadjimichalakis is the author of *Modern Macroeconomics: An Intermediate Text* (1982) and numerous journal articles on monetary theory and policy, expectations, and economic dynamics.